Urban and Regional Planning

Urban
and Regional Planning

A SYSTEMS APPROACH

J. Brian McLoughlin

FABER AND FABER
London

First published in 1969
Reprinted 1970
by Faber and Faber Limited
24 Russell Square London WC1
Printed in Great Britain by
Western Printing Services Ltd, Bristol

ISBN (paper edition) 0 571 09534 8

ISBN (cloth edition) 0 571 09005 2

In memoriam I.G.M.

Acknowledgement

I am grateful to the Council of the Town and Country Planning Summer School for permission to adapt material from the paper 'A systems approach to planning' which was read at the 1967 School at Queen's University, Belfast and published in the School's annual report.

Contents

Preface   *page* 15
1. Man in his Ecological Setting   19
2. Modifying Actions and the Environment   38
3. Location Theory: A Foundation for Planning   58
4. The Guidance and Control of Change: Physical
   Planning as the Control of Complex Systems   75
5. Planning as a Cyclic Process   92
6. Goal Formulation: Identifying Objectives   104
7. System Description: Information Needs   125
8. System Simulation: Forecasting and Modelling   166
9. Plan Formulation: Charting Possible Courses
   of the System   231
10. Plan Selection: Choosing the Desired Course   263
11. Plan Implementation: System Guidance,
    Control and Review   279
12. Implications of a Systems Approach to
    Planning   297
References   313
Index   325

Illustrations

4.1	A system	*page* 76
4.2	Error-controlled regulation	86
4.3	Error-controlled regulation applied to planning	88
7.1	Land parcels	134
7.2	Traditional land use map	152
7.3	Activities	153
7.4	Spaces	154
7.5	Communications	155
7.6	Channels	156
8.1	Simple graphical population projection	177
8.2	Ratio method (graphical): Step from nation to region	178
8.3	Ratio method (graphical): Step from region to sub-region	179
8.4	Apportionment method (graphical): Step from nation to region	180
8.5	Apportionment method (graphical): Step from region to sub-region	181
8.6	Cohort-survival: Female table, first quinquennium	186
8.7	A survivorship matrix	191
8.8	Diagrammatic representation of planners' information system	229
9.1	System trajectories	232

8.2 The essential argument of Lowry's 'Model of a
     Metropolis'   *page* 247
9.3 Formal/manual simulation process as applied to
     a sub-region   248–9
9.4 Simulation process output   258–9
11.1 Control process   293
12.1 Staffing: traditional and suggested frameworks   303

Preface

In recent years physical planning has begun to emerge from a
long sleep. Since its inception as a respectable activity of
government in the early years of the century in parts of Europe
and in North America it has had a chequered history. On the
one hand some remarkable successes can be claimed, among them
the British achievement since the Second World War–for example the rebuilding of Coventry, the new towns, the conservation of areas of fine landscape, the maintenance of a large
measure of public faith in the world's most intricate and comprehensive planning system. On the other hand, very serious
doubts have begun to arise–not only about the effectiveness of
the means for planning, but much more fundamental doubts
about the ends which institutionalised planning is supposed to
serve, about the nature of the process as a whole, about professionalism, skills and education. Within the space of four years
in Britain, government has undertaken a complete re-examination of the nature of the instruments of physical planning and
has begun enquiries into the relationships between physical and
economic planning, and into the question of public participation; meanwhile the Town Planning Institute has completed
a major overhaul of its membership and educational policies.
These events are surely only a beginning and reflect a greater
degree of awareness of the significance of planning and self-
awareness by planners than at any time in the past.

These seemingly distinct developments have a common factor. As the urbanised regions become the dominant human
settlement form, so do many of life's problems and opportunities
arise within them; but in recognising this we have become

acutely conscious of the lack of good theoretical foundations for their study and guidance. So planning in Britain, whether seen as an instrument of modern government or as a field of professional study and action, has had to try and build a larger and more complex structure on a fragmented foundation. For the component parts of such a foundation have become more abundant: economists, sociologists, geographers, political scientists and many others have intensified their studies of the spatial aspects of human activity; the boundaries between 'disciplines' become ever more blurred as studies starting from varied origins impinge upon urban and regional life, mingle, coalesce and reform. Americans, unable to rest on many laurels of physical and statutory achievement, have not surprisingly been fertile in speculation and analysis, spurred on by the practical problems of their burgeoning wealth and mobility. From various quarters of the 'western' world new and exciting attempts at synthesis have appeared: for example the work of Webber and Foley on urban form, social processes and values; of Isard, Haggett and others on spatial structure; of Lichfield on evaluative methods; of Harris on simulation. But some of the most important work has remained little known to most planners in Britain, partly because of its being scattered throughout many different sources, partly through problems of communication between disciplines and also, one suspects, because many people hold the mistaken view that all this theoretical stuff is of little relevance for practical men.

There is a need to bring the developments in both theory and practice (many of them closely linked) to the attention of a wider body of people and to provide a framework whereby it can be related to the emerging problems of understanding and planning of cities and regions; this is the first objective of this book.

Despite the great advances made in the last two decades there remain formidable problems in the theory and practice of physical planning. It is not yet possible to see obvious pathways between such growing fields as regional analysis and the new 'urban sociology'; between decision theory and the practical world of data-processing or between these and questions of resource management, food supplies and land conservation. And yet there are hints of the higher-order framework we need so much. Beginning in strategic studies in the 1940's we have seen the growth of operational research into almost all fields where complex systems are managed, including industrial and commercial activities of all kinds. Increasingly such tools are being used to solve problems in the public services. The identification and description of complex situations has been greatly aided by the techniques of systems analysis which itself rests on the foundations of general systems theory. Perhaps the most exciting prospect of synthesis is offered by cybernetics, the study of the processes of information transfer, communication and control in very large and highly complex systems, especially those found in living matter. For it is now clear that the fundamental principles of control in complex systems are universal, irrespective of the actual nature of the system—real or conceptual, animate or inanimate.

Can we apply these general tools of study, analysis, evaluation and control to the spatial elements of human life—to the patterns of living, working, recreation and movement? In the belief that not only are we able to do so but that for many reasons we *must*, the second aim of this book is to provide an approach to this task—as the title implies.

This book is neither a new theoretical statement nor entirely a practical manual. Rather it is an attempt to provide a framework by which interested people may relate the new tools from many fields to the problems of planning cities and regions. It also outlines the application of the general principles of systems analysis and control to the planning task, showing by example how 'traditional' and new methods my be fused within a systems framework of understanding and action. Finally, it is hoped to encourage the reader to penetrate more deeply to the roots of the new synthesis and especially to look forward beyond this book to the long haul of more detailed working out of principles and methods.

The extent of my debt to the published work of others is obvious from the references and bibliography. My direct and personal indebtedness to many other people is at least as great. The struggle with these ideas (so painfully evident in the following pages) began when I joined the staff of the Department of Town and Country Planning at the University of Manchester, shortly after the appointment of Professor Roy

Kantorowich. My re-education there is due to all my colleagues and students in varying degrees. H. W. E. ('Lyn') Davies showed me by example the virtues of logical dissection and clear synthesis; David Robinson cautioned with a dalesman's shrewdness against jumping to conclusions and opened my eyes to many human landscapes as did Ian Melville who also introduced me to new aspects of perception; Michael Yates and Mervyn Schonegevel were invaluable in trying to make me convince them—both with great patience and sympathy. George Chadwick showed me much of the ways of scholarship and the craft of teaching, and it was he who encouraged me to write this book and who gave me a wealth of advice and constructive criticism on its layout and content. Many other colleagues both in the planning school and elsewhere, research assistants and students, have contributed however unwittingly to the development of my ideas. My friend David Gill has been a source of comfort, hospitality, encouragement and advice throughout and gave valuable comments on certain sections. Peter Hall gave me a great deal of practical advice and encouragement at a crucial time. None of these friends or colleagues is in any way responsible for the faults in the book whether of form, content, fact or opinion—for these I am wholly to blame.

The preparation of the text has been helped greatly by the labours of Elizabeth Goepel and Maggie Churchill in preparing the typescript, and by Frank Coleman who drew all the illustrations.

My wife, Marie, supported me in the decision to take a job where I might try out some of my ideas in practise and have solitary evenings away from home to carry on writing. Her cheerful sacrifice, looking after a house and four children alone each week for two years, has in large measure made this book possible; I dedicate it to her with great affection.

Bramhall, Cheshire: Summer 1968

I

Man in his Ecological Setting

The animal *homo sapiens* has existed for somewhat less than half a million years – a small proportion of the time during which higher forms of life have developed and a tiny fraction of the lifetime of the planet. For most of that time *homo sapiens* was a rare animal living in sporadic but intense competition with other animals and subsisting by hunting and food-gathering (Childe, 1942). In the last ten thousand years he has been increasingly successful in adapting his environment to his own needs and in the creation of artificial habitats. In the last few hundred years only he has gained a position of almost complete domination over all other forms of life on earth, greatly expanded his sources of food and energy and his ability to modify the effects of nature on him. These unique skills and powers are evidenced by the great increase in his numbers and the steepening of the rate of that increase; currently the human population may be doubling itself within one hundred years.

Although in the first flush of the industrial revolution at the end of the eighteenth century Malthus issued his gloomy warning that the bulk of the rising population would always live at bare subsistence level, little attention was paid to his viewpoint once the initial fuss had died down. (The main reason may have been the absence of any reliable evidence about the numbers of human beings then living, let alone their standards of food, shelter and health.) The advanced nations of western Europe and North America bent to their serious purposes of transforming the condition of their peoples by way of technological innovation on an unprecedented scale. The grave problems of such rapid change were quickly apparent in the rural areas where peasant agriculture was becoming a food-producing industry, and in the burgeoning towns and cities—increasingly the habitat of nineteenth-century man in the advanced communities.

For the most part, such problems were recognised and tackled in isolation. They were problems of the coal industry to be resolved in long and bitter struggles between new groupings of human power—the entrepreneurs and the workers. Or they were problems of an area—of Manchester, London, Birmingham and Glasgow—to be worked out by new local and central legal powers and administrative arrangements. But already, the new transport technology was making apparent wider, planetary relationships between the diverse activities of men in all its corners. What men did with wheat and cotton in North America affected other men in Lancashire and East Anglia; the intricate social and economic system of the world-wide British Empire was sustained and grew by virtue of tea clippers and gunboats; the hardwood forests of West Africa could be depleted to provide sideboards in Cheltenham and Harrogate, Boston and Philadelphia.

The steamship, the railway and the modern gun were to facilitate the exploitation of nature in new and disturbing ways. Millions of buffalo were wiped out by the westward-moving railroads and rifles, and with them would vanish in a few years, *an ecological relationship* between plants, animals, soils and man which had grown up over countless centuries. The successors to Melville's Captain Ahab would come near to exterminating the big whales of the Arctic and Antarctic with their bigger, faster ships and harpoon guns.

Mechanised agriculture, and especially the tendency towards monoculture—large areas consistently used for growing one type of crop—would result in such disasters as the 'dustbowls' in the central and southern United States in the 1920's and 1930's. Fishing on the continental shelf of western Europe would become so technically advanced but ecologically backward as to threaten the depletion of many staple species of edible fish. Less spectacular but more widespread crop failures were to be a feature of large-scale mechanised monocultures during the late nineteenth and early twentieth century.

In recent years, more subtle and sinister outcomes of the

application of new knowledge are becoming apparent both in the human environment and in man himself. The use of chemical pesticides and artificial fertilisers are one cause of concern; the use of anti-biotic drugs, depressants, stimulants and chemical contraceptives is another. It is not so much the immediate or direct effects which give rise to disquiet, for often these are desirable. Rather it is the growing realisation that there are second, third, fourth, and fifth-order side effects of great complexity the 'kick-backs' of which may be understandable and sometimes disastrous.

The new awareness has led to a number of backward glances. We know what happened to highland Scottish farming following the deliberate introduction of the Red Deer, to parts of East Anglia after the accidental escape of a pair of coypus some forty years ago and to Australia after the rabbits arrived. But the decline of the ancient near Eastern civilisations is examined afresh also: catastrophic effects of earthquakes, political atrophy, religious wars—or perhaps these together with over-successful grain monoculture?

But for many people the present is alarming enough. The biological effects of above-ground testing of nuclear weapons and of the uses of drugs like thalidomide are sufficiently horrifying to draw world-wide attention and deep concern. But the less spectacular changes occurring all over the planet, although in themselves not so eye-catching, are perhaps more disturbing in combination. The most profound problems are also the oldest: the increasing numbers of mankind and the supplies of food and shelter. Beyond mere subsistence lie questions of the quality of life—bodily and mental health, happiness, fulfilment, joy. The ultimate source of all the benefits of life is the earth itself and man's relationship to all its life and resources.

One thing is becoming very clear: that man's life is intricately woven into the whole web of life on the earth (Wagner, 1960). His astonishing powers have not enabled him to 'control' nature in any categorical sense; merely to administer much more profound shocks or disturbances than ever before. But the interlocked nature of earthly relationships ensures at least the possibility of more profound *repercussions*—often coming from unexpected quarters and with long delays.

The idea that a more and more urbanised and artificial

human environment is less and less exposed to these repercussions is dangerously false. No matter how specialised our activities become, no matter how artificial their immediate environment, no matter how much local and immediate control may be exercised, we are part of the planet's ecology and we ignore this fact at our peril. The inhabitants of air-conditioned automated houses, the workers in electronics research laboratories, the riders in driverless trains, the users of international videophones, and those who play chess with computers need, as of old, food and water. They are also demanding second homes, huge areas of land and water for recreation and are moving materials, information and themselves about with increasing volume and frequency. 'Megalopolis' is here (Gottmann, 1961): the 40-million galaxies of human beings between Boston and Washington, Lancaster and Brighton are the emergent form of man's habitat (Hall, 1966). Visionaries like Doxiadis (1966) foresee an eventual link-up of these into the world-settlement, Ecumenopolis.

In many parts of the embryonic world-settlement, millions of men are living at subsistence level and below. Famine and disease are common-place in large areas of Africa, Asia, Southern and Central America. Both the migrations of some of these people to the wealthier areas and the support given by these more fortunate nations to those in distress make no appreciable difference. The awful truth is that most human beings on earth are very poor; a few are by contrast very rich and the gap is widening as the poorest multiply most rapidly while increasing their food supplies too slowly. Let us hope that the paternalistic and guilty concern of the few rich nations for the multitudinous poor is only the beginning of a long, sustained and more fundamental attack on the problem.

The solution must come about in two ways: in the first place there are the enormous ethical problems raised by the need to make choices and decisions affecting the relationships between men and all other forms of life and between different human groups; secondly there is the problem of understanding the nature of all those relationships in order to create more effective and sympathetic controls over the problem. This book is concerned with the aspect of understanding the complex systems of man's activities in the whole context of the planet's ecological systems. We must hope that greater understanding will be of help in the continuing debates and dialogues about the vexed ethical problems which are involved. For these latter super-vene: superior knowledge of how the world's ecology and man's place in it is structured, and the better control that should follow serves only to sharpen the points of the ultimate problems of value. The means beg the question of ends.

Fortunately there are now a number of signs of awareness, even though expediency may cause progress to be halting. Writing of the International Biological Programme, Anthony Tucker (1968) said that it 'has been described as the most am-bitious scientific programme ever undertaken for peaceful pur-poses. In a grand sense it is geared to the increasing need of mankind to understand and nurture the environment, rather than exploit it for means that are opportunist or, ultimately, out of the desperation of hunger. There is an astonishing lack of detailed knowledge of the interdependence of living systems, or of the impact of human activity on established systems. We do not know how to make use of the potential abundance of the sea, nor understand what it really means when apparently incidental species die because of some man-wrought change. But biologists and naturalists alike are unswerving in their certainty that before interfering any more seriously with existing complex living relationships an effort must be made to under-stand them . . . this is not simply a matter of learning, it is a matter of survival'.

All this may seem somewhat removed from the day-to-day problems of housing developments, parking, open spaces, the location of industry or the renewal of shopping centres. Quite the reverse is true. Whilst town and countryside were physically distinctive in the past, increasingly we live in a more regular and intimate contact with the whole of the earth's surface. For practical convenience we may distinguish 'urban' planning from 'regional' planning but in reality the problems we face are so integrated as to make it dangerous to take too circumscribed a view. The challenge is the need to *manage* the resources of the whole human environment, for man to 'create for himself a better relationship within nature if he is not to have an irre-trievably adverse impact on the environment' (Arvill, 1967).

This kind of awareness is now growing in the ranks of the

planning profession and among its client groups. But the fullest recognition of the nature of the problems and therefore of the means to tackle them are hindered to some extent by an accident of history. At the beginning of the present century it was becoming clear that there was a need for a new kind of professional skill, or a milieu for existing skills, to cope with the nineteenth-century towns and their continued rapid growth into the twentieth. In Great Britain, the most vociferous, articulate and well-organised bodies concerned were those with the construction and design skills of architecture, engineering and surveying, together with their colleagues in the legal profession. Although the recent infusion of other persons from different backgrounds—and especially geography, economics and the social sciences—has caused some changes of attitude there is still a considerable intellectual and practical inheritance from construction and design.

An underlying theme of this book is that a fundamental reorientation is needed in both the conceptual basis and the practical operations of planning. Whilst retaining the vitally important understanding of the operations of building, engineering and the measurement and transference of land, the profession needs a far greater awareness of the processes of change in the human environment, the underlying reasons for them, their manner of accomplishment, the complex web of interactions between human groups and much greater skill in the techniques of *foreseeing and guiding change*.

It is perhaps significant that one of the great sources of inspiration for physical planners was a biologist—Patrick Geddes—and that the title of his major work was 'Cities in Evolution' (Geddes, 1915). But much of his message has become garbled and, in the intervening half-century, man's habitats and his societies have undergone profound change; the time is ripe for a reassessment. The image of planning in the future must be drawn not so much from building as from gardening.

The idea of competiiton is central to ecology. Evolutionary theories of the development of species have concentrated on the struggle for survival and shown that long drawn-out processes of change in living creatures involving greater specialisation of skills in adaptation have produced the plant and animal kingdoms we know today. The process is still continuing and is likely to go on as conditions change and especially as man increases his powers.

Plants tend to multiply in conditions favourable to their growth whilst many animals have specialised their behaviour patterns and exhibit some locational specialisation in their activities. They have burrows and nests for domestic and reproductive functions, 'work areas' for food-gathering (in predators, these will be areas occupied by their prey), some animals, e.g. dolphins, monkeys and others seem to select or adapt areas suitable for play. Because different aspects of the creatures' life tend to occur in separate locations, they must travel between them and quite complex tracks or channels of communication can be discerned. These take a rich variety of forms: the salmon uses rivers to commute between the deep sea where he spends most of his 'working' life and the middle and upper reaches of fresh-water rivers where he breeds. The rabbit has well-marked tracks between his grazing areas and his living quarters.

The animal world displays a rich complexity of activities, locations and communications but if we consider any individual species the range of behaviour and spatial patterns is quite small. Relatively small brain-power and a consequently heavy reliance on instinctive response gives all but the 'highest' animals a very limited range of adaptability.

The evolution of *homo sapiens* shows a strong contrast. Possession of prehensile forepaws and a large brain has enabled man within less than half a million years to outstrip all the rest. The last ten thousand years has witnessed the rise of our species to a position of ecological domination. In the dawn of human development it seems that the differentiation of behaviour patterns and the adaptation of and to spaces was limited. Similarly, path habits would be restricted to linking areas for hunting and food-gathering with the living quarters.

The advance through cultivation and stock-rearing to civilisation was associated with and made possible by two linked developments. First, the emergence of the division of labour or specialisation of function whereby individuals and groups *within* a large unit (typically a kinship group, clan or tribe; later the urban community, still later the nation-state) were allowed and required to perform specialised duties, at first part-time and later on a full-time basis. Second, physical space was differentiated by man to accommodate these specialised activities and communications.

Thus some of the earliest villages of the barbarian farming communities show a social structure based on leadership and the release from hunting and farming duties of certain specialists, (e.g. artists, priests, magicians, potters, metallurgists). Equally we notice spatial separation of activities; dwellings, workshops, burial sites and other ritual locations. No doubt there were the inevitable communications in the form of *trails* and pathways both within and outside the settlement.

The first cities (Tigris-Euphrates, Indus and Nile valleys) show the process at a very advanced stage with highly specialised divisions of labour (usually in a hierarchical system) and equally rich and diverse buildings, spaces and communications channels.

Consider the situation now in the world's most advanced societies. The human animal has a very high degree of labour specialisation and the processes of further specialisation continue. Social organisation is similarly complex, so much so that an individual may play a large number of different rôles in different contexts of work, as well as in recreational, political and cultural groups and in domestic life. The specialisation of functions and rôles, changes in status, function and rewards, the power structure of societies, the relationships between individuals and groups, between themselves and of both with larger (e.g. national and supra-national) groups resembles an evolving kaleidoscope of great richness, diversity and complexity.

In parallel with this we observe the continued growth of greater specialisation in the use of the environment. Partly as a result of the successive specialisation of human activities and partly to enable it to occur, we are creating more and more specialised spaces. These are typified by buildings and enclosures of all kinds but include many other kinds of space. The varied kinds of forestry, farming, fishing, quarrying and mining are themselves specialised activities which either locate themselves (inevitably with e.g. fishing and mining) or adapt space to suit (e.g. ploughing, shelterbelt planting and fencing). Manufacturing and processing is demanding and obtaining very specialised and complex spaces, some of them highly differentiated and yet integrated into large and complex systems such as the modern vehicle assembly plant, chemical works (especially petroleum refining) and steelworks.

Similarly, distribution to wholesalers, retailers and consumers exhibits rapid change in methods and the differentiation and re-integration of activities whilst personal, social and domestic aspects of life are becoming very diverse indeed, particularly where real incomes are rising quickly.

Highly specialised activities carried out in specially suitable or adapted places at large numbers of separate locations have to be connected together. If they were not, man's economy and society would collapse in the extreme case. Where connections are poor, or temporarily absent, serious dislocations occur and the lives of individuals are reduced in scope.

Communications can be seen both as the consequences and the prerequisites of spatial separation of activities. The footways within the village and between the village and places outside become the streets of the early city, the great rivers, the conduits, the pipes and the written documents. From these times onwards we have successively improved communications and substituted one form for another. More efficient forms have ousted the less efficient which either disappeared or became used for less demanding purposes as when the railway replaced the canal as a bulk carrier for most, but not all purposes. A more important type of change is the substitution of non-material communications for those which involve the movement of people or goods as when telephone messages replace a personal journey or the carriage of mails. We should notice especially the *reciprocal* relationships between the location of activities and the growth of communications; spatial separation of activities requires communication between them, but the introduction of a means of communication may itself encourage that spatial separation.

We have identified three facets in the ecological process with particular reference to human affairs. First, the successive diversification and increasing complexity of rôles and functions and the contexts within which these are performed; second, as a consequence our great ability to create special 'habitats' for this very large range of activities whether by adaptation *to* physical space or the direct adaptation *of* space (typically building and engineering works); and third, the evolution of a rich

27

variety of communications which we need and enjoy in order to interconnect the locations of activities.

We must be quite clear that this division is made for discussion only—in fact these facets are intimately connected. The production and use of special spaces and places in which particular activities can be carried on is closely linked with the division of labour or specialisation of roles in human evolution; similarly, communications arise directly out of those processes and also enable them to proceed further.

So far we have partly outlined an ecological system (or *eco*-system) from the human standpoint. But to state that it evolves leaves an important question unanswered; why and how does it change? What provides the dynamism for its evolution? The answers derive from a look at an essential feature of eco-systems—*competitive behaviour*—which we shall interpret in human terms.

All living creatures, plant and animals, compete for the survival of their species and compete for conditions which will favour survival. A snake, to find food, must seek out those areas which his prey inhabits. He must find shelter from the rodents and birds which prey on him. He will use certain paths along which to range in search of his prey and which minimise his chances of being preyed upon. The complex set of relationships which exist is the ecology of that area. Consider now some disturbance of this system, let us say an increase in sparrow-hawks. More snakes will be eaten, the creatures on which the snakes prey will tend to survive and multiply. The increased numbers of small voles and shrews, frogs and mice will have their effects on grubs and insects, grasses and other plants. This may reduce the food supply and habitats of other creatures and plants and so on. The reader will be able to think of many other real or imaginary examples drawn from his own experience or reading.

Several points must be noticed. First the primary action of competitive behaviour (the sparrowhawk's search for meals), second, the sequence of responses in the eco-system which followed and third, that whilst the hawks, acting with self-interest, started the ball rolling the repercussions become quite complex and far-reaching, affecting many members of the living community who had perforce to make adjustments themselves. In fact, eco-systems tend to be self-regulating and reach equilibrium states known as *climax ecologies* in which the whole community of plants and animals, predators and prey, co-exist in a state of mutual interdependence. Climaxes can be disturbed by major forces only, such as climatic or geographical upheavals, or by the rise of a very superior animal. The Ice Ages provide examples of the former, the (geologically) recent rise of man exemplifies the latter.

For countless ages the world probably consisted of climax ecologies or eco-systems in which change was so gradual and protracted that they were for all practical purposes climaxes. Human evolution is so advanced and rapid (and apparently accelerating) that our species not only dominates the planet but, apart from a few isolated and inhospitable areas (e.g. the polar ice caps) and areas of very sparse population (e.g. central Australia, Northern Canada) eco-systems, with humans dominant, are evolving very rapidly indeed.

But the human species itself, in a position of almost complete dominance over the planet, is richly diversified. Our millions of individuals, with their complex groupings and multitudinous functions, needs, aspirations, our many activities and their locations, richly cross-connected and involved, in fact form a human *eco-system*. This, too, is driven forward in its evolution largely by competitive behaviour. Let us see how this happens. It will be helpful to use one or two cases as examples and then to conclude in general terms. Let us imagine first of all a small clothing manufacturing firm, With-it Weatherwear, Ltd. This is a highly competitive business and experience of the trade will have taught the proprietor, Mr. A. that certain things are important to him: he must be near wholesalers and retailers serving a large market; he must be in touch with the quicksilver process of changes in fashion; he must have raw materials in great variety and small or large quantities close at hand and there should be a large pool of partly-skilled casual labour (usually women) nearby.

Mr. A will always be scanning the world around and evaluating his position in it. We have already seen that the human eco-system comprises located activities occupying spaces which are interconnected by communications flowing in channels. Mr. A's part of the system consists for the most part of a suite of workrooms (1845 houses knocked about, Mr. A the seventh non-residential occupant since 1927) which he rents annually from an 80-year old widow. The most important and regular communications which flow to and from this space are (a) a daily trip by Jaguar from Mr. A's suburban home 4 miles away (b) a similar trip by Mini-van used by his 19-year-old son, A junior, who works in the business (c) about 20 trips by bus, bicycle and on foot by his all-female staff, most of whom live in obsolescent housing within a 2-mile radius (d) innumerable trips in the van by A junior to inspect materials in mills and warehouses and collect sample cloths etc. and also trips to wholesalers and retailers to show them With-it Weatherwear's latest offerings on the market. Most of these trips are of less than 2 miles, many of them are in and around the large city centre 1 mile away (e) a large number of telephone calls to mills, warehouses, wholesalers, retailers, mostly within ten miles (f) sense-data flowing into the premises include the ceaseless noise of traffic, the usually drab grey sky, air which is full of pollutants, altogether a dispiriting, even depressing environment. The A's and their workers seldom notice all this—having been inured to it. Their activities impinge on the passerby in similar fashion; there is a whirr of machinery, the building itself is drab and badly maintained, though its visual offence, being at the general level of the area, passes almost unnoticed. The coming of the Mini-van is more obvious.

There is much else we could describe; inputs of water, electricity, mails, parcel deliveries, outputs of sewage, garbage and so on. But we have sufficient for our purpose. We have in fact sketched in outline the *activity system* of With-it Weatherwear (Chapin, 1965).

Mr. A, like all of us, behaves competitively, scanning the world around and adjusting in an optimising fashion (or so he thinks). Many of these actions have little direct effect on his activity system; our concern is with those that do. Let us assume for example that over a period Mr. A has noticed that it has become increasingly difficult to recruit and retain his workers. He has tried increasing wages but this has had only a temporary effect. He now finds that the problem arises from local authority housing clearance and redevelopment at lower densities. Not only are there fewer women within easy reach of his factory, but they are paying more rent for their houses and have been pushed to seek better-paid jobs. Also, some of his most loyal employees have found housing much further away and face increased costs of bus transport to work. They will stay with him only until they can find work nearer their homes.

It also occurs to him that his rent is likely to be increased on the next renewal of lease since commercial values are rising as the city centre activities spread in his direction. There is the similar threat of parking meters. What is he to do? He must adapt somehow and in an optimal way. The changing pattern of home locations of his workers or potential workers suggests a move. But can he afford to move far away from the fashion-forming central area, from the wholesalers and retailers? An increased rent will cut into his profit margins. He must move —and in the direction of lower rents. To build new premises is out of the question—far too costly and 'tying up' of capital. Moving outwards would shorten his journey to work but the cost of this is trivial in relative terms. He would still have the telephone contacts, the postal services and so on. Parking for the Mini would be easier and trips by A junior would be only a *little* longer.

Yes, his mind is made up. Having weighed up all the likely alternatives and (for the most part intuitively) estimated the costs and benefits to the firm of each, he plumps for a move slightly further from the central business district, slightly nearer his labour supply and to an area of lower rents and much easier parking. From a number of possibilities he selects two adjoining terrace houses, spaciously built in 1870, knocks some party walls through and concretes over the scruffy garden at the front. Fortunately, the local Planning Authority was prepared to grant planning permission for five years for his light industrial use; the Housing Committee has this area next on the list for renewal.

Mrs. B, a widow in her late sixties, lives next door with her son and daughter-in-law. She was in fact born in the house and remembers that it was near the tram terminus and that 'you could look out over fields at the back as far as the hills'. The late Mr. B senior was manager of a small branch insurance office and since he died suddenly seven years ago, Mrs. B has supplemented her income by working in a confectionery shop in the centre of town. Her son, B junior, was apprenticed at a big electrical engineering firm six miles away and has worked there since. He is now 29 and his 24-year-old wife is expecting their first child. He travels to work by motor cycle and to the local College of Advanced Technology where he is studying for a diploma in management three evenings a week. He wants to 'improve himself', to buy a car and have holidays abroad. His wife gently suggests to him that they should buy a house, adding (out of her mother-in-law's earshot) that the area is 'going down' rapidly and it would be nice to have a garden for the baby.

Mrs. B senior is not unaware of the problem but hesitates to give any hint that she may wish to live with the young people. Moreover, any move would be a big wrench for her; she would not like to travel further to her job in the city, she is getting older and it is tiring enough, she has church, old friends and neighbours, the over-60's club and a lifetime's attachment to the area.

The arrival of With-it Weatherwear forces these and many other issues to a head. The area clearly is going down, the noise is increasing, women in curlers are seen arriving at 8.00 a.m., a Mini-van seems to be forever racing its engine to park outside or to roar off on dozens of seemingly life-and-death missions. Young Mrs. B (now the proud mother of a month-old child) is distracted because the baby is always being woken by these disturbances; Mr. B is so unsettled that his studies are suffering and he is increasingly concerned about his mother's future. A series of family conferences is held. A great deal of debate results in the decision to look for a modern 3-bedroomed bungalow at a price they can afford and in a convenient location. Weekends of searching and consultation of newspapers and estate agents ensues. Eventually everyone is satisfied. A local builder has a new bungalow in course of construction some seven miles from the centre of town. Public transport to the centre is not very good but there is the possibility that old Mrs. B will find a similar job in the growing shopping area on the estate. This is within walking distance. The longer journey for Mr. B to work (he has passed his exam and confidently expects promotion in the firm) is a little onerous being a somewhat tortuous and very congested ten miles. There was another bungalow, only slightly more expensive, rather closer to the works but what finally clinched the issue was the news that a new dual-carriageway road was shortly to be completed. This would lead from the vicinity of the new house to within 3 miles of his work, making his daily 'commute' much easier. (Also, thought the shrewd young B, house values would tend to rise.)

Before her marriage, the young Mrs. B was a keen tennis player and now that the baby was six months old, and the weather was fine she began to think of playing again. A neighbour invited her to join the local sports club. The club committee had a problem. In the 1920's when it was founded it had been rather 'exclusive', enjoyed a fine site, and had invested steadily over the years in pavilion, changing rooms, bar and dance floor, pitches, turf, courts and the like. Now population in the area was growing and new membership applications poured in. Tennis was a particular problem. It was increasingly popular and members were having greater difficulty in booking courts. The debate in committee ranged widely. Lay out another court? Out of the question, it would encroach on either the car park or the cricket field or both. Obtain facilities at another club? Unthinkably difficult and fraught with danger. Build more courts on a new site? Land was running short and being sold at 'very fancy' prices to builders and speculators—in any event it would cut down the social contact between members and involve players in journeys from the overflow court, back to the club headquarters. Sell up the whole site and start afresh? No, they would never recoup their great investment in the ground, and never find so attractive a location.

One committee member, an operations research manager, pointed out that many bookings were in fact never claimed and the club rules sometimes prevented the courts being used by others in the queue. He had done a little work on the problem and came up with a provisional solution. He explained that it was arrived at by 'linear programming', not many of the other members understood this but were swayed by his convincing assertion that in fact a revision of timings, the booking rules and a slight reduction in the playing of singles games could almost double the capacity of the present courts! The motion that this scheme be tried out for a season was carried unanimously. So Mrs. B had no difficulty in getting a game with her neighbour, though she heard older members grumbling about the revised booking arrangements. . . .

Our experience of the everyday world confirms the view that human relationships with the environment can be understood as an *ecological* or *eco-system* (Wagner, 1960). In terms of human behaviour we identify the components of the system as activities located in spaces. The activities interact or are connected by means of physical or non-material communications which flow through channels. The behaviour of individuals and groups is clearly competitive and is motivated by a constant scanning of the environment which from time to time results in action to modify either activities, spaces, communications, channels or some combination of these or their relationships.

Obviously these processes are complex both in themselves (i.e. for an individual or group) and in the ways in which they may be interwoven. But some structural simplification is necessary and possible. Chapin suggests that the individual or group is possessed of a certain set of *values* concerning relation-ships with the environment. These lead to *needs and wants* on the basis of which *goals* are formed which lead to the consideration of *courses of action*, a *decision* and *action*. This, when carried out modifies the relationship between the individual and his en-vironment but it may also alter the environment and the de-cision-maker. Values are thus modified and the cycle begins again. This complete cycle Chapin calls a *behaviour pattern* (Chapin, 1965, pp. 29–39 and 62–8).

We are concentrating here on the actions which individuals and groups may take. The imaginary examples we related, whilst sketched in simple outline, remind us that such actions are not simple but nevertheless certain elements can be dis-tinguished (McLoughlin, 1965).

First, in relation to the spaces within which activities occur, three elements are apparent:

(a) People may adapt their behaviour to enable them to improve the suitability of an existing space as did the sports club in relation to the tennis court problem. We will call this element of change *space-behavioural*.

(b) A more suitable space for the activity may be sought as in the case of With-it Weatherwear; this necessarily involves a change in location and is usually motivated by a desire to alter the pattern of spatial relationships between the activity and others with which it must interact. We will call these elements *space-locational* (Luttrell, 1962; Goddard, 1967).

(c) Building or engineering works may be used to modify or to construct afresh a space suitable for an activity. Examples abound: factories, warehouses, shops, offices, garages and residential buildings of all kinds; also playing fields, parks, stadia, and other outdoor works. The B family happened to resort to this in buying a new house (the builder having speculatively anticipated their 'commission'). We will call such elements *space-developmental*.

In similar fashion we can consider the connections or communications:

(a) A very familiar aspect of our lives is the way we adjust to the communication channels available to us. We drive on the left (in Britain), slow down in congested conditions and try to use the 'phone in off-peak periods; given a certain route we may change modes of transport in order to optimise e.g. we may abandon the car in favour of the bus; or we may use a combination of modes rather than one, e.g. train or aeroplane for part of a journey, car for the remainder. This element of change in communication behaviour we will call *channel-behavioural*.

(b) We are accustomed to seek the easiest path through a network of communications in order to minimise either distance or time or to increase the pleasurable qualities of the journey. The young Mr. A in his Mini-van would be an adept at this, knowing the city 'like the back of his hand'. He would undoubtedly adjust his routes to changing conditions, e.g. new traffic lights, one-way streets, a change of address by a customer and so on. When With-it Weatherwear moved he would have to adjust almost all his trips to new routes. So would the staff and Mr. A senior in his Jaguar. We will call this element of change *channel-locational*.

(c) Finally, for many reasons, new channels of communication are needed from time to time. Transport technology may require them (railways in the nineteeth century), new materials or energy may have to be shipped (e.g. pipelines and the electricity grid in the twentieth century). More familiar is the build-up of demand for movement along certain paths requiring expansion of channel capacities (e.g. the dual-carriageway road which young Mr. B will use when it is completed). We will call this element *channel-developmental*.

We must stress that these six elements are drawn out for convenience of exposition only. They are very seldom found in isolation; our examples indicate that. For instance, whilst the A's firm made what was predominantly a space-locational change some space-developmental change was present (knocking down walls, concreting the forecourt), and a good deal of channel-locational change ensued, especially in the van trips and the machinists' journeys to work. The B family plumped for action that was partly space-developmental and partly space-locational but obviously many other elements were associated. The sports club's alteration of the way in which the tennis courts could be used was almost purely space-behavioural.

In reality the actions we take in modifying the environment and our relationships with it are mixes of a great number of elements. These mixes vary greatly according to who is taking action, in what sort of society, how powerful and wealthy or weak and poor he may be, whether the action is taken by a family, a social club, a firm or an individual. These mixes will also contain varying amounts of irrationality; in other words not all aspects of human behaviour can be explained in formal terms, there are usually irrational and random elements in our activities. But we believe that the six broad elements we have given are sufficient to help in a preliminary understanding and we encourage the reader to interpret his own actions and other aspects of the world around him in these terms.

One final point must be stressed which derives directly from the eco-system approach we are using and which is essential to much of the later material in this book: the chain-reaction manner in which the system evolves. We saw how the increased numbers of hawks triggered this off in our earlier examples. In the later discussion of With-it Weatherwear etc. we saw how the introduction of Mr. A's workshops next door to Mrs. B and her family finally brought about a move and how, partly in consequence of the young Mrs. B's liking for tennis the club had to modify its internal arrangements. Let us be clear about this; we are *not* saying that With-it Weatherwear's action was the sole cause of Mrs. B moving house, or that, had it not been for young Mrs. B's desire for a game of tennis, the rearrangements in the club would never have come about.

What we *are* saying, and the point is vital, is that *optimising action taken by an individual or group at a particular time has repercussions which alter the context for decisions to act by other individuals or groups at subsequent times*. Whenever we take action in our environment in our own interest (or appoint agents to act for us) repercussions spread out like ripples when we throw a stone into a pool. These ripples are effects on communications, channels, spaces and activities. They merge with the ripples persisting from other previous actions, they ebb and flow, compound and dissipate in complex ways. But they *alter the state of the system* and thus they alter the basis on which the next action will be made, or they push someone over the threshold of taking action, or they affect the type of action taken.

Very large numbers of decisions are being made by the multitude of individuals and groups compromising human society. Their actions set up complex repercussions in the ecological system. We may think of these actions and repercussions (and further actions based on them, ad infinitum . . .) as forming a ceaseless flow of change through time (Hoover, 1948, Chapter 9). Since this is boundless and occupies the whole of the eco-system we will call it *systemic change*. This affects all members of the human (and animal and plant) community for good and ill since we are all involved in our own eco-system. We shall say later that planning must seek to guide and control systemic change but before we do so, we must look more closely at how individual and group actions to modify the environment are motivated and constrained and how they are carried out.

2

Modifying Actions and the Environment

The objectives of action

Chapter 1 discussed in general terms and by the use of imaginary examples some of the motivations people feel towards the environment and their relationships to it and some of the actions they may take to improve their relationships. We identified three main elements in the whole spectrum of change which people undertake or consider – developmental, locational, and behavioural – and we saw that these could be applied to people's activities and the spaces in which they occur on the one hand and to their communications and channels in which these flow on the other.

In this chapter we go a little deeper into the underlying motives for such actions, the range of possible courses of action (as seen by the 'actors'), the opportunities and constraints which define those possible courses, the actual methods by which actions are carried out whether by the actor himself or by agents whom he appoints and the ways in which the actor (either alone or on the advice of his agents) evaluates the alternatives which appear to confront him and chooses which course to pursue.

This chapter is concerned first with the objectives which the actor seeks. It was clear in Chapter 1 – and everyday experience suggests – that human actions are extremely complex in their motives.

As planners we are interested in only a small segment of the motivations which drive individuals and groups. They wish to be educated, to earn a living, to marry and have children, to enjoy their leisure time, to express themselves in creative activity. To a greater or lesser degree much of the vast canvas of an individual's life is 'place-related'–that is, certain activities and communications occur at certain locations and along certain routes in a regular and patterned way. The more regular and patterned (i.e. in both time and space) human activities are, the more they are susceptible to certain kinds of analysis and the more they are the concern of the planner.* We are concerned then with the motivations which people feel because of dissatisfactions (however slight) with these *place-related* aspects of their lives: with the suitability of the spaces within which they carry on their activity (house, school, factory, shop etc.) by virtue of the benefits they enjoy as compared with the costs that are incurred; with the suitability of the location in relation to all other located activities with which frequent interaction is necessary thus incurring a set of interaction costs which may be compared with the resulting benefits.

Put another way, any particular activity (residence, work, recreation, etc.) being carried on at a particular location (this house, this office, that sports club) has a set of costs and a set of benefits at any time. Both the costs and the benefits have two elements: those which arise from the nature of the activity and the kind and quality of the space in which it is carried on we refer to as *activity costs and benefits*; those which relate to the interactions with many other activities at other locations we shall call *communication costs and benefits*. We shall deal a little later with the problems encountered in defining and measuring these costs and benefits and comparing them. Our present purpose is simply to suggest that activities which people decide on by way of altering their relationships with the physical environment (as discussed in Chapter 1) arise because they believe that in carrying on their particular activity in the present space and at the present location the ratio of total benefits to costs is moving in their disfavour (Lichfield, 1956, Chapters 1–11).

We have seen that there are a number of elements in the form of action that arises: behavioural changes alter the nature of the

* Many activities are regular and patterned–eating meals, going to bed, having a bath, the playing of a football game (the patterning of the activities *inside* the stadium)–yet are not the direct concern of the planner but rather of the architect, the engineer, the football club manager and the lawyer.

activity itself or the 'mix' of communication modes employed for interaction with others, developmental changes make physical-form alterations to the space (building, etc.) within which the activity is housed or to the channels which carry communications whilst locational changes occur when the activity seeks a new location or the communications are re-routed through the network of channels.

We stressed in Chapter 1 that these were elements which usually occur in many different combinations and seldom in a 'pure' form. Here we would add that the type of modifying actions considered or chosen and the sequence in which a number of elements in the total action are carried out will depend on the nature of the activity itself and the space in which it is housed, the social, political, legal and economic context of the activity and the 'actor', the precise nature, dimension and incidence of the relevant costs and benefits, the nature and quality of the communication opportunities which are available and the personal collective tastes and whims of the individual or group 'actor'.

For example, a family man who feels his house is too small has the choice of building an extension (developmental change), re-organising the household's activities within the existing house (behavioural change), or moving to a larger house (locational change). A wholesale grocer faced with a similar problem has a similar range of choices open to him. But the choice of type of action or of the sequence of actions for both of them depends on the type of activity (what sort of family is it, in terms of size, ages, income, etc., what sort of wholesale grocery?) the nature of the spaces (number of rooms, quality of structure and so on in the house, floorspace, hoists, lifts, ventilation, refrigeration and so on for the warehouse) the alternative houses and warehouses available, the communications available at all those alter-natives, the social and economic background within which both men must operate and their personal ('subjective') preferences about place-related and other aspects of their lives.

Identifying the possible courses of action
It is very difficult to generalise about the ways in which house-holds, firms and other corporate bodies identify the possible courses which are open to them when they seek to change their

situation because of the very great diversity of activities and people we are trying to consider. It is this diversity which makes the human environment complex. In the long term we must hope for much more research into decisions of this kind and the human motivations behind them. But even though we are ill-suppliedwith such knowledge we should remember that it is the *effects* of the subsequent actions with which the planner must deal. This being so, it is perhaps sufficient here not to attempt anything like a comprehensive review of a very wide range of activities and decision-makers but rather to give a few illustrative examples.

By far the most numerous of decision-makers are households, and residential activity is the biggest single user of urban land. The householder or family man has a number of characteristic ways of reviewing the courses open to him. He may first think of developmental changes—buying an adjoining plot of land if he wants more garden space or selling (or leasing) if he has too much, building on an extension if he wants extra room in the house, installing a heating system and so forth. He identifies these opportunities largely on the basis of his experience and that of friends and colleagues, the influence of mass media urging or suggesting what he could or should do, consulting with professional advisers such as architects, and engineers and tradesmen of various kinds, all of whom give general advice as well as drawing up more detailed recommendations for the householder's consideration.

When considering locational change his problems are different. His field of choice at first appears vast but is quickly reduced by reference to the price-ranges of houses available, the areas which he regards as desirable in terms of access to his work, to shops, to schools and in terms of its social and aesthetic character (Wilkinson and Merry, 1965). Even when the problem is thus narrowed down the task of selecting a 'short-list' can be formidable. Information is the main difficulty here. Houses on the market are advertised in numerous ways: privately, by the vendor pasting a notice in his window or advertising in the press; or by the employment of an estate agent. Even in small or medium-sized town the person seeking accommodation must search through a multitude of different information sources to make sure he has covered the field. Many people accept that to attempt a comprehensive review would be too difficult and time-consuming and partially self-defeating since a good prospect which *is* known may be bought by someone else while the poor seeker is trying to find out if other suitable houses are available!

Clearly the 'classical' economic notion of perfect competition in the market, depending as it does on perfect *information* to all buyers and sellers simply will not hold water when one examines the housing market. A point we take up elsewhere (Chapter 3) is that, accepting this, the idea that house purchasers make 'sub-optimal' choices, i.e. ones which are admittedly not the best possible, is a more realistic one. Also such decisions can usefully be interpreted as moving away from an unsatisfactory position—making a tangible *improvement*—rather than the attainment of the *best possible* situation.

Behavioural change in the household is most difficult of all to discuss since it is so frequent and small-scale. But certain examples of more substantial change can be given. Rearrangement of activities within the house, the use of rooms for new purposes, the letting of spare rooms to lodgers or 'paying guests', are examples of decisions requiring some deliberation and which alter the way in which the space is used, perhaps obviating the need for altering the house physically or for removing to a new home. Such decisions are reached most often by discussion of a few alternatives within the household, with or without the advice of bank managers, solicitors or friends.

The small firm, in manufacturing, wholesale or retail distribution, personal or professional services goes about the problem of identifying possible courses of action in ways which are not dissimilar from those of the household, except that professional and other expert advice may more often be used (Luttrell, 1962). This is not only because being in business or professional life makes the firm more aware of the benefits of skilled specialist knowledge but also that expenditure incurred in obtaining such advice may be allowable as an expense for tax purposes—a remission not usually enjoyed by the householder. Furthermore, even for small firms the material risk inherent in making decisions is greater than for most households. As we saw in Chapter 1 small firms, like households, may consider physical development, relocation or changes in their operations and methods as elements in a number of alternative possibilities amongst which they will choose.

The large firms, with even more at stake in such matters tend to give more lengthy and elaborate consideration to these issues. The final decision will rest with the board of directors who will wish to have the essence of thoroughly worked-out alternatives presented to them. Such reports may have involved months, even years of internal debate and investigation backed up by expert study by specialists within the firm. Generally speaking, larger firms have more experts available within their staff—lawyers, accountants, the construction and design skills as well as their production, research and marketing staffs—but even they will have recourse to consultants over particular issues requiring highly specialised knowledge; for example, advice on the taxation laws of a foreign country in which investment is being considered.

Public bodies—local governments and departments of state, public corporations and the nationalised industries—tackle their problems in much the same way as firms of similar size. Differences arise in the isolation of alternative courses in so far as their motivations are unlike those of the private sector—the absence of a profit motive and of a market mechanism, reflecting supply and demand for services—and because much of the expert advice upon which they must call is available in other public departments who are charged with the responsibility for giving the necessary assistance (Lichfield, 1956, Chapter 18). For example, most acquisitions of real property by local governments must have the approval of the District Valuer of the Department of Inland Revenue who is able to give advice on what are reasonable prices for a number of alternative pieces of land which are under consideration. If a government department is seeking new accommodation, the advice of architectural and other staffs of the Ministry of Public Buildings and Works will be obtained on several alternative possibilities, perhaps including adapting, converting, buying or leasing existing premises, as well as tentative estimates for new building.

Constraints on possible action
Nearly all actions aimed at altering the environment, our relationships with it, or the ways in which we carry out activities

or communications are limited or constrained in several ways.

Some constraints on freedom of action are due to nature: the nature of rocks and subsoil, the slope and aspect of land, the incidence of strong winds, the presence or absence of sunshine and rainfall, the probability of flooding, of storms and of land-slips are all examples of natural constraints. Sometimes man's actions contribute to a 'natural' constraint as when mining causes subsidence or instability of the surface, engineering works increase flood hazards, and imprudent agriculture causes soil erosion.

Many natural constraints can be mitigated or even removed by engineering works–drainage schemes, flood prevention, and slope stabilisation, but obviously the climate of an area is not (as yet!) capable of being modified though its effects may be reduced by the appropriate design of works. Significant protection against natural hazards and the overcoming of major difficulties posed by landform and topography will always call for considerable capital investment. That is why such measures are usually taken by the community at large and also why a number of alternative schemes are commonly devised and tested for benefits and costs before a decision is reached (see the concluding section of this chapter, below) by both public and private developers.

Constraints or limitations on possible action also arise because of the presence of activities on the land or investments to enable activities to occur. It is more difficult to acquire land already occupied and used intensively (by housing, or shops or industry) than land which is either unused, derelict or in a highly extensive use such as grazing or forestry. To a very large extent these relative difficulties are expressed in the market price of land in the existing use (and leaving aside for the moment legal and administrative restrictions on its *potential* use which is mentioned below). The greater the intensity of the use of land and the higher the investments that have been made in the land and its associated structures, plant and capital equipment–in short, the higher the degree of 'adaptation' to a particular activity–the greater the price that must be paid either to convert it to another (and presumably more profitable) use or to re-use the investment for a similar activity.

Limitation can also arise because of difficulties with communications. A possible site may have much to commend it—it may be the right size, with suitable levels, aspect and local climate, be suitably drained and otherwise provided with a whole range of utility services, and yet so disposed in relation to other activities with which frequent interactions are necessary as to make it unsuitable for the particular use in question. Moreover, the site may be geographically near to the locations of those other activities and yet inconveniently placed in relation to road, rail, pipeline, telephone and other channels of communication which are needed. As before, these characteristics will be reflected in the price which is offered for the site by any intending user.

A highly complex web of constraints is imposed on the use of land by the law and administrative regulations of all societies—whether 'advanced' or otherwise (Heap, 1965). These have grown up gradually over long periods of time, usually in response to pressing problems as they arose. They form complex accretions of statute, 'common' law, case law and administrative precedent which require the exercise of incisive professional minds to unravel in many instances. Planning law and administration is a relative newcomer to this scene standing alongside a vast labyrinth of older forms of land law and regulation over construction and use.

Finally there are limits placed on the use of land which arise from a society's mores as applied to the environment (not all of which have been formalised as laws or regulations). Most of these govern the *manner* in which activities are carried on—the amount of noise they make, the fumes and smoke they emit, the vehicular traffic they attract, or the appearance of buildings and plant to house the activity. Many of these limitations are embodied in the common law (e.g. of torts, nuisances and misfeasances) and the statute law (e.g. on building standards and the emission of effluents). Planning in Britain has taken upon itself to regulate the appearance of certain developments by administrative procedures under the planning Acts and a great deal of negotiation is carried on about the design and layouts of buildings and other proposals between planning officials and intending developers.

There are two interrelated frameworks within which we can

study these various constraints on the freedom of action of the developer (or locator or actor): the market and the law.

The market price of a site will reflect the constraints imposed by natural conditions, by the presence of investment in the land to support present activities and the costs of removing or mitigating these limitations; the constraints imposed by law (and especially planning law) cannot easily be removed and these too will be reflected in the price of the land.

The intending developer must discover the extent of all these various constraints so that he knows the area within which he can manoeuvre and draw up his alternative schemes from which he will select a course of action.

Agencies and Methods

Whatever kind of change is contemplated–involving development, relocation, or changes in the nature of the activity whether singly or in combination–only those which are trivial will be carried out directly by the person or group concerned. Almost always a greater or lesser number of advisors, agents, contractors and others will be involved at some or all stages of the process of change.

We have already mentioned the sorts of advice which are sought in the period *before* change occurs–in the stage of exploring the possibilities of different courses of action. The lawyer will advise on both the precise points of law affecting different alternatives and give his considered opinion (or seek counsel's specialised advice) on more obscure issues; the accountant and the banker will give their support or advise caution in respect of various alternatives; the financier will indicate the extent to which he is prepared to provide funds for the project, other companies may be involved in complex operations together with their own advisers. In recent years specialised consulting firms have grown up offering 'package deal' advice tailored to individual problems and drawing on the skills of staff members qualified in economics, law, accountancy, operations research and many other fields. The duration, extent and complexity of these preliminaries will vary with the nature and scale of the project: a man seeking to build a private house may spend a few weeks discussing his problem with his bankers, his solicitor and his architect, whilst a chemical firm thinking of building a plant in a foreign country may well spend years in extremely detailed investigation and negotiation.*

Development cannot occur until a site is owned or a leasehold interest secured and all statutory and administrative procedures completed and impediments removed. At this stage the key advisers are still the lawyer and the construction and design professions, e.g. architect, landscape architect, engineer and surveyor. The building or engineering contractor will certainly have been consulted at the stage of site election among alternatives; once a specific site is chosen the contractor will have begun his own detailed appraisal of how to tackle the (possibly complex) job of organising his operations on the ground. Here too the 'package deal' is emerging whereby firms offer an integrated legal/economic/financial/design/construction/equipping and maintenance service to the client; the advantages of such 'one-stop' forms of service are obvious. Development of communication channels involves similar skills and advice though in many countries post, rail, air and road transport, power transmissions, water supply, drainage, etc., are to a very great extent publicly owned and controlled, and this results in advice being exchanged and evaluated within and between departments of the public service rather than between private individuals or firms and independent professional advisers and other commercial undertakings. Public developers (as mentioned earlier) either have a public department available to carry out the actual works or invite tenders from suitable public contractors in the same way as would a private developer.

Newer forms of communication (e.g. pipelines, telemetric control, closed-circuit television, radio-telephony, etc. etc.) have given rise to a great variety of new professional skills which are in a state of rapid evolution.

Locational change, removal or relocation must very often be preceded by similar sorts of advice as in the case of development. The new accommodation must be free from legal difficulties, economic appraisals will have been necessary, and finance available for the purchase of the freehold or a lease, and for any necessary adaptation (a 'developmental' change, of course). Again the simplicity or complexity of the process of gathering

* See for example *The Times* (Business News) 25 October 1967. 'The Brighton Marina case'.

the advice depends on the nature of the relocation or removal. A student or single girl moving from one bed sitting-room or flat to another may simply consult her parents, friends and bank manager, whilst a County Council with staff numbering 500 or 1,000 moving from city centre premises to a specially-built suburban office 'campus' faces a rather more complex operation needing considerably greater breadth and depth of advice and preparation.

The operation itself is performed by one sort of agency only – the removal contractor–but an agency which takes a great variety of forms.The single girl will 'contract' with her boy-friend or her father to transport her few personal belongings a few miles or street blocks; at the other end of the scale specialised firms with many years experience offer their services in moving a family's household effects in one smooth operation halfway round the world, involving packing, crating, storage, road transport to docks, loading, insurance in transit, unloading, transport to final destination and unpacking; often such an operation involves the use of agents and sub-contractors both at 'home' and in the country of destination.

There are, however, activities which can relocate with the greatest of ease where no physical movement of materials occurs. When a motor-cycling or car club changes the regular venue for its meetings from Mr. A's fields to part of Lord B's estate, little or no physical removal may be needed–yet the activity has been relocated just as surely as the 'bed-sitter' girl changed her residence or the County Council its offices.

Behavioural change is characterised by the use of rather more 'internal' advice. Families rearranging their pattern of living inside a house to accommodate Grandma or increasing amounts of homework, discuss the problem amongst themselves and may shift the furniture about, altering the heating and lighting arrangement, put up a few extra shelves and build in a cupboard with little or no recourse to 'outside' aid.

Behaviour in the use of communications systems perhaps illustrates the point in its purest form. We ourselves usually consider and decide a route to work in the car, or choose to telephone later, to catch an earlier train, to deliver the Christmas presents personally rather than to send them by post, without recourse to 'outside' advice.

48

But matters are not so simple in larger organisations where the internal workings of manufacturing and commercial firms, local government, universities and national legislatures may be the subject of increasingly sophisticated *operations research* advice. The acceptance of such recommendations may involve the organisation in considerable re-structuring of its whole pattern of operations (which may in part 'spill over' into subsequent developments and relocations) or internal behaviour. The executive agency for such changes is usually the organisation itself—the directors, management and staff of a firm, and academic and administrative staff in a university—aided to a greater or lesser degree by the operations research advisers who may themselves be either members of the organisation or (more frequently) consultants whose independent advice has been sought.

Evaluation and choice of modifying actions
We have now discussed the motivations which drive the actor to consider modifying his relationships with the environment, the ways in which he identifies possible courses open to him, the opportunities and constraints which influence him and the methods by which he seeks to carry out his intentions (either directly or through appointed agents).

It now remains to say a little about the way in which he chooses a particular course. Earlier we suggested that there are two sets of costs and benefits which apply to the actor carrying on a particular activity at a particular location: *activity* costs and benefits which relate to the activity itself in the particular space (building, area of land, enclosure) including rents, interest, depreciation, rates, repairs, wages and salaries, professional charges and so forth, and the benefits derived from that particular space, and *communication* costs and benefits (related to the location of the activity in relation to others) such as vehicle travelling costs, telephone charges, rail fares and air fares, together with the benefits or convenience associated with all these interactions.

We noted earlier that this is an arbitary distinction—for example the wages paid to employees might be regarded as an activity cost, but the fact that they may include a small element reflecting the difficulties of attracting workers to a location which is inconvenient to reach by various modes of transport suggests that this element is a communication cost—but it is nevertheless useful for purposes of discussion.

In general we have assumed that the actor's objective is to seek that location and that space for his activity which minimises his total (activity and communication) costs whilst maximising his total benfits; in other words, that *optimal* situation which maximises his benefits/costs ratio. It follows that his evaluation of possible courses of action and his choice will be made by assessing the costs and benefits of the alternatives which he considers.*

When a modifying action is contemplated the actor will begin by exploring, at a 'reconnaissance' level the opportunities that are available to him. The ways in which this is done are almost as varied as human activities themselves. One actor will begin by considering locational change and will ring up estate agents and ask them to report on suitable premises which are on the market. Another will just consider developmental change and call in his architect to discuss draft plans for rebuilding, extension or internal alterations. Still others will consider changes in their 'communications mix' issuing edicts forbidding long-distance telephone calls, consulting trade union representatives on the possible withdrawal of free transport services for workers, re-negiotiating rates and conditions with haulage contractors, seeking new sources (locations) of bulky raw materials. And yet others will first think of changes in the nature of their activity—volumes of production, office hours, range of services provided or goods traded.

The sequence and relative emphasis with which these aspects of change are considered will depend in large part on the nature of the activity itself but also to some extent on the personal (or collective or institutional) whims and fancies of the actor. One central-area small shopkeeper will first consider relocation when a rise in rents is mooted whilst his neighbouring competitor will stick it out by making different adjustments because he likes the view of the street from his shop window.

* What we have just stated (though using different terms) is in effect the foundations of the 'classical' theories of the location of economic activity or the location of the firm. We shall discuss these, and their inherent difficulties and the objections which have been raised in a more suitable context in Chapter 3 which follows.

In the 'classic' theories of location, an equilibrium condition was assumed in which each activity was optimally located. Thus, equilibrium was reached by a long series of individual moves in which each actor acted 'rationally' to optimise his circumstances. This rationality was based on the assumption of perfect information–that is, comprehensive knowledge of all the available opportunities for changing his situation. As objections to the classic theories have long since pointed out, and as common knowledge indicates, no one has such 'perfect' information. Anyone who has searched for a house to buy knows that of all the traumatic experiences which attend on this operation, perhaps the most extreme is being constantly haunted by the feeling that one simply cannot know of *all* the suitable houses that are on the market. This fear is frequently given sharp confirmation when, the day after concluding a deal (thankful the whole wretched business is over) one finds a superior house at a lower price on offer in the next street!

But there is another way in which information on alternative possible courses of action is imperfect. Consider the complexity of the alternatives (rebuilding, extensions, cutting down labour costs, moving etc., etc.) and the countless permutations and combinations which might *in theory* be examined; in practise the actor can consider only a very limited number of discrete possibilities. These will arise in a number of ways: in the matter of relocation they will be a selection of the suitable buildings or sites on the market, in the matter of conversions, adaptions or extensions of the present building or site they will be 'schemes A, B and C' which the actor and his advisers draw up, limited by time, error, energy and '*imagination*'. This latter point is important–the literature on decision theory points out that decision-makers have a field of choice which is in part at least circumscribed by their own range of experience, direct or indirect, and that this is a product of their upbringing, education and personal qualities.

In practice then, a limited number of alternative courses will present themselves for consideration and in general, evaluation will proceed along the following lines.

The lists of costs and benefits which follow are illustrative only and given to help understanding of the principles involved; an exhaustive listing for all activities is virtually impossible in any case.

(a) ACTIVITY COSTS
  (i) Mortgage redemption and interest charges.
  (ii) Chief rents, head rent or feuduty.
  (iii) Leasehold charges, interest on loans.
  (iv) Annual building rents.
  (v) Repairs, maintenance, decoration, etc.
  (vi) Heating, lighting, power, cleaning.
  (vii) Rates and other taxes.
  (viii) Professional charges.
  (ix) Raw materials, components, etc. (manufacturing, assembly).
  (x) Plant, equipment, etc. (construction, recreation).
  (xi) Wholesale supplies (retailing, etc.).
  (xii) Food, clothing, school fees, etc. (residential).
  (xiii) Wages and salaries (economic activities).

For any *established* activity (we shall consider the case of *changes* in a moment) some or all of these costs must be incurred though in proportions which vary between activities at a location and for the same activity at different locations. And since we are concerned at the moment with established activities, those not undergoing significant change by relocation, development, etc., all of the costs may be expressed as outgoings per annum or other unit of time. For any activity the total of these we define as the activity cost at that location and in that space.

Now consider the problem of change under the three headings derived earlier—developmental, locational and behavioural.

Developmental change: Here, the actor must take into account a number of costs for all of the alternative schemes which he and his professional advisers draw up. Lichfield (1956) has provided a useful listing of the costs which will have to be borne. These include: the acquisition of land; the legal preparation of the site; the physical preparation of the site; the construction of roads, sewers and services, planting; the construction of buildings and the interest on capital during the construction process. Against these costs he will be able to set the proceeds from the sale of his present premises if he is vacating them; in many cases however the development may be an addition, alteration or extension of his present premises. If he is considering alternatives, adaptation of his present premises and the construction of completely new accommodation may figure among them. He will also have to estimate the changed *annual* costs which these capital costs entail; indeed, he may usefully convert all estimated costs to a fresh set of annual costs for each alternative so as to afford direct comparisons with his current total activity cost.

Locational change: Many of the changed costs incurred by such change are obviously *communication* costs which we deal with later. The activity costs include the costs of the removal operation itself, the loss of business and trade, other disturbance costs such as the disconnection and reconnection of utility services, telephones, etc., the redirection of mail, advertisement of change of address and telephone number. Once again it will be necessary to consider the costs of rents, rates, mortgage charges, repairs, maintenance, legal expenses, utilities and all other relevant matters for the new premises in similar fashion to developmental change. As before all costs may be converted to annual costs.

Behavioural change: These include all the costs incurred by significant change in the nature of the activity itself or in the way in which it is carried on. For example–when a mineral operator changes to a new method of extraction (e.g. mechanised and automated coal mining), or when a manufacturer re-tools all or some of his processes, or when a wholesaler redesigns his storage space and methods of stocktaking and handling, or when a retailer converts to 'self-service', or when a large family decides to use the bedrooms as sitting-rooms for children–in all these 'behavioural' change occurs (with or without any development or relocation) and certain costs are incurred. As with other aspects noted earlier all such costs may be expressed in annual terms.

(b) COMMUNICATION COSTS
These include:
  (i) Shipment of raw materials to and finished products from the site of manufacture; transfer of components between sites.
 (ii) Shipment of wholesale goods to a retail outlet.
(iii) Deliveries of retail goods to consumers.
(iv) Postal, telephone and teleprinter costs.

(v) Radio and (closed circuit) television costs.
(vi) Part or full payment of costs of workers' travel from homes.
(vii) Household members' trips for business, school, shopping, social and recreational purposes.
(viii) Household postal and telephone costs, etc.

As with activity costs, some or all of these will be incurred because of the interactions which any activity must have with others at different locations – personal trips, mail, phone calls and so forth. The sum of these elements in a unit time (e.g. a year) we call the communication cost.

Consider now the problem of change:

Developmental change: this is an unusual element in change since most of us do not build roads, railways and airports but rely on public corporations or departments of government to do it on our behalf (and, indirectly at our expense by way of taxation). But those public corporations which construct communication channels – the Ministry of Transport's motorways, the Central Electricity Generating Board's major distribution network of overhead and underground cables – do face the problem of deciding on routes, construction techniques and specifications. In so doing they are under two sets of pressures which often conflict; 'internal' pressures deriving from their need to satisfy criteria of cost-effectiveness and possibly the demands of competitive tendering and 'external' pressures coming from all sides and including the interests of landowners, residents, amenity societies, schools, other public corporations and departments of state, all of whom may object that the chosen route for a motorway or overhead electricity line is harmful to their interests or to the common weal.

Such cases have given rise to some confusion over terms in recent years. Those who are charged with the (statutory) duty to supply electricity and build motorways, have often felt sincerely that the 'public interest' was best served by carrying out each development at minimum costs. To others, and especially to planners with their 'comprehensive' traditions and their 'synoptic' view of the environment, the public interest was served by having electricity and motorways, but not in disregard of a host of other values including the effects on people, on the location of other activities, on the way in which a town might evolve and on the aesthetic qualities of the whole environment containing the proposed channels.

In recent years the interpretation of the public interest by certain public corporations has become notably more liberal (this is especially true of the C.E.G.B.), but even so it is clear that the discharge of statutory duty at minimum cost (to the ratepayer, ultimately) is still the principal criteria used by most public bodies.

Obviously, measuring the benefit/cost ratio is the main criteria for choice among alternative designs for a channel by private developers—for example, oil companies' pipelines and private railways.

Locational change in the case of communications means taking a different route through a network of channels in order to try to improve a particular interaction. The most familiar example (and of enormous significance for city planning) is that of the behaviour of the car driver travelling between home and work or on business trips between several calling-points. Weather and traffic conditions, the time of day, the day of the week and the season, and also a 'personal whim' element affect the driver's choice of the particular route he takes among several alternative possibilities. His criteria are little understood and the traditional economic explanations of minimising cost are obviously inadequate since there is some evidence to suggest that car drivers especially respond to only part of their true costs— typically petrol and oil—and not to the whole costs of motoring as apportioned to each particular trip. But, moreover, convenience and especially *time* as well as other intangible elements such as the view from the road clearly enter into the choice of route through a network.

In different ways these remarks apply to commercial vehicle journeys also. Lorry or truck drivers choose routes which take account of congestion (and therefore time and convenience), and the presence of favourite cafés and stopping places where pleasant company and food add to the 'benefit' side of their personal calculus.

All decisions about choice of route through a network are affected by changing conditions in the network in so far as these are known to the driver. Persistent additional congestion on a particular road, prolonged road works causing delays, the closing down or opening of amenities along a route, the opening of improved stretches of road will tend to alter the choice of route.

In all cases, the decision is made so as to maximise the benefits in relation to the costs of the trip as known to, and as experienced by the particular driver.

Behavioural change: This is the element of change in interaction patterns which occurs when, given no change in the network geometry nor in the choice of route through it, the actor alters his communication behaviour in order to try and improve the benefit/cost ratio for that interaction. The most common examples are to change the *mode* of communication and the *time* at which it occurs. If a firm discovered that delays were occurring in its deliveries to customers by using public road or rail goods services it might buy its own fleet of vehicles and carry out its own deliveries. Or changing commercial conditions may cause a company to stop sending consignments by rail and to use air freight transport instead. A professional man may find that traffic densities on the motorway network have increased so much as to make his travelling more unpleasant and subject to embarrassing delays that he is persuaded to travel by train; after a number of months using trains the rail authorities discontinue cheap rates of travel before 09.30 and so he rearranges his professional life so that he travels after that time as often as possible, to take advantage of the reduced fares.

The costs of activity and communication

To carry out any form of activity–be it residential, commercial, recreational, industrial or educational–means that costs such as those discussed above must be incurred. In return, benefits–enjoyment, satisfaction, profits, the giving of service and the discharge of duty–accrue to the family, the firm, the corporation or the association. The lists and examples given are illustrative only; life is more complex and richly diverse than these selective examples suggest. But the general principle remains: whoever carries out an activity tries to keep the total costs of the activity (at its location) and of the communications with other activities at a minimum when compared with the benefits which arise. When circumstances change, whether 'internally' or 'externally', the individual or group tries to adapt so as to maintain or improve the benefit/cost ratio; at least to prevent a reduction. There is a very wide range of choice open to each actor in theory; in practise it will be limited by the necessity of studying a finite number of possible courses, by lack of information and by the *a priori* dismissal of certain avenues of exploration because of personal or institutional prejudice, superstition or whim. We can identify certain elements or facets in the changes which ensue resulting in physical development, relocation or changes in the ways of performing the activity or the necessary communications.

The criteria for all these decisions is the welfare of the individual or group as estimated (whether formally or intuitively) in terms of benefits in relation to costs; little or no concern is had for the public welfare or general good (and this is also true of bodies acting for a particular 'slice' of the public interest embodied in their terms of reference).

In trying to sort out and guide cities and regions towards better performance to give their inhabitants greater satisfaction, the planner should realise that it is these sorts of decisions– millions of them each year in a sizeable town–that are helping to shape its evolution and which create its problems.

Complexity of this kind cannot be met with brute force attempts at control–whether via utopian design solutions or by militaristic regulation. Subtlety and refinement in both the theoretical foundations and the practical superstructure are clear requirements; we shall deal with these in turn.

3

Location Theory: A Foundation for Planning

In the previous chapters we saw how dissatisfaction on the part of individuals and groups concerning their relationships with the environment led them to take modifying actions. These changes could involve the nature of the activity itself, the 'space' in which it was carried on, its location with respect to all other activities, the kinds of communications made with activities at other locations and (indirectly) the channels which served to carry or transmit them.

It is clear that these modifying actions to a greater or lesser degree cause repercussions on the world around—on other activities and spaces, on the pattern of communications and the efficiency of the channels. When a man decides to leave his car at home and travel to work by train his action causes repercussions, however small, on the pattern of road and rail traffic. No doubt these effects are trivial enough to pass unnoticed by the rest of the world but if several hundred of his neighbours were to change over from car to train and to do so persistently, the effects would be noticeable and would be of interest to the public at large and particularly to those responsible for road traffic and rail services.

Similarly, decisions by industrialists to change their volumes of production, the timing of shifts, the location or size of their enterprises, the type of power used and the business they do with suppliers or distributors may have significant repercussions on the use of land and communications networks over considerable areas. Moreover, some of these effects may immediately be felt whilst others will become apparent only after a lapse of time and may not be traceable to their original cause.

We know that the actions taken by individuals and groups in their own interests can bring about conditions which give rise to serious social, economic and aesthetic problems connected with the use of land. Planning seeks to regulate or control the activity of individuals and groups in such a way as to minimise the bad effects which may arise, and to promote better 'performance' of the physical environment in accordance with a set of broad aims and more specific objectives set out in a plan.

It will be obvious that no effective and responsible regulation and control can occur without the fullest possible understanding of the process of change we have been discussing. Such understanding cannot be confined to a knowledge of the behaviour of the individual or group taking the action; it must be extended to encompass the whole fabric of spatial relations between activities and the complexities of their interactions. In other words, we must strive to understand the environment as a changing back-cloth against which individual decisions are made, at the same time recognising that the effect of the subsequent action is to alter the back-cloth itself in complex ways! To refuse a man permission to build a group of houses for sale in the public interest is defensible only if 'the public interest' is specifically defined and if it can be demonstrated that the effects of the housing development would be injurious. Obviously this demands a knowledge of the ways in which the repercussions from a housing development (or a factory, a shopping scheme, a sports stadium, a 'one way street' system, a warehouse, a university extension, a motorway, an airport, etc., etc.) are likely to arise, in what order, with what magnitudes and in which places.

Practical knowledge of this kind must be related to sound theoretical principles. In this particular case the relevant principles are the concern of *location theory*. This chapter aims at introducing the planner to this still-evolving body of thought by giving a brief chronological review of the main lines of its development to date, the problems that remain unresolved and the principal directions in which location theory may now be moving. The treatment is broad and general and intended to serve as a link between the *individual actions* which the book has dealt with so far and the *social purposes* which stand behind the planning techniques discussed in the following chapters. The reader who is interested in pursuing his study of location theory further (and we would encourage him to do so if he is interested in the improvement of planning techniques and analytical methods) should consult the references at the end of this chapter.

The locational behaviour of the human is one of the great voids left behind the advancing front of inquiry. This is not to say that the area is unexplored but rather that, despite a great deal of work on facets and aspects, there has been no sustained attack on the general problem of locational behaviour. There are many reasons why this should be so. The brilliant advances of knowledge in the nineteenth and twentieth centuries was achieved by specialisation within narrowly defined fields. The search for integrations, for wider linking systems of order was desultory and unpopular. Holistic thinkers of the nineteenth century had to adopt the postures of revolutionaries. It is hardly surprising that no general theory of location appeared; as Toulmin (1953) reminds us, 'only when a regularity has already been recognised or suspected can the planning of an experiment begin: until that time the mere multiplication of experiments is comparatively fruitless ... and the accumulation of observations in large numbers will be as much a waste of energy in physics as in cartography'. A hundred years ago, even fifty years ago, the notion of order and pattern in the human use of the earth was novel and relatively unimportant.

In 1826 von Thünen, an agriculturalist, put forward the theory that concentric zones of different uses of land tend to form about an urban (market) centre. Ideal conditions were specified: an isolated state consisting of a featureless uniform plain of unvarying soil quality, equal transport costs and opportunities in every direction from the central point and so on. Land owners and renters are assumed to act 'rationally' to maximise profits; it is a largely deterministic theory of land use, the only variation admitted being the relative market prices of the various products. If long-term shifts obtained, the sequence of the concentric rings would alter. Perhaps the most important features of von Thünen's theory are its uncompromisingly 'classical' structure and the fact that it is an *equilibrium* theory. In other words it describes a static *climax* towards which the system will tend if no disturbances are applied; whilst it admits the possibility of change, such change is simple and discontinuous.

Thereafter, studies of location, and of agricultural locations in particular seem to be absent, for the remainder of the nineteenth century was dominated in Western Europe by industrialisation and urban growth of unprecedented speed. Towards the end of the century Launhardt applied geometric principles to the study of the location of certain industries and Halford MacKinder (1902) provided development of ideas which were to be carried further still by Weber (1909). The work of these men was dominated by consideration of the location of *the firm*, the key unit in the modern industrial economy. The locational decision of the (manufacturing) firm was seen as an attempt to minimise 'transport costs'. These costs are included within those we identified in Chapter 2 as 'communication costs' and in particular they are the costs of bringing raw materials or partly-finished products to the production or assembly point and the costs of shipping furnished products to the distributor or final customer. As Hoover points out, whilst Weber 'further developed the theory of relative attractive forces of materials and markets (he) made serious analytical errors and failed to appreciate the full significance of route layout, junctions, and long-haul economies' (Hoover, 1948, Chapter 3). Before the First World War location theory concentrated on the study of the imaginary individual firm, whose location could be determined by assuming 'rational' behaviour on the part of the entrepreneur who responded to the 'forces' exerted over distances by the 'masses' of raw materials and markets. The optimum location for the firm was then given by an 'equilibrium' point; the dependence of these theories on analogies with the physical sciences needs no emphasis.

In the inter-war years the focus of interest shifted quite markedly in two main directions. In the first place, the patterns of different land uses making up urban areas was subjected to similar sorts of analysis as that used by von Thünen a hundred years previously for agricultural 'zones'. The power-house of this school of thought was the University of Chicago where scholars like Park and Burgess (1925) were leaders in the 'ecological' approach to patterns of location within cities. Such studies became identified also by the labels 'urban geography' and 'urban sociology'. In complete contrast to the earlier work on the location of the industrial firm, these men took *land use patterns* as their starting point and attempted to produce explanations of them largely by analogous comparisons with agricultural land use arrangements, and with the 'zones' resulting from the ecological competition between plant and animal species. Possibe weaknesses in this work are its assumptions of a somewhat blind response by communities to ecological 'forces' and a certain selectivity in the use of data about the city in order to produce comparisons with 'Thünen's rings'. Their greatest contributions in retrospect may well have been the stimulation of ever-growing amounts of demographic, sociological and geographical studies of cities, on which better theories could be built, and the inherent need for 'ecological' approaches to account for *change* as a central fact.

This beginning bore fruit in the work of Hoyt (1939) whose studies of the process of change in the pattern of residential areas within the city clearly owes a great deal to the ecological notions of competition, 'invasion' and 'succession' in the dynamic situation of urban growth and change.

In the second place, the interest of the 'ecologists' in concentric zones of land use in cities focussed the attention of others on to the central area of the city (analogous with von Thünen's market place) and to the spatial arrangement of systems of 'central places', and their formation into 'hierarchies'.

The classic expressions came from Walter Christaller (1933) who showed the relationship between the 'rarity' of a service and the population needed to support it, the size of the 'field' or 'hinterland' within which such a population was contained and the size of the central place itself. In an elegant and rigorous statement, Christaller demonstrated how, under specified conditions, a nested hierarchy of central places would result, distributed in a hexagonal pattern of 'service areas'. In the same year Colby (1933) identified 'centripetal' and 'centrifugal' forces at work within cities, having the effect of concentrating certain activities and dispersing others respectively. In contrast with Christaller whose work suggests a static equilibrium condition, Colby and others were showing that although such assumptions of equilibrium may be necessary for the study of the phenomena, these were in fact highly dynamic if not inherently *unstable*.

The 1940's saw further progress along several lines deriving from earlier work. Outstanding among this was August Lösch's brilliant synthesis (1940) and further development of the general theory of location along the lines pioneered by earlier workers in studies of industrial location, central place hierarchies, networks and the size and shape of service areas. Ullman (1941) advocated the extension of central place theory to the study of the size and spacing of cities and to the disposition of land uses within them. Later he and Harris (1945) produced a seminal study of the patterns of land use distribution within cities, developing the earlier 'concentric ring' and 'sector' hypotheses into their 'multiple nuclei' theory. Hoover (1948) continued the development of work on the location of the firm but extended it significantly to include treatment of *locational change*, competition for locations and the influence of public policies on locational choice.

In summary, the state of affairs by the end of the Second World War was as follows: Despite a large number of studies made for many different purposes by people from widely differing academic and professional backgrounds, explanations of the location or spatial patterning of human activities shared two great common factors:

one, the idea of an *equilibrium* condition in which change was explained as an 'outside' disturbance after which a fresh equilibrium would be reached;

and two, that locational decisions made (whether by farmers, boards of directors, school governors or heads of households) were made *rationally* in order to select an optimal location for their activity.

Both of these foundations are open to serious objections which have been voiced over the last two decades. When we consider the world we live in, it is very hard to discern anything like an equilibrium condition. Change seems ever-present, an inescapable feature of our lives. Cities grow and multiply, decline and fall. Once-prosperous areas suffer hardship and poverty while formerly undeveloped regions experience burgeoning growth. The internal structures of many areas, especially the great metropolitan regions of the world, seem to be in perpetual flux, not just with diurnal or seasonal ebbs and flows, but with secular shifts and upheavals. True, if we regard the daily changes as pulsations, we might look on our world as being in equilibrium during short periods of time. Before the seventeenth century a man might discern equilibrium throughout his lifetime with major changes the exception (Amsterdam after 1609, London after the fire in 1666). Equally, in the undeveloped or sparsely-settled regions of the world now it is justifiable to think in terms of a stable order, changing so slowly that secular evolution is barely noticed. But for a growing number of the world's people the reverse is surely true; change is endemic, the normal condition, equilibrium a useful way of describing short periods of time, a convenient abstraction (Turvey, 1957).

Moreover, equilibrium-based notions of location decisions take no direct account of the flow of time as it affects decisions. Our discussion of the ecology of human activities in Chapter I of this book suggested that a decision may be explained at the time it was made only by reference to events in the past and those anticipated in the future. That is, the context of a decision is the past course of change in the environment, the net effect of past decisions and also the future decisions which might be taken by others, whether as consequence or not. In our *ecological* view, the decision-maker scans the environment and anticipates its future; in both aspects he is using *information*.

This brings us to the second group of major objections; attacks on the idea of the rational, optimising decision. Until the 1940's theories of economic behaviour, and the location of activities had rested on the assumption that decisions were reached 'rationally'. We do not wish to involve ourselves or our readers in lengthy discussion of the philosophical problem of rationality: it is sufficient for our purpose to say that a rational decision in this context means one reached by a systematic study of *all* relevant information, and that the decision taken was optimal, that is that the net benefits to the decision maker were maximised. In other words all other possible choices would result in a less satisfactory outcome.

These assumptions, the foundations of a whole world of economic and locational theory, received a rude shaking in 1944 from von Neumann and Morgenstern. Common sense had long since suggested that decisions are based on rather less than perfect information; furthermore that they are based on a degree of anticipation of competitors' responses; and, finally that a good proportion of decisions are demonstrably 'sub-optimal', i.e. *less* than the best possible outcome is accepted. Von Neumann and Morgenstern introduced two important notions into the theory of decision making; *the state of information* and the *attitude toward risk* of the decision maker. They likened the making of business, political and military decisions to *strategies in games* and in so doing they both relied on and stimulated developments in the mathematics of probability.

In twenty years, decision theory with its growing emphasis on gaming, probability and random processes, sub-optimal decisions and sequential decision chains has grown apace, transforming many military, commercial and industrial organisations. Since the 1950's the repercussions of this work fusing with older ideas of locational behaviour have sparked off increasing interest among planners and related professionals working in the field. Theoretical and practical advances have been very closely related, each stimulating the other.

For example, in the early post-war years, road engineers still approached their design problems in simple physical terms. Isolated problem areas – a congested junction, a length of road with bad alignment – were dealt with one at a time by 'improvements' conceived in isolation. But the concept of a road *system*, a network of links and nodes, was arising. In order to design improvements, system characteristics must be considered, such as the attraction of traffic to improved links and relative reductions on other links. Mitchell and Rapkin (1954) produced a major statement of the idea of traffic as 'a function of land use'. Put another way, vehicles moved along routes in order to connect activities at different locations. Commuter flows were directly related to the location and size of workplaces and of home areas; flows of goods could be seen to derive from the spatial separation of raw materials from factories, component plants from assembly points and finished products from market outlets.

In the 'transportation' plans for Chicago and Detroit, this idea had already been used as a design aid. If the appropriate ratios of trip generation (per unit of each land use) were derived and could be projected, if a future pattern of activities or land uses were supplied, then the engineer could predict the pattern of demand for trips from each of a number of zones to all other zones in the city. A road plan could then be derived by trial and error methods which could deal with the expected volumes of traffic. From the highway engineer's viewpoint, land use patterns were one of the prerequisites for his task, comparable with budgetary limits, topographical and soil surveys, and the availability of experienced contractors; for them the problem was essentially one of designing a future highway system *from* future land use.

For the engineering profession these new techniques represented a profound change in outlook. Traditionally approaching their problem as one of the *design of physical equipment* to satisfy functional and cost criteria the engineers were increasingly forced into studies of *human behaviour and choice* in the making of trips and the use of different modes of travel and possible routes through the network of communications.

Increasing refinements were made: separate treatment of different types of vehicles, taking into account many modes of transport both public and private, road and rail and studying the 'modal split' between them; superior original data deriving from interviews with samples of the populations of trip-makers; vastly better data-processing methods as computers and other machines came into general use.

Very often then, by the end of the fifties, highly sophisticated plans for integrated transportation systems for large urban and metropolitan areas were being developed on the basis of very crudely-derived land use patterns. It was rather like navigating a jet airliner with Columbus' instruments. Even though the exploration of alternative future land use patterns had been introduced, as in the Washington region, these were still produced by crude methods and subservient to transportation questions. At the time the relationship between land use and movement was regarded as one of dependence rather than interdependence; the profound effect of movements and transport facilities *on land use patterns* (themselves also the outcome of human choices and decisions) was either understated or ignored. Additionally, these plans were 'one-shot' efforts; whilst their authors and sponsors recognised that years, even decades, must elapse whilst the facilities were being built, they failed to account for changes in movement and location which would occur *through* such a period and beyond.

Location Theory: A Foundation for Planning

Wingo and Perloff were well aware of this in 1961 as they criticised the Washington scheme. 'Because of its impact on the locational behaviour of firms and individuals, urban transportation can be viewed as the basic spatial organiser of the metropolitan region. The distinction between transportation and locational behaviour, between short-run and long-run effects, is the crux of the difference between urban transportation planning as an engineering exercise on the one hand, and as the design of a framework of interaction ... on the other'. And they go on to add that 'once locational behaviour is admitted to be a part of the system, however, economic structure, land use, and the transportation system are seen to be locked together in a more general "system" in which the importance of purely transportation behaviour of firms and individuals is subordinated to the patterns of economic activity which emerge in response to changes in the conditions of interaction. Our view is that it is necessary to broaden the "system" – to recognise as central the critical interdependence between the use of space and the means for interaction, between accessibility and land use'.

Wingo and Perloff lay emphasis on this facet of interdependence; others in the early 1960's have been concerned also with the dynamic aspects of the problem, i.e. of trying to order our thoughts on how change occurs *through time* as well as in space. Mitchell's contributions are noteworthy, and whilst he did not set out to make major theoretical statements, his advocacy of a dynamic rather than a static 'picture-of-the-future' approach to planning in practice, clearly rested on evolving theories of *growth and change*. He was a leading figure in the setting up of the Penn-Jersey Transportation Study which, despite its title, was instituted as a 'permanent regional planning process'. The technical heart of Penn-Jersey was a regional growth model which could predict future land use and movement changes *incrementally*. By varying assumptions about public policy, values held by firms and households about location and movement, etc., a large number of different 'trajectories' of change were generated for study.

Thus the position at the start of the 1960's was one of rapid evolution in the development of theories of human locational behaviour. Emphasis was clearly shifting rapidly away from the earlier static equilibrium notions which, whilst accepting the existence of changes in land use and demographic patterns, made little attempt to offer *behavioural* explanations. In its place we see change assuming a central position in its own right both in the sense of ceaseless regular and random interaction between activities via communication and transport and in the sense of the evolution of spatial configurations in response to sequences or chains of modifying actions made to the environment by individuals, firms and institutions. This latter point in its turn has focused increasing attention on the processes of decision-making and the ways in which human values both derive from and modify the environment.

These theoretical developments were stimulated to a greater extent by the increased amounts of data–demographic, economic, 'land use', movement–collected by the big urban transportation studies and especially because the rapid development of the electronic computer enabled theories to be subjected to empirical testing on a scale and at a speed which was unimaginable a decade before. For the same reasons, theorists and practitioners have been forced to confront the awful complexity of urban and regional systems of activities and their interactions and the uncharted territories of human values as criteria for locational and communication choices.

Britton Harris, in a brilliant essay (1960), could thus conclude that 'by the logic of the development so far, there is an implicit assumption that the problems addressed must be solved within a systems framework, because the entire system of metropolitan function is the environment of the decision-making that shapes metropolitan growth. It would also appear that the analysis of the decision-units has lagged and will be a focus of future work . . . [but] . . . we are now well along the road to an adequate systems approach'. The main problems, as seen by Harris 'arise essentially out of the complexity of the system of metropolitan interaction, and out of the wide variety of modes of behaviour that are legally and socially permitted to the decision-makers whose actions influence metropolitan growth. . . . It would appear that this field of research will for some time offer a standing challenge. . . .'

In the last few years, further progress has been made, some of it consolidating and deepening earlier insights, some offering new views. Yet the challenge is still with us for as Chapin wrote in 1965, by rigorous standards, 'the present stage in theory-building relating to urban spatial structure is spotty, and in general the field has a long way to go. . . .' An important collection of essays, 'Explorations into Urban Structure', appeared in 1964 and the contents were summarised by John Dyckman who drew attention to the ground shared by the contributors. He found a common emphasis on the need to understand *processes*; that is on the ways in which change arises, occurs and in turn generates further response. Dyckman quotes the objections raised by one of the essayists, Herbert Gans, to ecological approaches. In Gans' view, such interpretations are of most value where 'the subjects under study lack the ability to *make choices*, be they plants, animals or human beings'—and in 'situations of extreme scarcity where all conditions tend to be marginal'. But in our view these objections cannot stand since both the freedom to choose and the existence of scarcity are relative terms and do not put the human and his environment in a separate category, subject to different 'rules'.

The whole world may be viewed as one ecological system (with a considerable number of hierarchical sub-systems). No matter that man, by virtue of his enormous brain power has (very recently) come to dominate the world's ecology, he is none the less part of it—a fact he ignores at his peril. His amazing abilities to adapt to environment and to modify it are only *relatively* great in comparison with those of all other living creatures; there are no different 'rules' for humans. As Orwell might have said, all powers to make choices are equal, but some are more equal than others.

Scarcity too is a relative term. The scarcity of food was reduced by neolithic agriculture, the scarcity of power or energy by the eighteenth- and nineteenth-century technology and scarcity of information is being augmented by twentieth-century 'information technology'. One man is short of food, another of symphony concerts; one family would like a new fireside chair, another a weekend house with a view of the mountains. 'Scarcity' is with all of us all the time, because (as Galbraith has shown us about work) *we keep on redefining it*.

Thus in our view Gans does not make out a case against an ecological approach; we shall suggest below that an approach to the study of human locational behaviour within an ecological *system* framework offers considerable potential for progress in the building of sound, testable theories.

The welter of work which has recently emerged on the locational or spatial aspects of human life is not easily summarised. Not only is the literature growing rapidly but it comes from a wide variety of individuals and disciplines with differing intellectual traditions and modes of expression. In his review of recent work, which we mentioned above, Stuart Chapin examines contributions from sociology, economics, architecture and civic design, transportation, communications and political science as well as the work of himself and his colleagues. Despite this diversity he finds that 'four emphases tend to crop up again and again in the work above:

The necessity of a system of analysis which is continuous rather than discontinuous.

The importance of the system taking account of activity linkages where change in one element has the effect of altering the climate for change in another element. Recognition of the feedback influence which gives rise to the need for modifying the change initially instituted.

Significance of the random aspect of human interaction and the importance of a probabilistic view toward development rather than a deterministic view.

The interrelation of policy, proposal, and action–phased to lead successively from one to the next.'

The existence of such common ground among such a variety of work prompts the question: is there some underlying rationale, some *single* framework within which human locational behaviour can be studied and understood? If so, the prospect is indeed exciting for it would suggest a means of approach to the problems control and guidance, that is to *the problem of planning itself*.

We believe that there is such a single framework that is a *systems view* of human relationships with the environment (Chadwick, 1966; McLoughlin, 1967). We have spoken of systems already, asking the reader's indulgence over definitions; it is now time to make this issue clear for the idea of systems is completely central to the whole argument of this book.

SELECTED CONTRIBUTIONS TO THE THEORY OF HUMAN LOCATIONAL BEHAVIOUR LISTED IN CHRONOLOGICAL ORDER

(These are repeated in the references at the end of the book)

1826 Johann Heinrich von Thünen, *Der isolierte Staat in Beziehung auf Landwirtschaft und Nationalökonomie*, Hamburg. (See Chisholm, 1962 and Hall, 1966.)

1902 H. J. Mackinder, *Britain and the British Seas*, D. Appleton Century Co., New York.

1909 Alfred Weber, *Ueber den Standort der Industrien*, Part I, 'Reine Theorie der Standorts', Tübingen. (See Friedrich, 1928.)

1923 H. H. Barrows 'Geography as Human Ecology' *in Annals of the Association of American Geographers, 13.*

1925 Ernest W. Burgess, 'Growth of the City' *in* R. E. Park *et al.* (eds.), *The City*, Chicago University Press.

1929 C. J. Friedrich, *Alfred Weber's Theory of the Location of Industries*, Chicago University Press.

1933 Walter Christaller, *Die Zentralen Orte in Süddeutschland*, Jena. (See Baskin, 1957.)

Charles C. Colby, 'Centrifugal and Centripetal Forces in Urban Geography', *Annals of A.A.G., 23*, 1–20.

R. D. McKenzie, *The Metropolitan Community*, New York, McGraw-Hill.

1935 Tord Palander, *Beiträge zur Standortstheorie*, Uppsala, Wiksells boktryckeri-AB.

1939 Homer Hoyt, *The Structure and Growth of Residential Neighborhoods in American Cities*, Washington.

1940 August Lösch, *Die Räumliche Ordnung der Wirtschaft*, Jena. (See 1954.)

1941 Edward Ullman, 'A Theory of Location for Cities' *in American Journal of Sociology*, May.

1944 J. von Neumann and E. Morgenstern, *The Theory of Games and Economic Behaviour*.

1945 Chauncy D. Harris and Edward L. Ullman, *The Nature of Cities*.

1948 Edgar M. Hoover, *The Location of Economic Activity*, New York.

1949 Richard U. Ratcliff, *Urban Land Economics* (esp. Chapter 2).

1954 Robert B. Mitchell and Chester Rapkin, *Urban Traffic: A Function of Land Use*, Columbia U.P.

August Lösch (see 1940), *The Economics of Location*, Yale U.P.

Edgar S. Dunn, jr., *The Location of Agricultural Production*, Gainsville, Univ. of Florida Press.

1955 Martin Beckmann and Thomas Morschak, 'An Activity Analysis Approach to Location Theory' *in 'Kyklos' vol. 8*.

Richard U. Ratcliff, 'The Dynamics of Efficiency in the Locational Distribution of Urban Activity' *in* Robert M. Fisher (ed.), *The Metropolis in Modern Life*.

1956 Walter Isard, *Location and Space-Economy*, New York, Wiley and Sons.

Melvin L. Greenhut, *Plant location in Theory and in Practice: The Economics of Space*, Chapel Hill, Univ. of N.C.P.

Gerald P. Carrothers, 'An Historical Review of the Gravity and Potential Concepts of Human Interaction' *in Journal of the American Institute of Planners*, Spring.

1957 Tjalling C. Koopmans and Martin Beckman, 'Assignment Problems and the Location of Economic Activities' *in Econometrica* January.

Kevin Lynch and Lloyd Rodwin, 'A Theory of Urban Form' *in Journal of the American Institute of Planners*, November.

Ralph Turvey, *The Economics of Real Property: An Analysis of Property values and Patterns of Use*, London, Allen and Unwin.

1958 Brian J. L. Berry and William L. Garrison, 'Recent Developments in Central Place Theory' *in Papers and Proceedings of the Regional Science Association, vol. 4*.

F. Stuart Chapin, jr., *Urban Land Use Planning* (1st edn.). (See 1965.)

1959 Berry and Garrison, 'The Functional Bases of the Central Place Hierarchy' *in* Mayer and Kohn (eds.), *Readings in Urban Geography*, Chicago Univ. Press.

Charles T. Stewart, 'The Size and Spacing of Cities' *in* Mayer and Kohn, *op. cit.*

1960 Albert Z. Guttenberg, 'Urban Structure and Urban Growth' *in Journal of the American Institute of Planners* (May).

John D. Herbert and Benjamin Stevens, 'A Model for the Distribution of Residential Activity in Urban Areas' *in Journal of Regional Science* (Fall).

William L. Garrison, 'Toward a Simulation Model of Urban Growth and Development', Lund, Sweden, Gleerup.

1961 Brian J. L. Berry and A. Pred, *Central Place Studies: a bibliography of theory and applications*, Regional Science Research Inst.

Britton Harris, 'Some Problems in the Theory of Intra-Urban Location' *in Operations Research 9* (Fall).

Walter Firey, *Land Use in Central Boston*, Cambridge, Mass., Harvard U.P.

Lowdon Wingo, jr., *Transportation and Urban Land*, Washington, Resources for the Future Inc.

1962 Walter Isard and Thomas A. Reiner, 'Aspects of Decision-Making Theory and Regional Science' *in Papers and Proceedings of the Regional Science Association, vol. 9.*

Michael Chisholm, *Rural Settlement and Land Use: an essay in Location*, London, Hutchinson U. Lib. (N.B. Chapter 2 summarises *von Thünen* (1826)).

Richard L. Meier, *A Communications Theory of Urban Growth*, Cambridge, Mass., M.I.T. Press.

F. Stuart Chapin, jr., and Shirley F. Weiss (eds.), *Urban Growth Dynamics in a Regional Cluster of Cities*, New York, John Wiley and Sons.

Richard L. Morrill, 'Simulation of Central Place Patterns over Time' *in Lund Studies in Geography*, series B, *Human Geography 24*, 109–20, Lund.

1964 William Alonso, 'Location Theory' *in* John R. Friedmann and William Alonso (eds.), *Regional Development and Planning*, Cambridge, Mass., Harvard U.P.

Edwin von Böventer, 'Spatial Organisation Theory as a Basis for Regional Planning' *in Journal of the American Institute of Planners*, May.

Brian J. L. Berry, 'Cities as Systems within Systems of Cities' in Papers of the Regional Science Association, vol. *10* (reprinted in Friedmann and Alonso, *op. cit.*).

Melvin Webber (ed.), *Explorations into Urban Structure*, Philadelphia, University of Pennsylvania Press.

Ira S. Lowry, *A Model of Metropolis*, Santa Monica, Cal. The RAND Corpn.

1965 Britton Harris (ed.), Special Issue on Urban Development Models of *Journal of the American Institute of Planners* (May).

F. Stuart Chapin, jr., *Urban Land Use Planning*, second edition (especially Chapters 2 and 6), Urbana, Univ. of Illinois Press.

Peter Haggett, *Locational Analysis in Human Geography*, London, Edward Arnold.

1966 Britton Harris, 'The Uses of Theory in the Simulation of Urban Phenomena' *in Journal of the American Institute of Planners* (September).

Peter Hall, *Von Thünen's Isolated State*.

4

The Guidance and Control of Change: Physical Planning as the Control of Complex Systems

The following chapters of the book deal with planning techniques: the planning process in outline, the identification of goals and objectives, information for planning, projection, simulation and modelling, the design of plans, their evaluation and implementation.

Systems in general

This present chapter lays the foundation with an introduction to notions fundamental to this book—*the environment as a system and its control by the application of cybernetic principles.*

In general usage a system is understood as a 'complex whole', a 'set of connected things or parts', an 'organised body of material of immaterial things' and as a 'group of objects related or interacting so as to form a unity'.* In recent years bodies of thinking have grown up known as *General Systems Theory* (von Bertalanffy, 1951) which deal with the notion of systems in general just as *Operations Research* (Churchman, Ackoff and Arnoff, 1957) applies systems thinking via *systems analysis* to real-life situations, whilst *Cybernetics* (Wiener, 1948; Ashby, 1956) is the study of the control of complex systems, both living and inanimate.

In Chapter 1 of this book we saw the relationships of man (and other creatures) with the environment could be identified in system terms—as an ecological or *eco-system* in fact. Stafford Beer

* Oxford English Dictionary.

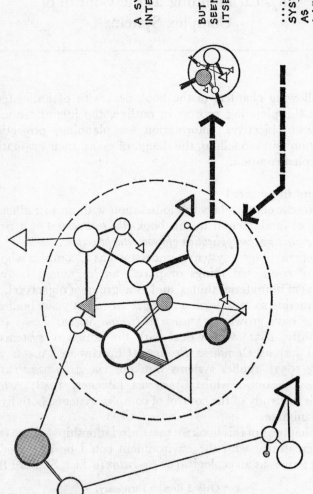

A SYSTEM IS A SET OF
INTERCONNECTED PARTS

BUT EACH PART MAY BE
SEEN AS A SYSTEM
ITSELF........

........AND THE WHOLE
SYSTEM MAY BE REGARDED
AS BUT ONE PART OF A
LARGER SYSTEM........

4.1 A system

(1959, Chapter II) reminds us 'that the definition of any particular system is arbitrary . . . the universe seems to be made up of sets of systems, each contained within one somewhat bigger, like a set of hollow building blocks [Figure 4.1]. Just as it is always possible to expand the system to a scope of wider perspective, it is also possible to cut down the system to a smaller version . . . the point to seize on here is that if we wish to consider the interactions affecting one simple entity, then we shall have to define that entity as part of a system. The system we choose to define is a system because it contains interrelated parts, and is in some sense a complete whole in itself. But the entity we are considering will certainly be part of a number of such systems, each of which is a sub-system of a series of larger systems. So the problem of stating the system we wish to study is by no means easy'.

The human environment as a system

We can now attempt to define the system with which we will deal in the remainder of the book. This we must do by identifying the parts or components on the one hand and the connections or interactions on the other. The parts of our system are persistent *human activities* and especially those that tend to occur and recur at specific locations or within particular zones or areas (Chapin, 1965, pp. 90–5). Within the vast range of human activity there is a continuous gradation between those activities that are very strongly 'place-related' and those which are totally random with respect to place. For example, family life, the nurture and care of children, the welcoming of friends, these are strongly place-related; by contrast a hobby such as taking photographs, where the whole environment may be grist to the mill, is of itself very weakly related to place. Although there is gradation between extremes, considerable shifts occur. Webber (1963, 1964) has given us a full and provocative account of the way some human activities are becoming more and others less place-related. Whilst the components of our system, being an *eco-* system, are those activities which are more recurrent and more strongly related to place, we must bear in mind the fluid nature of the distinction.

The connections between these parts are *human communications* and once again, our concern is mainly with those that are recurrent and spatially clustered (in 'channels'–see below) (Meier, 1962). The communications enable the various activities to interact, to link up and cross-connect so that necessary patterns of human behaviour can occur. These communications take many forms. Radio communication is a good example of interaction which is wholly unrelated to place whilst railway transport is obviously at the opposite extreme. Communication involves many types of interaction: the transmission of material goods, of persons, of messages and of impressions received by the sense-organs of sight, sound and smell. It is useful to distinguish *transport* as a sub-system of communications concerned with material interaction (goods and persons). Just as activities may be more or less place-related, so with communications. We are familiar with messages sent by letter, (material and so involving place-related transport) being substituted by telephone messages. Television enables the sense impressions of sights and sounds at a football game to be received almost anywhere on earth, (though it cannot convey the smell of grease paint from a theatrical performance). Once again our main concern is to see the system's connections in those communications which are more recurrent and strongly patterned spatially.

So, the first step in defining the system with which we deal is to recognise *activities* linked by *communications*. We can imagine this graphically–in the words of Beer (1959): 'We will now represent the "bits and pieces" which make up this by a series of dots of paper. The connectiveness of the system can now be introduced into this picture by drawing lines between the dots; some dots may well be connected to all other dots, but in some cases a dot may be connected to only one of its fellows. In this way, we come to look upon a system as a kind of network'.

Proceeding further, our system takes physical form. The activities occur within adapted *spaces*. These include buildings, arenas, parks, seashores, lakes, quarries, forests and airfields. The adjective 'adapted' does not necessarily imply physical construction or development; fields used by a motor-cycle club for 'scrambling' meets, seashores and sand-dunes by holiday-makers, a natural lake by sailing enthusiasts, and a mountain by hill-walkers are all examples. It is their conscious and regular use rather than building and engineering work which earns areas the title 'adapted spaces' (Lynch, 1960).

Similar remarks apply to the physical forms for communications—the *channels*. These too may be constructed deliberately as are roads, footpaths, railways, canals, pipelines, cables and ski-lifts; or they may be borrowed from nature as are rivers, air corridors, ridges and valleys.

Systems and Structure

The parts of our system are activities linked by communications, and many of these use the physical forms of adapted spaces and channels. But we must not think that there is a fixed, unchanging correspondence between these two aspects of the system (Buchanan, 1966, Chapter 3 and Supplementary Volume 2). Very many activities take place within adapted spaces which were originally intended for some quite different purpose and channels become used for new forms of communication (Cowan, 1966). The whole history of towns and the countryside is witness to this: churches become warehouses then bingo-halls; houses become shops, then offices; royal parks may become partly used for underground car parking. Equally, many different activities may use the same space or channel—a phenomenon sometimes called 'multiple use'. A lake is used for water supply, fisheries and water sport; roads are used not only for transport but also for parking, retailing and public assembly.

We must not be disheartened by these conceptual problems. The key point to remember is that a system is *not* the real world, but a way of looking at it. Definitions of systems therefore depend in part on the purposes and objectives for which they are to be used. The reader who is not accustomed to thinking in system terms should have patience; increasing familiarity will almost certainly bring great clarification. We believe that for planners, one of the main difficulties arises from an undue emphasis to date on the physical side, on spaces and channels. We would advise a corrective emphasis which whilst remaining fully aware of the great importance of the material equipment, lays stress on the *human activities and communications* which are the key to understanding and control of the system. In addition to giving understanding, the systems view helps in practical situations and many of the problems of defining our system, its components and its linkages will in large measure be resolved when discussing planning techniques in the chapters which follow.

We can further describe our system components and connections by *type or mode*. For example, activities include domestic, productive, recreational and educational types. If we adopt a finer 'grain' of typology we might wish to distinguish such activities as stock-holding for distribution, soft fruit-growing, youth clubs and carburettor manufacturing. Connections can be described by either the content or the medium or both. For example we might identify material goods movements, person movements and message flows; among modes there are road vehicle transport, radio signals, pipeline flows, telephone messages and visual sense-impressions transmitted from the objects to the human eye. Finer grain reveals private-car passenger movements for recreational purposes, pipeline-flows of natural gas, police VHF-radio transmissions and so on.

By way of illustration here, we can quantify both the components and connections of our system in varying ways. Activities have measures of *stock*, e.g. amounts of population, employment, fixed capital, standing timber, floor space, and of *density*, e.g. persons per acre, workers per acre, sales per square foot.

Communications are measured by *flow*, e.g. vehicles, messages, kilovolts, trains, passengers, and by *flow density* or *interactance*, e.g. passenger-car-units (p.c.u.) per hour, million gallons per day (m.g.d.).

Refinement of the systems view of settlements

The Detroit and Chicago transportation studies about fifteen years ago interpreted the city as this kind of system, a view which was confirmed by Mitchell and Rapkin (1954). In the view of those men and their colleagues the city was a system whose component parts were small zones of land uses or activity, and whose connections were all forms of communication and especially road traffic. A series of transportation plans was then based on this view since, it was argued, if a future land use pattern could be defined, then the resultant traffic pattern could be derived and a suitable transport system designed to fit it.

In the late fifties and early sixties fundamental objections were raised to this view (Wingo and Perloff, 1961). In essence, they amounted to this: because land uses and traffic flows are interdependent, each affecting the other, we cannot push forward land use in one giant stride of, say, twenty years and derive a traffic flow pattern or vice versa; for the simple reason that traffic flows alter in response to changing land use patterns while at the same time (though at different rates of response), land uses tend to relocate themselves in relation to the movement opportunities that are available; the city evolves through time in ways which depend upon the sequences in which changes in land use and movement facilities are introduced (Beesley and Kain, 1964).

Within a decade, then, we moved from a view of the city as a machine-like system—a system that *works*—to a view of the city as a system that evolves. To analyse the city as a complex system that evolves has profound consequences for many aspects of planning thought and practice.

When we seek to control any dynamic system we must try to foresee how that system might evolve—how it would develop if left severely alone, and also what the outcomes of many different kinds of stimuli and intervention might be. Anyone who seeks to control anything must ask the question, 'what would happen if . . .?' Effective control must be based on understanding and is often gained through learning by experiment.

But it is not always possible to experiment with the actual situation—sometimes it is too dangerous, sometimes too costly, sometimes too slow. In such cases we have to simulate the situation as best we can and carry out our experiments and learn to know the system's responses by way of analogues or models of real the thing (Harris, 1965). Examples are numerous: wind-tunnels and model planes in aero-engineering, the water-tank models in hydraulic engineering and naval architecture, experiments (which many people deplore) in which living creatures are used as 'models' in order to discover more about possible human responses. If the model is a good one (and often time alone will tell) it will reproduce the behaviour of the real thing with sufficient accuracy to answer questions of the 'what will happen if . . .?' kind.

Of course it has long been possible for planners to foresee

aspects of the future of the city–we can project population, employment and spending power, we can forecast complex travel patterns and shopping centre sales. Many professions and skills have contributed greatly to our ability to make such forecasts.

But until recently it has not been possible to foresee the city as a whole, its future shape, the disposition of its activities and linkages, and its resulting character in the round. Thus, we have been lacking in our ability to answer the 'what would happen if . . .?' questions in the most important way–with a synoptic view of the future. We should like to know the city-wide effects of certain policies or trends–of green belts, green wedges and conservation areas, of different programmes and patterns of road construction and parking policy, of expansion or entrenchment of central area shopping and employment, of different timings of similar proposals.

We want to experiment within the whole range of the possible in order to discover what is most desirable. Of course to some extent we have always tried to do this sort of thinking. We have considered alternative policies, and different likely responses, we have approached the private sector's industrial, commercial and residential developers to find out their aims and to test their response to various public policy alternatives. The trouble is that when we try to take into account the inter-relations of more than about a dozen or so of these issues, their scores of immediate side effects, their hundreds of indirect effects all merging and overlapping with different time-lags, we find the human brain cannot cope without assistance. We cannot model the city in our heads–its complexity overwhelms us.

We know that the city is comprised of a myriad relationships, but if we have the vision to identify and describe these in the right way they can be expressed in mathematical terms. The way changes occur through time can be built into the equations, and the computer, handling the instructions provided, can in a matter of minutes enable us to observe decades of growth in a large city. In effect, changes in the location of many kinds of activity in the city, the flows along roads and railway lines, the accompanying shifts in land values, clearance and renewal operations, the growth, change and shifting of manufacturing and commercial enterprises, the evolving life of the city in outline is mirrored in the model or 'family' of models. We can study the results for any point in time–asking 'how will things be in 1985 on this basis?'–or we can see a whole trajectory of the city's evolution like a series of frames in a cine-reel of the future. The extent to which we have a correct and appropriate method of forecasting the city's future depends on how clearly we have been able to describe the system we are simulating in the models. Simulation exercises have the very salutory effect of forcing us to find out how the real world actually works. Projection and simulation are discussed in Chapter 8.

The system view of plans

So, if we see the city as a dynamic system that evolves in response to many influences, it follows that plans for it must be cast in similar form; as Mitchell (1961) says, they

'will be plans for the nature, rate, quantity and quality of urban change–for a process of development. They will be expressed in dynamic rather than in static terms. They will start with present conditions and point the direction of change'.

Following experiments about the stages through which it could pass plans will essentially show the steps through which the city ought to pass–they will be the charts of a course to be steered. We will thus focus our attention on the well-being of the city at all times and not simply at some distant future date.

The basic form of plans should be statements which describe how the city should evolve in a series of equal steps–of say, five years at a time. These statements would be a series of diagrams, statistics and written matter, which would set out for each five-yearly interval the intended disposition of the principal activities–agricultural, industrial, commercial, residential, recreational–together with the intended communication and transport networks. The land uses and the flows on the networks would be described in quantitative and qualitative terms. There would be enough information about such matters as the distribution of population, car ownership, spending power, industrial and shopping floor-space, car parks and traffic volumes to make clear the intentions and expectations of the plan. Also the information should be in such a form as to be directly usable in implementation and control (a very important point which will be developed in some detail later). The figures would be expressed as probabilities over a range—narrower in the near future where we can be more certain, widening out as the 'horizon year' is approached to broader ranges in acceptance of the fact that forecasting of human behaviour is a hazardous job.

Of course, all this refers to the basic plan documents only—they would be supplemented by a host of more detailed studies of land development, redevelopments, road construction, school-building and housing programmes. In some areas dereliction and restoration, in others holiday development and tourism would be the subjects of special studies. They would in part derive from and in turn help to refine and correct the broad and general view put forward here; such detailed studies would have already helped in the construction of models to simulate the growth of the study area as a whole. The mapped or diagrammatic part of the plan should also resemble a cine-film of the future—each frame showing a picture of the city as it should be at some future date, the whole reel showing a process of change which we want the city to undergo. Using the same metaphor, the statistical and verbal parts of the plan are the sound track giving a full commentary on the city's planned course; Buchanan (1966, foldout sheets 7–13) has provided a splendid example.

Such plans are the necessary description of the course or trajectory we wish a dynamic system to follow. They bring together land use and communications at all times; they show where the city should go and how it can get there. Methods of formulating plans and the details of their form and content are dealt with in Chapter 9, whilst Chapter 10 discusses problems and methods of choosing between a number of alternative possible plans—that is with plan *evaluation*.

Implementation, guidance and control

The implementation of such a plan falls within the general province of control—control as understood in systems engineering and in the biological sciences; not in the narrow and restrictive sense of the use of the veto but in the fullest sense which includes 'positive' stimulus and intervention. Control has been defined as

84

'that ... which provides direction in conformance to the plan, or in other words, the maintenance of variations from system objectives within allowable limits' (Johnson, Kast and Rosenzweig, 1963).

This is a general definition and can be applied to any control situation whether biological, economic, industrial or political and whether the system is simple and determinate or probabilistic and highly complex (Rose, 1967). We shall see how it can be applied to urban and regional systems. To implement a plan of the kind described here requires that the city shall follow 'within allowable limits' the course which the plan has charted in all important aspects. Such control processes are very familiar. They occur in such simple devices as thermostats where the heat source is controlled by deviations from the prescribed temperature, in more complex industrial processes and in highly complex man/machine systems such as driving a car.

The general principle involved here is called 'error-controlled regulation' (Ashby, 1956, Chapter 12); the system is actuated by a control device which is supplied with information about its *actual state* compared with the *intended state* (Figure 4.2). There are four common features of all control:

1. The system to be controlled.
2. The intended state or states of the system.
3. A device for measuring the actual state of the system and thus its deviation from the intended state.
4. A means of supplying correcting influences to keep the system within the limits set.

In our own situation, the city of course is the system we wish to control, the desired states are expressed in the plan, we measure the actual state at any time by all forms of survey and can thus compare the actual conditions with those intended by the plan. So far, so good, but what about the correcting influences to keep the system on course? By the nature of the city, it is influenced by the addition, removal or alteration of component parts or connections–that is, land uses and communications. It follows then, that the evolution of the city can be influenced by regulating the flow of additions, removals and alterations to land uses and communications (McLoughlin, 1965). This can be done in two ways: first by directly carrying out changes and here we think of the very wide range of public

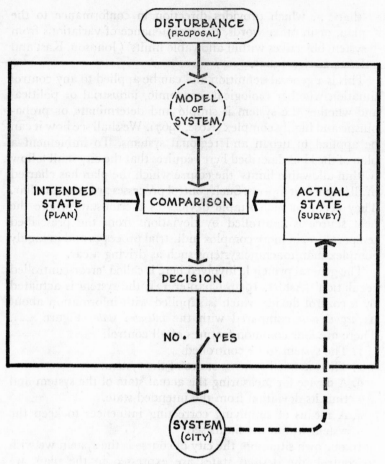

4.2 Error-controlled regulation

influence over hospitals, schools, housing, utilities, roads, bus services, railways, car parking, airports and so on; and second, indirectly, by regulating the flow of changes proposed by others through all the processes of development control—the power to say 'yes' or 'no' to a very wide range of private (and certain public) proposals (Llewelyn-Davies, 1967).

We can picture the planner now as a helmsman steering the city. His attention focuses on the plan—the charted course—the future states through which the city should pass—and on the survey observations which indicate its actual state. In order to steer, he has two main controls—one is his influence over public investment, development and policy, and the other can be visualised as a switch marked 'on/off' of 'yes/no' by which he releases or blocks private proposals for change (Figure 4.2).

One problem remains: how does the planner know at any point whether he should say 'yes' or 'no', or what his response should be to public proposals? The car driver must see the road ahead—he has learned by experience what sorts of response to expect from steering, throttle, brakes and gears. As the PAG report said,

'the planning authorities must consider whether the development proposed would advance or hinder (or have no effect on) the policies and objectives set out in the plan' (Planning Advisory Group, 1965 p. 46).

Now such questions can be answered partly by experience as in driving a car, but to control more complex systems like the city we once again need help of analogues or models. Just as these devices helped us to experiment in the drawing up of the plan, they will help in its implementation; in control and implementation we are asking, 'what would happen if we approve, or refuse this application? Will the city continue on course or not?' We must have the means to foresee the possible effects because by the time they occur, the system may have gone outside the limits set in the plan and corrective action may then be too late (Figure 4.3). We can refer such questions to our models which can simulate the responses in the city over a period of time. Single large proposals for change or the aggregate of a number of smaller proposals can be treated in this way.

These models augment or amplify the planner's experience. They can also be an early-warning device, indicating needs for corrective action that may lie ahead and enabling the planner to experiment with different forms of public intervention or policies which would keep the system in control or put it back on course again. Thus, because time is simulated in the models we can see the different effects of short, medium and long-term actions. As Mitchell (1961, p. 171) has put it,

'this continuous planning process of the future will incorporate a feedback of information on community change and on the results of planned and programmed action. In this

87

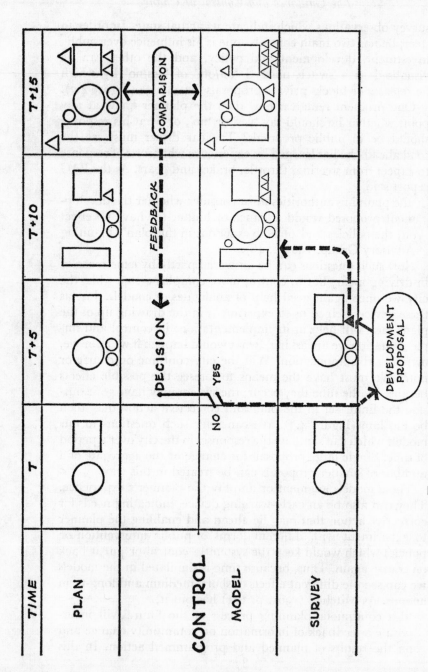

4·3 Error-controlled regulation applied to planning

way, as progress is measured, the planning process can adjust to guide development, much as the course of a missile is guided by a feedback of information on its deviation from a projected course.'

He goes on to say that,

'the planning process thus becomes time-oriented in three ways:

(a) it is continuous, without termination in a "final plan";

(b) it seeks to affect and make use of change, rather than to picture a static, future condition; and

(c) it is expressed partly in long-range and short-range programmes of action to be taken and of capital and other resources to be utilised.'

Finally, serious deviations and the discovery that major interventions are necessary might well suggest a review of the plan because its aims and assumptions may be due for overhaul. This could result in the charting of a modified course to be followed; and so the endless cycle is closed. The detailed treatment of these issues–implementation, control and review–is to be found in Chapter 11. Control depends on the handling of appropriate *information* about the system's intended and actual states, and in the form of models of its possible behaviour. The kinds of information needed in planning are the subject of Chapter 7.

The promise of cybernetics

But let us return to the view of our system as a whole, with its property of 'connectiveness', to use Beer's word. In Chapter 1 we showed that our system was ecological in nature. By any standards it is extremely complex. Beer (1959, p. 10) shows that a system of n components can take up $2^{n(n-1)}$ *states* if we define a state to be the pattern produced when each of the connections is either 'on' or 'off' (a gross simplification). Thus a system of seven parts could have 2^{42} states!

It is no good our being either impressed or frightened by this realisation; in any case, we know already that human relations with the environment are complex. But it must surely make us realise the nature of the planner's position. The largely intuitive and informal methods with which we have grown up cannot in honesty survive the admission of the complexity of the task.

But is it not hopeless? Should we not simply admit defeat and throw up our hands at the futility of it all? We think not, and for a number of reasons. Until very recently science has attempted to deal with complex systems in ways which were almost doomed to failure from the start. Situations in which complexity and randomness were inherent (e.g. that of most living organisms) have been studied by varying one factor at a time. Unfortunately for scientists (and they knew it) *many* factors of the system under study were varying at once in mutual interactions. In recent years the new science of cybernetics has grown up defined by one of its founders, Norbert Wiener (1948), as 'the science of control and communication, in the animal and the machine'. Cybernetics, rather than shrinking from complex systems has made the study of complexity and control its own field. Astonishing progress is being made. Cybernetic techniques have enabled us to postulate the structure of control mechanisms in living tissues (e.g. the connections between the retina and the optic nerve) which have later been confirmed by improved microscopic examination. Lord Snow, recently addressing the Historical Association, expressed his view that we are now living through the latest of three spurts of progress. The first was the agro-urban revolution which resulted in the first literate cities supported by advanced agriculture about 10,000 years ago. The second was the dramatic increase in available energy in the eighteenth and nineteenth centuries which enabled us to transform the earth with machinery and create undreamed-of material wealth. Now, says Snow, we are experiencing the 'Cybernetic Revolution' in which we are beginning to understand complexity and its control for human purposes. He believes that this will be by far the most significant change of all. Dr. Ashby (1956, pp. 5–6) tells us that 'cybernetics offers the hope of providing effective methods for the study, and control, of systems that are intrinsically extremely complex. It will do this by first marking out what is achievable (for probably many investigations of the past attempted the impossible), and then providing generalised strategies, of demonstrable value, that can be used uniformly in a variety of special cases. In this way it offers the hope of providing the essential methods by which to attack the ills–psychological, social, economic–which at present are defeating us by their intrinsic complexity.'

In medicine and in management, in astronautics and in biology, cybernetics is showing its astonishing and growing powers. It is able to do this because its field is the study of complex and probabilistic systems and their control. We have tried to show in this and the preceeding chapter how the study of human location behaviour, originating as a facet of work in many other fields, has recently been regarded as a study of a system in its own right. This has happened because of closer links between theoreticians with a systems approach and practical projects in which personnel, with or without a systems view, found it an increasingly useful and powerful aid to understanding action. The latest insights (which we would stress are completely untried in practice) concern the evolutionary character of the system which is the planner's concern and the potential offered for its control by the methods of cybernetics.

These are difficult notions. Many attitudes of a lifetime may have to be modified, even rejected, if the systems view is adopted. We put this framework forward then simply because it is our belief that it solves far more problems than it creates and is at the same time an elegant and beautiful means to understanding the man-environment relationship, and a potentially powerful means for its control and guidance.

We would urge the reader not only to study the works we have listed but also to relate these notions to the world around, to his own daily experience. Only by making this attempt to relate these insights to the 'real world' will the fullest benefits be gained. From here on, this book is concerned with planning techniques. Many of these are well-tried and familiar, others are new, even experimental; we shall always make the distinction clear. We hope that many of the points discussed in this section will be better understood in retrospect when the following chapters have been read.

5
Planning as a Cyclic Process

Previous chapters have shown us man in his ecological setting and how he modifies his circumstances in order to make improvements in his relationship with the environment. We know that we are dealing with a complex and probabilistic system in which changes in activities, the spaces which accommodate them, or in communications or their channels, result in repercussions which modify the system. These changes in the system motivate others to change *their* circumstances, and so on.

From the beginning of recorded history we can discern attempts to interfere with or control this process. Usually the intervention is made on behalf of society as a whole if democratic and on behalf of a small powerful *élite* if autocratic. There are many gradations between these two extremes but always the intervention comes from some individual or group *in power*, some organisation with responsibilities and sanctions greater than any other section of society. The Athenians built flanking walls to protect the route to the port of Pireaus, elaborate traffic regulations were introduced in the city of Rome at the height of its powers, the entry of produce and merchants was strictly controlled by medieval cities, and the monastery and the feudal manor are timeless examples of finely balanced mechanisms for controlling the relationship between people, land and animals. More recently, the establishment of Karlsruhe and Versailles show what can be done to modify the environment when power and wealth are highly concentrated, whilst the seventeenth-century plans for Amsterdam (1609–10) and London (1666–7) illustrate more democratic and co-operative enterprises. One feature we should note especially and that is the highly-localised direct effects of these great works and the much longer time-span involved for their repercussions to take effect. Enterprises such as we have mentioned were wrought by huge effort but the limited transport and communications of past times limited their impact to confined spaces in the short run.

In eighteenth-century England, transformations of a different kind arose. On the one hand, an increasingly wealthy aristocracy and the nouveaux-riches aspirants to its ranks were reshaping thousands of acres of England into fashionable landscape parks as settings for their fine houses. Whole villages were moved if they spoilt the view as at Milton Abbas in Dorset, and new ones constructed to frame the park entrances and to house estate workers as at Harewood in Yorkshire. On the other hand, more down-to-earth work was forging ahead. Science, allied to agriculture was inducing men like Coke and the Collins brothers to increase land productivity and improve animal breeding out of all recognition. In the last twenty years of the century, and the first two decades of the nineteenth, whole tracts of England were reformed by the Enclosures as a direct result of the need to increase productivity and take advantage of these highly successful methods. Notice two important characteristics of the Enclosures for later reference: their widespread incidence and the direct involvement of the state through Acts of Parliament (though direct control was localised in the parishes).

As Hoskins (1955) has pointed out, the early stages of the Industrial Revolution were characterised by small-scale extractive and manufacturing enterprises in rural surroundings. Until larger-scale activity grew up and until transport and communications were transformed, their impact was localised, their side-effects slow to develop. But this was not to last for long. The fast coach on Telford's and Macadam's roads and then, above all, the railways linked together activities and enabled further interaction to be generated and multiplied in ways which knew no precedent. The telegraph, the news room and the national daily newspapers did the same with flows of information.

The catalysmic effects of these developments in 150 years are fully documented and discussed. So, too, are the myriad governmental attempts to keep pace with and control these changes through Acts of Parliament and other measures to regulate transport, communications, industry, housing, commerce, recreation, public and many other facets of life. A great deal of this effort was concerned with the physical environment. We need not recount the details here as excellent accounts are available (Ashworth, 1954), but there is one point we would like to stress. The essence of nineteenth- and early twentieth-century legalisation is direct control of the action itself. For example, permission to build houses had to be sought from local sanitary authorities following the 1875 Public Health Act. The local byelaws made under this and other Acts were specifically designed to enable control to be exercised in a simple 'yes/no' fashion; the proposal *conformed to the standards* or it did not. Whilst the relationship in simple terms between damp-proof courses, street width and ventilation and the health of the community was appreciated, the complex ecology of human settlement was not. In ecological terms, it was a matter of ruthlessly cutting plants to size (byelaws, Factory Acts, School Boards) and later of rigid compartmenting of habitats (land-use zoning under the early planning legislation).

The control mechanisms developed in Victorian and Edwardian England involved the application of police-type regulation, of 'thou shalt nots'. These methods had served mankind well in the thousands of years in which settlements had been small and interaction drastically limited. They were (and are) very unsuited to dealing with large, complex, richly interconnected systems of human ecology (Beer, 1959, Chapter 3 and Chapter 5).

We have seen the power of a systems view in *explaining and understanding* human relationships with the environment; it is possible that such an approach would help in *controlling* such relationships? The underlying theme of the remainder of this book is that *deliberate control of the man-environment relationship must be firmly based on a systems view*. Simple deterministic systems like clocks and steam engines can be controlled in simple ways by levers, governors and valve gears; but a very complex probabilistic system such as human ecology must have a rich and varied set of controls. These controls cannot be simple, coercive and 'policeman-like' as we have mistakenly thought in the past, but subtle and persuasive; in other words, our controls will have to be cybernetic. Chapter 4 showed how the control devices for any system have to be isomorphic with the system to be controlled, that is, they have to be of similar form.

This enables us to say that the *planning process must have a similar 'shape' to the human eco-system* which it seeks to control. The chapters which follow discuss in detail the construction and operation of a planning system. Because of the importance of the statement just emphasised above, and in order to introduce the detailed chapters which follow we shall now outline the planning process.

In Chapter 1 we saw how the human eco-system was 'driven forward' by modifying actions taken by individuals and groups within society. These actions of many kinds are merely the critical points in cycles which Chapin (1965, page 33) has called *behaviour patterns*. In essence, the cycle is as follows:

1. *The environment is scanned* and on the basis of values held by the individual or group, certain needs or wants become apparent, some of which might be satisfied through the physical relationship with the environment.

2. *Goals are formulated* in broad terms and perhaps at the same time certain more precise *objectives* (which must be reached in order to move toward goals) are identified.

3. *Possible courses of action* to reach the objectives and move toward the goals are examined.

4. *Evaluation* of these possible courses occurs by reference to the means available, the costs likely to be incurred in overcoming constraints on action, the benefits likely to be derived, and the consequences of action, so far as can be seen.

5. *Action* is taken on the basis of these considerations. The action modifies the relationship between the individual or group and the environment; it will also alter the environment itself and, in time, the values held about it. The environment continues to be scanned and new goals and objectives may be formed.

Thus the cycle is completed and begins afresh.

Planning, the means for controlling the complex systemic changes which give rise to, and arise from these behaviour patterns, must have a similar form. For reasons which will be clearer when we get down to detail, the relationship will not be a perfect, or *iso-morphic* one but nevertheless the correspondence must be as close as possible. In order to regulate and guide the results of actions taken by sections of the community, the community must adopt a form of control which has a 'shape' which is similar to the behaviour patterns of its members. Let us look again at the cycle outlined in paragraphs 1 to 5 above and interpret it in terms of the public interest.

Stage 1, in which the environment is scanned and in which needs and wants are experienced which might be satisfied by action in the environment, has its counterpart in the *decision to adopt planning*. As we have noted, this process has been going on throughout recorded history but has been highlighted in recent years by the dramatic rise in human populations and the corresponding impact of human actions on the life of the earth. Planning as we understand it today, the regulation of the use and development of land and of communications, including the deliberate promotion of development, is of very recent origin. For instance, in Great Britain and Germany it dates from the late nineteenth and early twentieth century. The decisions to adopt planning cannot be pinned down; they are not identifiable as sudden moves by governments or municipalities. Rather, decisions to invoke planning form steps on a gradual progression which is a long drawn-out evolution from a society dominated by *laissez-faire* principles to one which accepts the need for a certain measure of intervention by the state. Nor has planning superseded earlier controls which, on a detached view, might seem to fall within its province. Typically, planning has been 'tacked on' to earlier means of control such as housing legislation, control of extractive and productive processes and controls over means of transport. Great difficulties have arisen because of this. Both the formulation of policies and their execution have often been confounded because planning, in Dyckman's words, 'has come into being in part to fill gaps left by other kinds of decision-making' (Dyckman, 1961). The foremost problem as we see it is the need to define not only the planning system, but first to identify the 'real world' system with which our sort of planning deals. We have gone some way towards this in earlier chapters and we shall have more to say about the administrative frameworks in Chapter 12 of the book. For the present, however, we note that the first stage in the planning process is the decision to plan and that this is not a finite step but one which needs continuing thought and effort. Societies cannot rest on the laurels earned by adopting planning. To remain still in a moving stream is to be left behind; the need for planning, the definition of its roles and purposes, the relationships of 'physical' to other kinds of planning, the administrative means for doing the job; these and many other questions must be kept under periodic review by all sections of the community.

Stage 2, the *formulation of goals*, is very closely paralleled by individual, group and community behaviour. None of us likes to think that he takes purposeless action though it is often difficult to say precisely why we did a certain thing. We are distinguished from other animals at least by this; that we are able, through language, to discuss goals and objectives with friends and family, with professional advisers, or through the medium of the written word. Governments, and the political parties which seek power, offer to their potential supporters some idea of the goals which they would pursue. To do so, they must have ways and means of 'sounding out' the needs and aspirations of those people whose support they value and require. Public planning then must identify the goals which it seeks. This is a logical progression from the first stage of adopting planning since that in itself needs justification by a set of aims. The goal-formulation stage is thus in one way simply an extension of stage 1, a sharpening-up of the notion of purpose. Goals are typically somewhat vague and general, though this is not inevitable. Usually, progress towards a goal will require the attainment of certain objectives which are more precise and clear. For example, a goal might be 'the increase in opportunities for all kinds of outdoor recreation in and around the city' and some of the objectives on which this goal depends would be 'double the acreage of parks within ten miles of the city centre' and 'acquire 5,000 acres of river, stream and lakeside land within half-an-hour's driving time of the majority of households'.

The formulation of goals is of great importance since much of the planning process depends directly upon them. Once goals and objectives have been determined, thousands of decisions and sub-decisions will follow from them until such time as they

97

are reviewed and amended. Without a clear idea of goals and objectives, the choice of courses of action to be followed is indeterminate; purposeless planning may result or the planning machine may become a sort of weathercock blown by the winds of change emanating from other sources, the whipping boy for other (public or private) errors or a convenient lever for the arguments of other agencies. Talk of goals is common at the present time, not because planning has always operated without them (though there are instances where this would appear to be true) but rather because goals have been very poorly defined, or inconsistent with other public goals, or the goals of the planners rather than their 'customers'. We shall develop these and other themes fully in Chapter 6. It is sufficient to note here that both for the individual or group and for society as a whole, it is neither possible to discuss courses of action nor to evaluate them except in relation to goals and objectives.

The next stage, stage 3, in the planning process, is the derivation of *possible courses of action*. Individual and group action usually appears tightly constrained by financial difficulty, legal requirements, personal or group tastes and preferences and so on. In fact, a great deal of choice is often possible. The process of moving house as we saw it in Chapter 1 is riddled with variety; a very wide range of possibilities may exist even in cases which appear at first to be tightly limited. The decision-maker often arbitrarily limits his own range of consideration in order to bring the problem of choice within a manageable range. Also (an important point), it is apparent that the range of choice is limited by the fact that possible courses of action *outside the chooser's experience* are discounted. Had it not been for the specialised knowledge of a member of the committee, the sports club mentioned in Chapter 1 would have failed to consider the possibility of amending the court-booking arrangements.

In public planning similar considerations apply to the problem of 'generating' possible courses of action to consider but the situation is far more complex. What has to be recognised is that the plan will both impinge upon and make use of thousands, perhaps millions of decisions made through time by a multitude of public and private agencies both large and small. These decisions arise in a great variety of ways in response to many kinds of stimuli. Large public-body decisions reflect public policy to a great extent; medium-scale units such as local authorities and firms will be responsive to government policy, the money market, changing technologies of manufacture, distribution and communication, but will also exhibit a great degree of randomness and unpredictability; the smallest-scale decisions, the multitudinous number of acts by individuals, households, clubs, societies and the like will be responsive to different political, economic and social 'climates' in ways which are only partly explained by those climates, partly by local eco-system conditions and are partly random.

The 'generation' of possible course of action requires a model of the system which will show *changes of state through time* under the influence of a range of 'policy variables'. These are matters which are under public control directly or indirectly and which can influence the system in major ways. For example, in Britain the supply of development finance, railway policies, road building, slum clearance, the release of land for housing, the location of industry and offices and many other matters are all examples of policy variables which might be tested in consistent 'bundles' against a model of the system. Each 'bundle' of assumptions (e.g. one bundle might be: steadily available capital funds, slightly accelerated road programme and slum clearance, abandon Green Belt and substitute country park principle, subsidise commuter rail travel, etc.) would tend to generate a 'family' of physical outcomes in terms of distribution of population and activities and a main network of communications and flows. Of course, these plans will not be expressible in entirely spatial (i.e. cartographical or diagrammatic) terms. Many of the courses of action to be generated for study will have to be expressed in figures and in words. We should note also that some goals and certain elements in plans will have been 'passed on' by other authorities, either 'downwards' from higher-tier planning authorities (central government to regions, regional to local planning authorities) or 'upwards' for consideration and testing, or 'sideways' from other public agencies such as national utility organisations or industries and representative bodies or private industry and commerce.

These and other detailed considerations of developing, refining and the preliminary testing of alternative broad courses of action will be fully dealt with in Chapter 9.

The fourth stage in the planning process is to *compare and evaluate the range of alternatives* which has been developed. This can be done in exploratory stages in successively greater detail. A range of very broad and general plans will be evaluated in approximate terms and as the process of refinement continues the 'fittest' plans will 'survive' for further refinement and testing until a small number of internally consistent courses remain. These will be expressed in sufficient detail for a full evaluation. The evaluation itself must be preceded by two important questions: first, what elements of the plan are to be used in the evaluation and second, how are these to be measured? Just as individuals and groups attempt to optimise on their own behalf, so must the planner on behalf of society. This is a very tall order indeed. The individual knows his own goals and objectives and this leads him directly to a 'checklist' of points for evaluation. Thus a prospective house buyer will list accommodation, structure, garden space, access to work, countryside, entertainments, relatives, schools, shops, quality of immediate and neighbourhood environment and compare these with capital and running costs and non-quantifiable measures of satisfaction. He will be aware that his resources, needs and tastes will change in the future and to some extent he allows for these elements in making his decision.

The planner has a more difficult task. He must devise a 'checklist' of elements to evaluate and measures for evaluations but on behalf of a large and heterogeneous community. Furthermore, since he is evaluating not one decision at a point in time, but *a trajectory of change through time* (albeit expressed in steps of 1, 2 or 5-year intervals), he must try to relate his evaluation to changing needs and preferences (e.g. for transport methods, space standards, recreation types) at various points in the future. This may seem a frightening prospect but on another view it is a challenge. It reminds us that we are dealing with the control of a complex and probabilistic system and that this particular problem is one of the implications. But one thing is certain and that is that the elements chosen for evaluation will derive directly from the goals and objectives identified earlier; so here again we can stress the one-ness of the process we are discussing. Although the state of the art of evaluation is in its infancy (reflecting the growth of planning as a feature of the twentieth-century world) enough progress has been made to warrant a fuller treatment and this is given in its proper sequence in Chapter 10.

The fifth stage in the planning cycle, as in the individual or group behaviour pattern, is the *taking of action*. Again, an important distinction must be made; whereas the individual takes a single action which he hopes will improve his position for some considerable time (since it uses scarce resources and involves other upsets and troubles) the planner is trying to control the outcomes of a large number of actions which result in a continuous *flow of change through time*. It follows then (from the cybernetic principle of iso-morphism) that the *control mechanism must be continuous*. In other words, the 'action' phase of the cycle is a permanent feature of planning. This does not mean that the planner must mount a 24-hour watch, seven days a week like the crew of a sailing vessel, but rather that like his fellow-cultivator, the gardener, he must pay regular and periodic attention to his changing care, pruning here, weeding there, planting from time to time, and at certain intervals taking a larger and more thorough look at the situation to see whether or not it is developing broadly along the right lines.

The heart of the mechanism will therefore be development control – the making of decisions on the kinds of changes which were classified in Chapter 1. For these modifying actions in the environment are the principal shapers of systemic change – the changing state of the human eco-system. Judgements on proposals for such changes will be made by reference to models of the system, the same (or similar) models as were used to generate the courses of action or plans themselves. By introducing a simulation of the proposed change into the model of the system it will be possible to estimate the effect, if any, which the change would have on the system to deviate from the course charted for it in the current plan. Large-scale public and private developments (power stations, steelworks, motorways, reservoirs) which were known in advance will have entered the system in the plan-formulation stage but will be tested as they occur. This is for two reasons; first, the proposal may differ considerably from that originally envisaged and second, the environment which it 'enters' may well be different from that predicted by the model in earlier stages.

As time passes the environment changes. Some patterns of change, perhaps the broad outlines, will have been foreseen, others, mostly the details, will have been foreseen with uncertainty. The economic, political and social backcloth to the whole operation will have altered with it, the tastes and preferences, needs and desires of individuals, groups, communities and the whole of the society.

Thus to complete the cycle, the control mechanisms need overhaul, *the plan must be reviewed* and modified to suit these changed circumstances. The whole process will be repeated in the sequence we have described. We must be clear that this action phase of the planning process is not simply a two-level or two-part affair of continuous control and major review. As we shall show in more detail later it is a nested hierarchy of major reviews at longish intervals which mesh with more frequent minor reviews and special action exercises of many kinds until finally the day-to-day process of control is reached.

We can now summarise the planning process as a series of steps or phases in a cycle:

1. (Strictly outside the main cycle of the control mechanism.) *The decision to adopt planning* and as to what methods of planning to adopt. This has a cycle of its own with a relatively long time-span in which the administrative methods and techniques are reviewed and the education and professional organisation of planners are considered afresh.

2. *Goal formulation and the identification of objectives* for physical planning by appropriate agencies of all kinds, including the clarification of the ways in which physical planning will relate to other forms of communal action.

3. *Possible courses of action* are studied with the aid of models of the environment. These studies show how the system might behave as it changes through time under the influence of a variety of influences arising from private actions and public activities and interventions.

4. *Evaluation* of these courses of action in order to select an operational course by reference to assumed social values and the estimation of costs and benefits.

5. *Action* to implement the plan including both direct works and the continuous control of public and private proposals for change. The essence of such control is to study the impact on

the system of proposed changes in order to see whether or not they would deflect the system from the course charted for it in the plan. Again, the models of the environment used in Stage 3 are employed. As the process goes on it becomes clear that we must. . . .

6. *Review* the plan and its control mechanisms from time to time, in minor ways at shorter intervals and in major ways at larger intervals. This is necessary because we are dealing with a probabilistic system, one in which changes cannot be foreseen with certainty. Reviews must take account of both specific proposals which are different from those expected, of changes in the political, social and economic context in which the plan operates and which generate new needs, desires and aspirations in the community and its members.

Thus the cycle returns to Stage 2, and periodically to Stage 1 also. The stage is now set for the more detailed technical treatment in the chapters which follow.

6

Goal Formulation: Identifying Objectives

The previous chapter showed the position of the goal-setting stage in relation to other parts of the planning cycle. Though each part is interdependent with all the others – the form of survey is affected by the type of plan and the type of area, the review of a plan may bring about re-examination of goals – it can be argued that the goal-setting stage is of paramount importance since the decisions taken here affect a widening and deepening stream of smaller-scale decisions which follow from strategic agreement on goals. Stuart Chapin (1965, pp. 349 et. seq.) has called this the 'hierarchy of policy decisions' and given examples of its operation. Imagine, he says, that the top-level decision is 'a choice between urban development stabilised at a certain level . . . and urban development proceeding on an indeterminant [*sic*] and non-containment basis. Conceivably there could be gradation of several choices here rather than these two extremes. In any case, involved in this illustrative choice are a variety of social, economic, and public interest considerations relating to public finance, health, safety, convenience, and the general amenities of urban living. A decision on the first alternative – containment of urban development at a particular level – would involve in the planning implementation of the decision an emphasis on balance within the limits of a known size of ultimate growth. A decision on the non-containment alternative would involve an incremental approach . . . which accommodates the needs of growth as and when they occur, but still according to a plan'.

Chapin illustrates second-order policy decisions as being concerned largely with broad physical structure or form alternatives—concentration versus dispersal, a few large nuclei or several smaller ones—with possible dispositions of land uses and with related transport systems. Third-order choices get down to questions of local residential densities, street-access systems, 'homogeneity *versus* heterogeneity among functional use types and among various activities within each use type'.

There is no suggestion that the ways in which policies are made follow such a neat and tidy sequence, nor that it should. It is given in order to show the logical structure or 'decision tree' within which choices are made.

Goal-setting is important too in order to provide frames of reference in the making of day-to-day decisions. It follows from the hierarchical or tree-like nature of choices and alternatives that lower-level decisions tend to require higher-order choices to be clarified (Young, 1966). For example, it is often found that a particular proposal such as the rebuilding of a row of older shops and houses cannot be resolved without consideration of the question of the future width and alignment of the street, which itself cannot be decided until the circulation and access system for that part of the city (and thus perhaps for the whole of the city) is decided upon; this in turn forces attention onto the land use patterns which the transport system is to be designed to serve.

Wingo and Perloff (1961) show how such issues tend to escalate: 'To choose among sets of long-run developmental consequences requires a criterion not of transportation efficiency but overall socio-economic effectiveness. It seems clear that one of our concerns must be with the productivity of the region as a producer of goods and services for itself and for the rest of the world . . . (and) . . . the competitive standing of local industries in the regional and national markets.'

This argument does *not* mean that decisions on each and every small proposal must therefore await a plan for the region, the nation and the continent as the attitude of some planners occasionally suggests, simply because the 'upward' effects of lower-level decisions or choices is limited. What it does suggest, however, is that more detailed choices are greatly facilitated by the existence of broader and more general plans which have taken account of inherent detailed ramification. The discussion on goals must therefore be conducted with a full awareness of the wider, longer-run detailed consequences which follow from broad alternatives.

It follows that broad and general *goals* must be supplemented by fuller statements of the *objectives* which must be attained in order to move toward the goals (Young, 1966). There are two reasons for this. First, by their very nature goal-statements are somewhat vague and general – 'political' people and the electorate which supports them may find it very difficult to form a clear picture of what is involved in reaching a goal and planners may be disappointed, even disheartened at the lack of response (Meyerson and Banfield, 1955). However, when a broad goal is translated into more detailed objectives or actions politicians and their public are likely to show greater interest, response and desire to participate in discussions. Secondly, when a plan is prepared on the basis of any particular goal, there must be means of measuring the rate of progress towards the goal otherwise the whole of the planning process becomes arbitrary through lack of a measure of error to guide implementation and controls; more detailed objectives provide such operational measures.

Two simple examples might be helpful. Consider the goal of 'providing the most convenient pattern of major shopping centres for the people in the area'. This statement is not capable of providing a clear basis for the design of a plan nor an operational basis for its implementation. It lacks the more precise statements of objectives and standards which are needed. These might take the form of 'minimising the total amount of personal travel involved in reaching major shopping centres' (plan-design objective) and 'containing the average distance of households from major shopping centres at no more than 4·3 miles' (implementation/control objective). (Compare Friedmann, 1965.)

Consider also the goal of 'increasing the spaciousness of housing conditions in the area' which might give rise to the objectives of 'reducing the overall density of the area from the 1961 figure of 12·9 persons per acre to about 11·0 persons per acre by 1985 and the average nett residential density from 42·6 persons per acre to 28·5 within a range of 10-60 persons per acre'.

It is obvious that the same goal may give rise to quite different objectives – either because they are framed by different planners or they relate to different areas or because they are deliberately varied by the professional planner in order to stimulate the 'dialogue' between professionals and politicians from which mutual understanding and clarification may emerge or be enhanced (Leven, 1964). Different objectives (or sets of objectives) may lead to the same goal but with varying costs and benefits. The objectives will comprise sub-objectives or specific programmes of action such as investment in utilities, land reclamation, construction of buildings and highways. Each will have not only different capital costs but operating costs also. Approximations to these costs and benefits will greatly assist in initiating and sustaining the dialogue between planners, politicians and the public and the clarification of goals.

The importance of thinking-through and talking-through from long-range general goals to shorter-range objectives has been stressed in recent years by a number of writers. Altshuler (a political scientist with a special interest in planning) has said 'that truly comprehensive goals tend not to provide any basis for evaluating concrete alternatives. It is thus difficult to stir political interest in them and impossible to plan rationally in their service. Recognising this many contemporary planners claim to practise middle-range planning—planning for the achievement of goals that are general, but still operational' (Altshuler, 1965a).

There are many types of goals in physical planning. Some date from its inception and others are more recent; some are common in growing and developing countries, others in older more mature societies (Young, 1966, p. 77).

The *aesthetic qualities*—and especially the visual qualities—of the urban or regional environment is one of the oldest goals of planning. We can observe its influence in the classical Greek towns (especially the 'Hellenistic' cities of colonial expansion) and their enlarged image in the Renaissance towns of Italy, France, Spain and Northern Europe. Its influence is most apparent in Baroque planning where the dictator expressed his power in an elaborate stage-setting for his dramatic leading rôle. The modern city planning movement, originating in Europe and North America at the beginning of the present century was strongly influenced by visual aesthetic goals. Indeed in the United States one aspect of modern planning's birth has been called the 'City Beautiful' movement.

Another goal which can be traced to the origins of the modern planning movement is concerned with *healthy and sanitary living conditions* and especially as these apply to residential areas. Ashworth (1954) has shown in detail how the late-Victorian middle-class revolt against housing conditions in the mid-nineteenth century British towns provided one of the foundation-stones of statutory planning and professional practice in this country. Webber (1963b) says that the American 'Congressional objective of "a decent home and a suitable living environment for every American family" properly remains a high-priority goal to which our profession is dedicated'.

In more recent times the *economic health* of cities (and regions) has come to the fore as one of planning's principal aims. It is often maintained that economic growth as such is more properly the business of other kinds of planners (i.e. economic planners). Some maintain that economic planning should be carried out in agencies specially set up for such tasks, whilst others maintain that they should work alongside physical planners within the same agency. These questions are explored in more detail in the last section of this book but it is sufficient for our present purpose to note the increasing importance of economic development, economic 'health' and growth, however defined, as goals which are at least *part* of the concern of physical planning. This is so because economic activities occupy land areas and are sensitive to locational relationships, both of which affect the properties for economic growth and which are susceptible to the actions of physical planners.

This question of locational relationships or *'accessibility'* has itself recently emerged as a leading goal of physical planning–so much so that there is concern lest it should overshadow other important criteria of planning. But the importance of accessibility or the opportunity for interaction cannot be denied. 'This is because bare physical distance works as a barrier to human interaction. . . . Metropolitan areas have flourished in this age precisely because that type of spatial arrangement has expanded people's opportunities to find fruitful associations with others . . . we seek, then, to induce those patterns that will effectively increase accessibility to the diverse opportunities for productive social intercourse that are latent in an advanced association'.

These are only some of the more important goals which planners have set out to achieve by their work. An important characteristic of both the philosophy of the planning 'movement' and the precepts of its practitioners has been to strive for many of these goals, if not all of them, within the same plan. In other words, *comprehensiveness* is one of the defining characteristics of physical planning—a striving for the total welfare of the public in so far as living conditions are affected by and through the physical environment, rather than a partial or sectoral welfare related to health alone, or to the urban and regional economy alone, or to opportunities for interaction alone, or any other aspect of life taken in isolation. As Dyckman put it in a notable essay, 'the main gaps in rationality which institutionalised planning has been asked to fill are the presumed deficiences of other decision mechanisms in dealing with the future and the extensive repercussions of limited goals. Specifically, these deficiencies are the alleged undervaluing of the future by short-run decision and the lack of attention to "neighbourhood effects" or system-wide consequences of the behaviour of parts. Institutionalised planning thus is obliged to be both long-range and comprehensive.' (Dyckman, 1961.)

In less formal language, the comprehensive ideal of planning, and thus its desire for comprehensive goals, is founded on the belief that private decision-makers (households, firms, etc.) and public decision-makers with a particular mission (road construction, power generation, public transport, housing, hospitals, etc.) are concerned primarily with the welfare of their own family or business or part of the public service. The planner seeks to co-ordinate, integrate, design and decide on the basis of the total public welfare over all (or most) aspects of the life of the city or region, and with a longer time-span in view.

For a long time such a comprehensive basis for physical planning passed almost unchallenged but in recent years the study of decision theory and its applications in politics, business and public administration has brought forth one or two serious challenges to the logic of comprehensiveness, and thus to the possibility of comprehensive planning goals. Altshuler showed that comprehensive planners claim to guide work of specialists, to evaluate specialist proposals and to coordinate the work of specialist agencies in the *overall* public interest all through the vehicle of the 'master plan'. He maintained that in order to do so, comprehensive planners must 'understand the overall public interest, at least in connection with the subject matter (which may be partial) of their plans . . . (and) . . . possess causal knowledge which enables them to gauge the approximate net effect of proposed actions on the public interest'. In a general discussion high-lighted by case studies he illuminated the dilemma of a profession committed to a synoptic view: true comprehensiveness could result in a superficial knowledge of the work of specialists that the planner claims to evaluate for its effects on the general welfare; but a deeper concern with a partial goal (e.g. economic growth of the central area or 'downtown') must mean an abandonment of the comprehensive position.

In a response to Altshuler's arguments, John Friedmann (1965) admits that comprehensive city planning on a deliberately loose and open definition may include 'all the subject concerns for which the city claims responsibility' including economic growth, social welfare, education, housing and redevelopment, public transport, public health, recreation and culture, land use control and urban design. 'Professional fields of competence have grown up around all of these concerns. It is thus no longer possible for any single person to pretend to the universality of his technical abilities . . . the technical expert is replacing the comprehensive planner in influencing the decisions that guide a city's development'. Whilst admitting that (American) experience bears this out, nevertheless the planner 'may agree that this fragmentation among technicians of the power to influence decisions sacrifices *the view of the whole which has been the traditional claim to the legitimacy of planning*' (my emphasis).

Friedmann then resolves this central dilemma with a brilliant shift of conception showing that it arises from a mistaken view of what 'comprehensive' means. The dilemma is real and formidable so long as we think of the planner as the man whose job it is to tell all the other ('specialist') chaps how to do their jobs because he knows so much about them and can 'coordinate' them into a 'master plan' which is based on a superior view of the public interest.

Friedmann resolves the dilemma in a manner which is completely in accord with our systems view of the city and of planning. 'Comprehensiveness in city planning', he says, 'refers primarily to an awareness that the city is a system of interrelated social and economic variables extending over space. To uphold the principal of comprehensiveness, therefore, it is sufficient to say, first, that functional programmes must be consonant with the city-wide system of relationships; second, that the costs and benefits of these programmes must be calculated on the broadest possible basis; and third, that all "relevant" variables must be considered in the design of individual programmes.'

Just so: goal-setting in planning as in any other similar operation requires *the establishment of performance criteria for a definable system.* We have already established that all systems are hierarchical in nature and that the city is no exception. Single components of the planner's system (e.g. a housing neighbour-hood, a sewage works) will be systems in their own right to the city architect and the city engineer respectively who will seek optimum solutions for them. But these optima may be sought within limits (e.g. 450–500 dwellings; 9·5–10 million gallons per day). If they are adhered to the planner's system may be un-affected whatever particular design solution is arrived at by the 'specialist' agencies for housing and sewage disposal. Provided then that the planner defines the units or components of *his* sys-tem (the city or region as a whole) in such a way as to maximise the freedom of the public and private decision-makers to op-timise *their* systems within his components; and provided that both he and the public and private 'specialists' realise the nature of the relationships ('It matters little to me precisely how you design this shopping centre so long as it is around 250,000 square feet and has parking space for 400 cars . . .') *it is possible to consider comprehensive goals for a city or region, that is, performance requirements for a spatial system of interacting activities.*

The whole of this discussion is thrown into relief when we con-sider the establishment of *national* rather than urban metropoli-tan or regional goals. Leaving aside questions of the adequacy of the methods of discussion in establishing national goals, say, in socialist and communist countries, or more recently (1964) in Great Britain for the National Plan, one point stands out clearly and that is the relative ease with which the 'performance requirements' can be spelled out for the nation as a whole by way of quantifying the goals. National planners have a rich variety of measures to choose from in giving dimensions to goal statements: population, income levels, production in various sectors, consumption, ownership of consumer durables, investment in plant, savings, etc., etc. These measures may be subsumed within or derive from some broader indicator – typically Gross National Product which was used in the British National Plan. (The operation of the 'goal hierarchy' is well illustrated in that document which indicated the rates of growth in sectors which were needed to achieve the goal of a 4 per cent per annum growth in G.D.P., and which in turn required the gaining of objectives in defined sub-sectors of the national economy.) As Altshuler (1965a) says 'we are still lacking a set of social accounts for urban units that would permit policy planners to measure the current state of the city by a few simple indices. Planners are consequently unable to say when the city is performing optimally and when it is not. . . . This failure to evolve a widely accepted system of urban social accounts reflects the absence of a theory of the city'.

In the meantime what can we do to make the best of such data as does exist, which will have to serve as proxy for the ideal 'set of social accounts,' remembering that they must be indices of the performance of the whole area as a system? Previous chapters suggest that we must look for broad measures of the 'efficiency' or 'utility' with which activities and communications occur, with which spaces and channels are used, and with the 'goodness of fit' of activities to spaces and communications to channels. Also we might look to system-wide indices such as Gross Urban (or Regional) Product and average net *per capita* income, gross rateable value or average rateable value per head (Hirsch, 1964). And we might consider measuring indices of concentration or dispersion (Haggett, 1965, pp. 229–31), overall indices of accessibility or specific indices of accessibility to work, to schools, to shops, to recreation for the system as a whole (Farbey and Murchland, 1962, p. 33). And we must face the problem of making assessments of the quality of the environment as experienced by the senses of sight, hearing and smell, and considering to what extent these may be expressed in quantitative or in qualitative terms. Finally, we are dealing with an evolving system which must be capable of evolution under different sets of circumstances arising 'outside'; we must try to specify a degree of adaptability or flexibility which the system should attain—the ability to function well under different kinds and rates of external stimulus.

Some examples which indicate the sort of operational (i.e. measurable) objectives which might be adopted to serve goals in an imaginary area may be useful.

Criteria for activities and spaces may take a number of forms. Considering economic activities first, an objective might be to maintain area growth in gross urban or regional product at a rate comparable with that of the nation. In most parts of Britain at present this will not be measurable and the objectives may therefore be expressed as growth in total employment or in nett incomes or in the output of manufacturing industries. Alternatively, the objective might be to achieve a rate of growth which is x per cent *above* the national (or regional) rate, or above the past rates experienced in the planning area. It has been common in many parts of Britain to state a regional or area objective in terms of reducing the rate of unemployment. Whilst this is no doubt a praiseworthy objective in general, doubts have been cast on its soundness for small areas and on the validity of the operational measure because of the ways in which the data are collected. A more positive and very common objective is to maximise employment—one which has great appeal for many politicians and officials at both national, regional and local scales. But Leven (1964) has argued that this single objective is fraught with problems and enters a strong plea 'that coherent policies can and should be constructed on the basis of multiple objectives if planners are to make serious headway in approaching an optimum development strategy for regions'. He outlines a multiple-objective strategy for regional development which takes account not only of total employment but also the costs of government services, value added (by manufacture), total production and nett migration. He rejects the issue of work *versus* leisure on the grounds that working hours are determined institutionally (but this would not seem to be true where 'moonlighting' and the employment of married women are concerned).

Objectives for residential activity and space may take a number of forms: maximising total rateable values or rateable values per head of population or per household could be a popular measure in that rateable values, being related to a hypothetical rental values may be held to reflect a host of other variables—'amenity', convenience, quality of the buildings themselves, etc. A very common British objective has been the removal of specific numbers, proportions or areas of 'unfit' dwellings within certain time periods; yet another is the provision of a separate dwelling for every household in the area—i.e. the 'reduction (or removal) of overcrowding'.

Recreational activity or 'open space' objectives are, like those for residential activity and housing, part of the history of planning. They have negative and positive aspects—the reduction of congestion and monotony in living and working environments and the provision of green space generally, and facilities for outdoor recreation including 'organised' sports and games in particular. For a long time simple space standards have been in use in many countries such as the familiar '7 acres per 1000' in many British plans. Such objectives have recently come in for increasing criticism on grounds of inflexibility (in failing to reflect different area needs and social composition) and of inaccuracy—that is, notwithstanding the question of whether a simple ratio is the appropriate *form* of the objective statement, are the particular *standards* commonly adopted based on empirical evidence of present demands? In Britain and North America the great upsurges in recreational activities have been largely accounted for by growth, not of 'organised' team games such as football, hockey, cricket and baseball, but of individual sports such as mountaineering, sailing, fishing, golf and general family car-borne outings for picnicking and viewing. For these sorts of activities simple space standards or ratios are singularly inappropriate and with increased personal mobility almost meaningless for all but very large areas.

The limited but growing amounts of research into recreational behaviour and demands suggests a focus on the *provision of opportunities* rather than on the achievement of space standards; this is a point best taken up below in the context of *accessibility or interaction*-based objectives.

Objectives for standards of interaction or communication—the ease or difficulty with which people may pass messages, move about, and transmit goods by many different means and through a variety of channels—have long been a feature of physical plans. Phrases such as 'the need to reduce journeys to work', the 'improvement of traffic circulation' and 'the diminution of congestion along the main radial roads' are old friends to the planner. They are good examples of goals which are bound to be acceptable and by that token excite little discussion and interest – especially if they are not further developed and put into *operational* form as guidelines for policy and 'warning levels' for day-to-day implementation.

For example, an operational objective for journeys to work may be cast in a form such as 'the average journey to work should not rise significantly above 5·3 miles'. Improvement in traffic circulation might be stated operationally in terms of average speed within a certain area; central London's traffic planners have worked on this basis for a number of years and they have measured the success of their work by increases in average speeds. Reduction of congestion might also be expressed in terms of reducing the time taken to travel between stated points in the peak traffic period; alternatively the objective could be to spread the peak loading (perhaps by 'staggered' working hours) and this would be measureable as the proportion of all movements occurring in the peak hours, – say 8–9 a.m. and 5–6 p.m.

Objectives for quite complex movement can be reduced to simple measures as Haggett (1965, pp. 248–9) has shown in quoting work done in Wisconsin. The objective was to minimise the total distance travelled by children to school (subject to a number of other practical criteria). Supposing that x_{ij} is the number of children living in zone i who go to school in zone j and that d_{ij} is the relevant distance, the objective is to minimise the function:

$$\sum_{\text{all } i} \sum_{\text{all } j} d_{ij}, x_{ij}$$

In the case quoted, the problem was to redraw the school 'catchment boundaries' so as to minimise travel; the principle is, however, more general and could be applied to the journey-to-work problem by adjustments to the size and location of job opportunities in relation to residential areas and *their* disposition.

Communication of course is a general term, and *transport* is merely a part, though a very important part of it. Increasing use is being made of non-material communications, especially for the transmission of messages or information. Certainly in the future we may expect that objectives for opportunities to communicate by telephone, teleprinter, closed-circuit T.V. and the like will assume greater prominence. But to the extent that geographic location is nowhere near as important to activities which make great use of such communication channels as for those which use physical means (roads, ports, airfields), to that extent such objectives are likely to be less significant in physical planning exercises as we know them today.

Sometimes it may be that a general system-wide objective is to decrease the concentration (or simply to disperse) the jobs, or the population of an area. Again, this complex issue can nonetheless be measured fairly simply. Stewart and Warntz have developed a measure of the degree of dispersion of a population which they call the 'dynamical radius'. This is measured by

$$\sqrt{\left[\sum (pd)^2\right]/P}$$

where p = the population of each of many small sub-areas
     d = distance of each small sub-area from the mean centre (see below)
    P = total population

The mean centre referred to may be located by methods developed by Warntz and Neft which extend the common statistical measure—arithmetic mean, median, mode—into two dimensions. The mean geographical centre of any distribution (of people, or jobs, for example) is given when

$$\int d^2 \cdot G(gA) \text{ is a minimum}$$

whilst the median centre is located so that

$$\int d \cdot G(gA) \text{ is a minimum}$$

In both cases 'G is the density . . . over a very small part of area gA and d is the distance from each part to the mean or median point in question. In the same way the mode can be defined in terms of the high point on the density surface'. By making use of these measures, the present degree of centralisation of dispersion can be measured, standards for the future established and progress towards the objective monitored from time to time (Haggett, 1965, pp. 230–1).

It would be difficult to find any physical plans which did not include some goals for the quality of the environment. In many cases operational objectives are clearly indicated too. The goal of 'raising the quality of the environment in the coalfield area of the region' might be developed into operational statements including 'the levelling, soiling and planting of old spoil-heaps A, B, C and D in the first five years' and 'establishing artificial mounds and planting them so as to screen the view of pits E, F, G and H from the main road'. Good examples of such a general goal being translated into operational form are provided by some of the English coal-mining area plans–Durham, Lancashire and Nottinghamshire.

By contrast, goals and objectives in more fortunate areas– towns of exceptional architectural character, rural areas with highly attractive landscapes–are more concerned with preservation and conservation (Smith, 1967). Objectives will take the form as statements like 'the preservation of the unique aspect of the town from the south across the River Y and the prevention of any development likely to interfere with or detract from the quality of that view'.

But environment-quality objectives are not always as simple as these. Difficulties arise in innumerable ways: accepting that changing agricultural technology will produce changes in the *character* of rural landscapes how can levels of *quality* be defined? How many holiday caravans can be absorbed by a rural landscape before becoming 'excessive' from the purely visual point of view? And what can be done to clarify in operational terms such objectives as 'new private and public housing developments shall be attractive, orderly and well-designed'? or, 'in keeping with the scale and character of their immediate surroundings'?

Questions of value, of subjective judgement and preference are obviously to the fore in such cases. This does not mean that such matters cannot be stated clearly; on the contrary, it is just as important to be as specific as possible when expressing qualitative objectives as with all others. To some small extent, matters of environmental quality can be measured–especially the non-visual ones such as levels of noise and atmospheric pollution and where possible this should be done. Some interesting experimental work is in hand, leading towards the measurement of visual quality, but it is too early to report on this now (Lynch, 1960; Appleyard, Lynch and Meyer, 1964). Accepting then the primacy of subjective values in these cases it is incumbent on planners to be as specific as possible and in particular to say *whose* opinion will be used to determine particular questions which may arise in the implementation of a plan and to what extent general public opinion will be invoked on certain issues.

In matters of environmental quality, more than in all other kinds of planning objectives, noble sentiments are only a beginning; if they are to be capable of fruitful discussion and subsequent operational use they must be put into a form which makes these possible.

Finally, to conclude this illustrative list, we might consider one of the newest (and most fashionable) planning goals–that of 'flexibility'. The novelty of this goal obviously reflects the growing consciousness of planners and their clients of the accelerating pace of social, economic and technological change and the resulting increase in the rate of obsolescence of much of the physical environment–the 'structure' for our system–both of its component parts and their arrangements in relation to each other. 'Flexibility' can be termed that characteristic of a system (and its structure) which enables it to respond to secular changes with the minimum degree of disruption or disturbance to the system as a whole. Biological notions of adaptability and survival are obviously useful mental analogues here.

Buchanan (1966, Supplementary volume 2, p. 20 et seq.), considering the problem of organising a programme of substantial growth which might vary considerably both in size, timing and locational dispositions, adopted five criteria for judging three idealised urban 'structures'–centripetal, grid and directional grid. His criteria were:

'i. ... maximum freedom of choice, communications, and association for people throughout the area ...

ii. As the structure grows it should be possible for each phase to function efficiently and not to be dependent upon further growth taking place.

iii. The structure should lend itself to change and renewal in its elements, once they have been brought into existence.

iv. The versatility of the structure should not be limited by rigid standards in such matters as transport or housing groupings.

v. The structure should be capable of growth without the risk of deformation or distortion.'

Cybernetics and information theory have developed largely from study of living systems, highly complex non-living systems and 'man-machine' systems which combine elements of both. Flexibility in living systems – the ability to adapt to changes in the environment or changes in the system induced by illness or injury – is provided by *redundancy* (Ashby, 1956, p. 181; Beer, 1959, p. 47). In simple terms, more elements and more connections are provided than are strictly necessary for the functioning of the system (provided no faults ever occur).

Physical planning, inheriting the principles and practices of the building and engineering professions has tended to allocate land for activities and channels for movement on an exact basis by fairly rigid standards (e.g. 7 acres per 1,000, 800 vehicles per hour per 12 foot lane). But higher orders of complexity in a system require greater degrees of flexibility and some measure of redundancy is necessary. (In practice even the most rigidly-designed town has some redundancy, and this is in the adaptability of *people* in their usage of spaces and channels.)

How can redundancy be deliberately introduced into a plan and how can we measure it and thus compare the relative flexibility of a number of different plans? Clearly we can try to assess

(i) the flexibility of spaces with respect to activities;

(ii) the flexibility of channels with respect to communications.

In the drawing-up of plans the rights of land-owners and others must be safeguarded by giving some kind of indication of where and when changes will occur and what activities are to be permitted. But flexibility can be introduced in a number of ways; for example, one recent plan on discussing flexibility said 'land that will be required for long term use should be reserved by permitting an appropriate interim use'. But it is in the networks of channels that redundancy or flexibility is best introduced. This is very well exemplified by living systems: the human arterial and veinous system exhibits a moderate degree of redundancy whilst the brain exhibits redundancy of an extremely high order.

The practical application of this principle in urban communication networks can be considered in one example–the road system. It is obvious that if only one road is provided between points A and B any failure–an accident, a collapsed bridge, malfunction of traffic lights, etc.–will cause a serious problem. If redundancy is present in the form of alternative routes the problem will be much less severe. Buchanan's criteria quoted above show awareness of this principle and especially the importance of building in opportunities for quick and easy change *within networks* for each mode of transport and *between modes* by persons travelling.

Haggett (1965, pp. 238–9) has discussed ways of measuring and comparing certain characteristics of networks. One which is relevant is the measure of 'connectivity', *Beta*, which is found by dividing the number of connecting links (or 'edges') by the number of nodes (or vertices). Obviously the higher the number of connections between any given number of nodes–i.e. the greater the value of β, the coefficient of connectivity–the easier it will be to move through and within the network.

It now remains to discuss ways in which planning goals and objectives may be formulated in practice. In doing so a contemporary British context will be assumed; obviously some details will be different if the context is a society which is significantly unlike a modern north-west European democracy. Also for simplicity, we will assume a situation where a fresh start is being made–i.e. either at a major review of an established planning programme or where a new planning authority or exercise is being set up and a 'clean slate' approach is justifiable and necessary.

Goals and objectives cannot be clarified easily. It will take time, patience and understanding. The essential characteristic should be *a dialogue between the 'professionals' and the 'politicians'* (Bor, 1968). These terms are used in a broad sense: 'professionals' may include not only physical planners as such, but also many others involved in advising the 'politicians' and in administering and implementing policies from day-to-day – medical professionals, engineers, architects, lawyers, teachers, recreational specialists, transport operators, personal welfare professionals and many others; the 'politicians' are not only elected representatives but also many other groups, both formal and informal – trade unions, management associations, churches, welfare organisations, sporting interests, neighbourhood groups, religious minority groups and, in certain instances, 'the public at large'.

Nevertheless, the dialogue has a focus which results in a direct confrontation between the planning professionals and the elected representatives of the political unit or units for which the plan is being prepared and all the information, views, aspirations, comments and questions will ultimately be channelled towards that crucial point of contact between the planners and their 'clients'.

The first stage is one in which the planner casts his net very wide indeed to gather as much information as possible on the aspirations of the client groups. A thorough study of relevant press, radio and television material is one element, the public statements of representative groups through annual reports, proceedings, meetings and so forth is another. Obviously matters which receive a deal of discussion in local council chambers are of prime relevance. The published reports provide 'straight' information whilst a good local paper which is sensitive to local opinion will provide in its news reporting and editorial matter valuable 'slants' on the issues of the day.

From a wide variety of sources, by assiduous 'monitoring' of current material and by digging into past material, a great deal of information can be gathered. It is then necessary to sift this very carefully to see which matters are of persistent concern rather than being 'nine day wonders', and also which are issues and problems which can be tackled within the framework of physical planning. For example, the local newspapers may have been full of letters for a period of years which complain of the difficulties of travelling between certain residential areas and the city centre as well as equally vociferous letters about dogs fouling footpaths: both are clearly matters of public concern; one is capable of being dealt with by physical planning, the other is not.

We noted earlier in this chapter that aspirations have both positive and negative ways of becoming manifest. People either express their wish to have ills remedied or their desire for better conditions and opportunities. But many aspirations are latent and do not present themselves to view. They are vaguely felt and difficult to express, or, if expressed are not voiced in the supposition that there is little hope of their achievement.

Thus it is very important for the professional to cultivate the ability to 'sense' these latent aspirations which for one reason or another are not openly expressed, and to consider adding them to his shortlist of goals and objectives. To go further, it may be his professional opinion that certain goals *should* be striven for, even if they are neither manifest nor even latent. In such cases he should add these too to the shortlist.

Following these investigations the time will come when, by discussion among themselves and their professional colleagues in other fields, the planners are ready to present their list of goals and objectives to the 'politicians' for the first time. Great care should be given to the presentation. For reasons given earlier in this chapter a bald statement of goals is to be avoided at all costs. Each broad and general goal should be worked out into more specific objectives, or rather into a range of alternatives each of which might serve to advance towards that goal. The assumptions on which each statement rests should be clearly expressed. Those objectives which are mutually consistent and inconsistent should be identified and the implications of resolving inconsistencies must be spelled out.

Time spent on design of presentation will be well rewarded (Joint Program, 1965). Great care should be given to brevity consistent with full explanation and to clarity of communication. The judicious use of simple graphs, maps, histograms and other devices for 'getting the message across' will be well worth the effort involved.

For each goal and set of necessary objectives the expected effects should be described not simply on the whole community, but also for significant sections within it—that is, whilst the content is largely matters of physical planning, the form and 'style' should be readily understood by the recipients who are people playing a political rôle.

The subsequent stage involves a gathering together of initial reactions from the 'political' side of the dialogue. This can be organised in a variety of ways. It may be that the elected representatives ask the planners to receive and consider their comments, criticisms and suggestions only with a view to returning with a modified goals-objectives package. Alternatively, the representatives may take over for a while and disseminate the original statement themselves to a wider audience representing many key sections of public opinion, in order to gather responses. Or they may instruct the professionals to do so on their behalf and to report back. The precise way in which this stage is carried out will depend on particular circumstances—the nature of the area, the background of the planning programme, the political 'style' and history of the area, even the individual personalities of key figures on both the professional and political sides.

Eventually a further direct confrontation will occur at which the planners and politicians discuss a reformulation of the goals and objectives based upon further clarification which might well have been aided by further technical work (e.g. pilot demographic, economic and land development implications by the planners and more detailed 'soundings' of opinion by the politicians).

The whole of the process described here may be greatly aided, the dialogue and debate clarified and discussion made more fruitful by enlisting the aid of *simulation* in one form or another. The precise form will depend on the skills, resources, and data available, but if the growth and development processes of the area can be simulated and especially their sensitivity to different public policies for land development, economic growth, conservation, etc., it will be of great benefit (Webber, 1965). With the aid of suitable models or analogues the outcomes of different policies and their relationships to various goals-and-objectives packages can be more quickly assessed. Simulation and model-building are discussed fully in Chapters 8, 9 and 10; it is sufficient here to note that it may be some time before full-scale mathematical and computer-based simulation or urban and regional systems is possible and such analogues may be inherently more adapted to detailed work in the planning office than to the dialogues we are discussing. Some form of gaming simulation, suitably aided by 'quick, cheap and dirty' models of e.g. population growth, employment demand and supply, land development patterns, are likely to be more readily attainable and perhaps inherently more suitable to the goal-setting dialogue.

In due course, perhaps after a number of cycles of presentation–discussion–reactions–reformulation–re-presentation, it will be possible to reach agreement on a package of goals and objectives which will form the basis or starting-point for work on the planning programme proper. These should be clearly documented and given some formal recognition as terms of reference for both the politicians and their planners. Preferably they should be made public by means of press, radio and television coverage, indicating that the authorities concerned have adopted them and instructed the planning (and other) professionals to proceed accordingly.

From time to time, as the subsequent plans are implemented and as progress of the outcomes is monitored together with public and institutional opinion and reaction to that progress and the changing environment, major reviews will be undertaken (see Chapter 11) at which times the processes described here will be repeated.

In conclusion we should resist any temptation to think that goal-setting for physical planning can be put into a precise form, even in general terms let alone for any particular area. Johnson, Kast and Rosenzweig (1963, pp. 310–11) maintain that 'under the systems concept, planning occurs at three different levels: (1) master planning for the establishment of goals, objectives, and broad policies, (2) resource-allocation planning for the project and facilitating systems, and (3) operations planning for each of the project systems. A substantial part of planning involves discovering and defining problem areas. . . . Master planning, which includes establishment of broad goals, objectives, and policies, is usually unstructured. Many of the variables are unknown or uncertain. It is difficult to quantify them. . . . Imagination and creative thinking are required. It is an innovative process and requires a relatively unstructured frame of reference which is typical of human processes.'

7

System Description: Information Needs

Preliminary considerations

All purposeful action is based on the possession and use of information and planning is no exception. What kinds of information does the planner need, how does he obtain it, organise it and put it to use? What connections are there between the use of information and other parts of the planning process we have just outlined? These are some of the important questions we shall deal with in this chapter.

Twentieth-century planning has been information-conscious. Patrick Geddes (1915), one of the major prophets of the planning movement, stressed the need for wide and deep information to clarify problems, understand the context in which the plan was to operate and provide a sense of dimension, scale and the limits of the probable. His message was very clearly stated in the now-famous cycle of 'survey, analysis and plan'. The approach revolved around simultaneous awareness, or 'synoptic vision' of 'Place, Work and Folk'. His influence has been extremely powerful both for good and ill. The great benefit of the Geddesian heritage is a very healthy concern for his principle of diagnosis before treatment, understanding before action. But on the debit side, misunderstanding and unimaginative interpretation of his message has led to a tendency towards collecting information for its own sake, unselective and uncritical wallowing in facts and figures, impressions and maps, charts and diagrams, trends and influences. Worst of all, many plans seem to bear little if any relationship to these great catalogues of information; it is almost as if survey or information-collecting was a kind of ritual behaviour, an appeasement of some planning god to ensure his blessing on the plan itself; but how the word is made flesh (or the survey into a plan) is a mystery too deep to be plumbed; unlike other sacraments, this transubstantiation lacks outward and visible signs of the inward and spiritual process.

We have seen that planning can be regarded as the control of change in a system, the system being composed of those human activities and communications which have a locational or spatial element. This being so, we have a clearer notion of what information is needed in order to plan. In general, our information must be *a description of the system we seek to control*. This general requirement can be expanded: since our system is dynamic, i.e. changing irreversibly through time, we need to know *how its parts and connections change* and therefore *how the system changes as a whole*; also, we must try to identify *what has caused these changes* since this will be vital to our hopes of effective control.

The problems of describing the changing state of the system is the concern of this chapter. Questions of identifying the structure of changes and particularly their causes (so that the future behaviour of the system may be estimated) are dealt with in Chapter 8.

The description of our system

How do we begin to describe our system? In common parlance, how do we go about the job of carrying out a 'planning survey'? It will be helpful if the reader (especially if he is a practising planner) puts out of his mind all customary ideas about the job and approaches the problem afresh from first principles.

For many practical purposes (and stepping over certain philosophical difficulties), phenomena which are subject to continuous change can be described by taking observations *at intervals*. This is exactly what we do when we plot a graph of temperatures and pressures taken at a small weather station; we plot discrete points in relation to the two axes (temperature or pressure and time). If we join up the points with a smooth curve we are to some extent deceiving ourselves since we do not in fact know the temperatures between observations. But the approximation may be sufficient for the purpose in hand and known to be so from experience.

Similarly the height of a growing plant could be set down:

Time	0	12	24	36	48	60	72	84	(hours)
Height	110·0	110·2	110·5	110·8	111·2	111·6	112·0	112·7	(mm.)

From this simple statement much else could be derived which might be of value. For example, the average rate of growth of the period = 0·032 mm./hr; average rate during the first 12 hours = 0·017 mm./hr. and the average rate during the last 12 hours = 0·058 mm./hr.

But in many cases we wish to know about more than one aspect of change; in other words we want to measure a number of variables with respect to time. A child's growth can be studied by monthly measurements of height, weight and chest girth. Thus:

Age (yrs./months)	10·0	10·1	10·2	..	..	..	12·0
Height (in.)	58·0	58·3	58·6	..	..	..	63·8
Weight (lb.)	84·0	86·0	88·0	..	..	..	113·0
Chest (in.)	27·5	27·7	28·0	..	..	..	30·2

Here, an extremely complex system (a human being) undergoing constant change is represented by a *vector* consisting of three variables (height, weight and chest girth) at intervals of one month. Notice that we can observe the growth in height as distinct from the growth in weight (row vectors), we can compare them, or combine them in the form of a 'body index' such as

$$\frac{\text{height (in.)}^2}{\text{weight (lb.)}} \times 100$$

or we can observe the change in the system as a whole expressed by the column vectors.

Of course, the usefulness of such descriptions is limited by the number of variables considered. The three we have mentioned might, however, suffice for a child health clinic where the records of thousands of children are maintained and compared. Clearly we gain no understanding of the child's intellectual capacity, the colour of his eyes, his friendliness, his creativity, his hobbies or his father's occupation. A careers master, wishing to advise a group of one hundred sixth-form boys would need quite different information from the athletics master picking out a school team for competition purposes.

Complex systems may adequately be described for particular purposes by a relatively small number of variables (Ashby, 1956, p. 106). The set of variables at any given time we call a *vector* and this vector describes the *state of the system* at that time. A sequence of such vectors for a series of times, describes the way the system changes or its *trajectory* (Ashby, 1956, p. 25). Thus:

Time:	t_0	t_1	t_2	t_3	t_4	$\ldots$	t_n
	a_0	a_1	a_2	a_3	a_4	$\ldots$	a_n
	b_0	b_1	b_2	b_3	b_4	$\ldots$	b_n
	$\cdot$	$\cdot$	$\cdot$	$\cdot$	$\cdot$	$\ldots$	$\cdot$
	$\cdot$	$\cdot$	$\cdot$	$\cdot$	$\cdot$	$\ldots$	$\cdot$
	$\cdot$	$\cdot$	$\cdot$	$\cdot$	$\cdot$	$\ldots$	$\cdot$
	z_0	z_1	z_2	z_3	z_4	$\ldots$	z_n

Where t_0, t_1, t_2 etc. are times and a_0, b_0, etc. represent the values of variables a, b, etc. at time 0; a_1 b_1 etc. their values at time 1 and so on. The state of the system at, say, time 3 is given by the vector

$$\begin{bmatrix} a_3 \\ b_3 \\ \cdot \\ \cdot \\ \cdot \\ z_3 \end{bmatrix}$$

whilst the trajectory of the system is given by the complete matrix (Jay, 1967).

Now we can turn from generalities to the specific case of the planner's system—one of activities in spaces linked by communications in channels. A description of this system must therefore have these characteristics:

(a) descriptions and measures of the various types of *activity* within each of a number of sub-areas comprising the area studied

(b) descriptions and measures of the various types of *adapted spaces* within each of those sub-areas

(c) descriptions and measures of the various types of *communications* between each located activity and all others in the study area and/or between each sub-area and all others and between these sub-areas, the study area as a whole and the 'rest of the world'

(d) descriptions of the dispositions, types, capacities and other characteristics of the *channels* for communication linking the sub-areas of the study area and the study area with the 'rest of the world'

(e) the ability to show *how* the system as in (a) to (d) changes, for instance by describing *a sequence of states or trajectory*,

(f) the ability to suggest *why* activities occur in particular spaces and communications in certain channels thus relating the system directly to human values and motivations.

In the pages that follow we shall deal with the principles by which the planner should be guided in setting up adequate descriptions of his systems. Different practical problems–the making of plans for different types and scales of area–will require different levels of detail to be identified, each appropriate to the task. It is therefore necessary to discuss various levels of detail in describing our systems. Because highly detailed information is capable of being summed or 'aggregated' in order to yield greater generality (but not, be it noted, vice-versa) we shall move from the detailed and particular to the broad and general.

Activities and Spaces
Let us deal first with *activities*. How shall we satisfy the criteria for describing these, the component parts of our system? We have seen that a system may be described at any point of time by a vector, that is a list of variables, each with its appropriate value.

As Clawson and Stewart (1965) put it, 'since every action of man takes place at some point in time and space, one could thus conclude that everything which happens in the career of a person from the cradle to the grave involves activity on the land, or a form of land use. However, some of man's activities– agriculture, for instance–are closely related to land, while others are much less so. There is a continuum, from the very closest to the most remote relationship between man and the land which he uses; . . . we shall consider only those activities of man which are more or less directly related to land, with perhaps more attention to those which are closest and less attention to those which are less directly related.'

Guttenburg (1959) has warned us of the need to clarify our

notions of 'land use' which he feels we are tending to make more and more uncertain. Clawson and Stewart echo his theme, concentrating on the twin objectives of flexibility and clarity. A good classification of activities, they say, should satisfy a number of points.

First, it should deal with *activities only*—a 'pure line' classification. It should not mix up the idea of activities with the land on which they occur, the buildings in which they take place or the human motives for carrying on the activities. This is often difficult but it must be attempted if information on activities is to be of value. They remind us that 'data on improvements to land, on land tenure and on other concepts relating to land may be collected at the same time and by the same procedures' as for activities themselves and handled subsequently by the same data-processing methods.

Second, they say, activity classification should be flexible in that it can be used either in great detail or in summary form, and be capable of many different kinds of re-combination without altering the classification itself.

Third, the classification should be based on what the observer sees on the ground so that he records it with the bare minimum of classification himself.

Fourth, the data should relate to 'the smallest recognisable and geographically identifiable parcel or tract or unit of land'. For example, a farm would be distinguished by fields in different crops, woodlands, the farmstead itself, etc., whilst an area of uniform residential activity would be subdivided by units of tenure.

Fifth, the classification scheme should make the data suitable for machine processing.

Sixth, it should be possible to expand and modify the classification without altering its basic features and without rendering past records useless.

As Clawson and Stewart conclude, 'compromises with these ideal characteristics are likely to arise in one or more of several ways': the multitude of existing data sources which the planner will perforce have to draw upon will not conform to the ideal singly, let alone when many sources must be borrowed from and used in combination; planning authorities and other government and local agencies already have data which have been collected for many years and 'new data systems must consider compatibility with old data systems'. But above all, certain compromises should be avoided like the plague–the temptation to do quick 'one-off' surveys which add nothing to the establishment of an ongoing system and the equally strong temptation to use broad groupings ('residential', 'industry' and 'open space') which can never be subdivided except by fresh survey at considerable expense.

Bearing in mind the principles set out above, what bases now exist for the construction of a classification of activities?

Economic activities are classified and listed by most national governments. Great Britain's Standard Industrial Classification is a good example providing 8 major 'Groups' which are then successively subdivided to give 152 'Minimum List Headings'.

Domestic activities are best treated in a rather different way. Whilst nearly all households or families have one or more members travelling to work daily, going to the shops, and to school, and whilst at some time or other most households and their members will go on recreational trips of many different kinds, the patterns of these activities vary considerably. In other words, the *effects* on the human eco-system produced by different families is very diverse. Study has suggested that their behaviour patterns are closely correlated with the occupation and educational level of the head of the household, with the family size, composition, income and racial or ethnic group. Therefore, in any particular area of study a typology of households may be produced which subdivides the 'domestic activities' group into subgroups with particular *sets* of activities. For example, we might find that households whose heads were in professional and managerial occupations, and where the family income was relatively high tended to spend a large share of their income on durable goods and services, to travel further to work and school, to travel more frequently by private transport and to make more recreational trips over greater distances, whilst at the other extreme families where the head was in unskilled manual work would spend a greater proportion of their income on convenience goods and very little on services, to travel relatively short distances to work and school, to use public transport and to make fewer recreational trips to a more restricted range of destinations.

In similar fashion, by reference to the differing *effects* they have on our system we can distinguish between the many kinds of 'welfare and social activities'. A fire station ejects at infrequent and unpredictable intervals a small number of large and powerful machines making a great deal of noise; a child health clinic collects at frequent and predictable intervals a large number of small and frail (but equally noisy) human beings. Both activities are for the general welfare, both are 'place-related' and thus of importance to the planner, but they can readily be distinguished by their different *effects on the* system.*

There is not to date in Great Britain any work on the classification of activities (and spaces) comparable to the recent work of Clawson and Stewart (1965) which we have cited. It would be inappropriate here to attempt to make detailed recommendations. Suffice it to say that the *principles* are of paramount importance; present methods used in most British planning

* We have just begged the big question: how is a component of our (or any) system identified? We have spoken above of quarries and factories, houses, fire stations and clinics as components in the system but surely they are systems in their own right and pretty complex ones, too? We faced this problem in Chapter 4 where we learned that 'if we wish to consider the interaction affecting one single entity, then we shall have to define that entity as part of a system' (Beer, 1959). We wish to know how a system affects, and is affected by, a residential activity, a fire-fighting activity or a child welfare activity, then these by definition must be component parts of the system and distinguishable in our description.

This in another way illustrates the need for flexibility because the 'activity' we define as one component part of the system could be one manufacturing firm or fifty in an industrial area, one household (in its dwelling) or two thousand in a residential neighbourhood. As we shall see, these different levels of *aggregation* or *dis-aggregation* will be partly a matter of choice (in defining the parts of the system) and partly a matter of necessity, forced upon us by the availability of data and by difficulties of collection, storage and processing. A great deal of information concerning people and households is available in the Census of Population. Certain agencies (planning authorities among them) can obtain the finest-grain tabulations, those relating to the Enumeration Districts–(E.D.)–areas covered by one enumerator on Census day and containing about 250 dwellings and 800 persons. If a finer 'grain' is required, a house-to-house survey may be needed and this is expensive. So the greatest disaggregation readily available for persons, domestic activity, accommodation and so on is the E.D. But these aspects are often readily described by groupings (or 'aggregation') of E.D.'s in cases where we choose to describe the system in coarser grain. But remember the earlier statement: we can observe the effects of the system on whatever we have defined as a component (and vice-versa) and on nothing 'smaller'. If we have decided that a particular group of 3,000 persons is to be one component in our system then we can study (and anticipate) the effects of transformations in the system only *on those 3,000 persons as a whole* and not on some sub-group of, say, 200 living in a particular street.

work fall far short of even a practicable ideal confusing as they do activity with land cover, with structures and with ownership (e.g. 'residential', 'woodland', 'office building', 'War Department land', etc.), lacking consistency in definition and degree of detail and being wholly unsuited to modern data-processing methods.

A major effort is needed to improve matters. The Standard Industrial Classification, classifications used by the Ministry of Agriculture and the Forestry Commission, the Censuses of Population and Distribution are obvious foundations on which a National Activity Classification Scheme could rest. Until that effort is made (and it should be made urgently) we can only refer the reader again to the work we have cited and hope that it will be emulated in Britain.

The special characteristic of the planners system is its *spatial or locational* aspect. This is of course true of all ecological systems, ones in which the interactions between the components occur *in space* and new components and communications are produced *in space*. It follows then that our system must be described in spatial or locational terms, as indeed we hinted by referring to 'sub-areas' in (a), (b), (c) and (d) above. This is necessary for two reasons. First, the system is transformed by human attitudes towards the spatial arrangement of activities as we saw first of all in Chapter 1. As planning seeks to control this process, the system must be described by its spatial arrangement. Second, communications are always between 'point A and point B' where one or (usually) both are in the study area; moreover, for the planner, communications are between *the activity at point A* (or within area A) and *the activity at point B*.

Location and extent of areal units

'Space' in our usage then is *that which accommodates or may accommodate activities*. It thus comprises the surface of the earth, including water surfaces, the airspace above the earth, and space underneath the surface. Our particular concern as planners is with discrete spatial units and there are several aspects of information which we need concerning them.

The first and foremost are *location and boundaries*. To quote Clawson and Stewart once more, 'one must know the boundaries or geographic location of every area to which data are applied, whether it be a nation, a state, a county, a city, a farm or a smaller parcel.' Since we are proceeding from detail to generality, we will discuss the content of surveys about 'spaces' first of all in relation to the *parcel* which is defined as 'the smallest unit or tract of land identifiable with the techniques used in a particular study'. In a residential area, the unit of ownership might be the parcel, but within a single ownership (e.g. a steel-works) the areas occupied by different activities – car parking, office activity, storage, in addition to steel milling – would define the parcels. In general, a map on which the subdivisions showing different areas of *activity,* of land *cover,* of land *ownership and tenure,* of *physiographic characteristics* (and so on for all aspects being considered) were drawn successively would reveal an intricate lattice of boundary lines; the small spaces enclosed would be the parcels for that particular study (Figure 7.1).

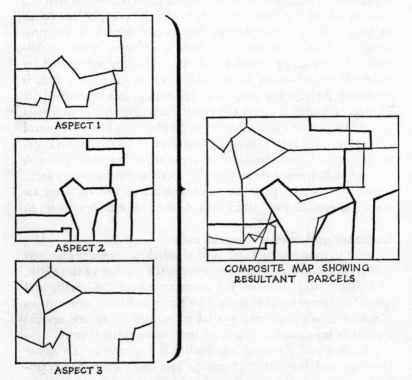

ASPECT 1

ASPECT 2

ASPECT 3

COMPOSITE MAP SHOWING RESULTANT PARCELS

7.1 Land parcels

The maps used for original field studies should identify the parcels used by inserting their boundaries clearly. In Britain we are doubly fortunate in the matters of recording parcel boundaries and geographic location, thanks to the superlative cartography of the Ordnance Survey. Any point in the British Isles may be located to an accuracy of one metre by giving a reference consisting of two letters and ten digits representing the coordinates of the point within the National Grid. Such accuracy is seldom necessary, however, and any square of 100 metres side may be identified by a pair of letters (signifying a hundred kilometre square of the grid) and a six digit number. For example, the main administrative buildings of the University of Manchester fall within the 100-metre square which is uniquely identified by the reference SJ 845965. On larger-scale Ordnance plans (1:2500 and 1:1250) parcels of land contained within physical boundaries are numbered and their areas in acres are shown.

But different users or compilers of data will find different types of parcel identification suited to their needs. Planners, engineers, and geographers will find cartesian coordinates and grid cells useful, but demographers, sociologists and economists will require tabulations for local government and other political units, trade areas and economic regions. 'Thus, it may often be highly desirable, if not essential, to describe the same tract of land in more than one way ... data obtained or recorded by one system can be translated rather readily to another, in most cases ... the smaller the units by which data are recorded, or the building blocks in a data program, the more accurately they can be made to fit any other geographic system of identification' (Clawson and Stewart, 1965).

The smallest parcel which planners are likely to need recording is the single dwelling or small shop. This can be precisely located on the 1:1250 Ordnance Survey plan and by a grid reference to ten-metre accuracy. For a restricted area the grid letters (e.g. SD) may be omitted since no confusion is likely to arise and the ten-metre reference given, e.g. 7316/8548. This reference will relate to *the centroid of the parcel*. (We shall see later that this makes subsequent analyses by larger units easy. For example, a parcel whose centroid reference was 7398/8562 might be partly in the kilometre square 73/75 and partly in

74/85 immediately to the east. For purposes of analysis no ambiguity arises; the *centroid* of the parcel is within the kilometre square 73/85 and all tabulations of the content (e.g. population, floorspace, trip origins, grocery stores, etc.) of that kilometre square would contain that parcel in question.)

Adapted spaces and improvements to land

The next characteristic of space we need to know is the type and quality of *adaptation or improvement*. Space is adapted in order to accommodate and facilitate activities and so there is often a very close correspondence between activities and adaptations (Lynch and Rodwin, 1957). The more specialised the adaptation of space, the more close is this association. One or two examples might help.

It is very difficult to conceive of an oil refinery or a steelworks being used for any other activities than those for which they were designed. A main railway station is a complex of track, signals, wires, platforms, restaurants, offices and shops contained within a large structure; considerable alteration at great cost would be needed to accommodate any activities other than those centring on 'terminal or interchange for rail trips'. For many different reasons, cemeteries, athletics stadia, public lavatories and nuclear power stations are *spaces* which cannot readily be used for activities other than those originally intended.

These are in the minority; most spaces we can think of can be used for a wide variety of activities. Churches become paint warehouses and warehouses television studios; old schools become workshops whilst houses relinquish their domestic activities to commerce, retailing, the professions, entertainment and education. Moorland 'waste' may become pasture, or a tank testing ground; a lake can be used for water supply, sailing, swimming and fishing, pasture land may change to forest or arable, arable to residential.*

* Similar remarks can be made on communications and channels. Channels include the 'ether' (as it used to be called) carrying radio and television signals, the air 'corridors' for aircraft, mountain paths for walkers, the sea, rivers and canals for water transport, pipes for fuel, water and waste products, wires for electrical energy as well as the familiar roads and railways. A channel is *that which accommodates or may accommodate a communication or a number of communications.*

Communications may use channels which were designed for other purposes: pleasure craft ply canals designed for industrial use; a motorway follows the line of a disused railway.

A very considerable amount of relocation of activities is always going on in which use is made of spaces which were originally adapted for other purposes. It seems clear that the decisions which users take about relocation are in large measure conditioned by the availability of such existing adapted spaces (as always we include buildings in the meaning). Where is space available? What kind of a site or buildings? How much of the present facilities could be used without further ado and how much alteration would be necessary at what cost? These are some of the important questions which intending relocators ask before committing themselves to a decision to move. Since relocation of activities has profound effects on the course of change in our system it is very necessary for us to record information about adaptations and improvements on the ground.

Guttenburg (1959) suggests a two-tier approach. First he would record 'general site development characteristics' under five heads: undeveloped land; undeveloped land otherwise used; developed land without structure; developed land with permanent non-building structure; developed land with permanent building. He goes on to say that 'the *type* of building, if one is present, is also a matter of interest, because it indicates the form and quality of internal space available to a user or potential user of the parcel'–thus justifying his second tier classification in which he distinguishes over 80 kinds of buildings.

Useful though it is, Guttenburg's scheme seems to place undue weight on the *building* element in adaptation and at the same time pays too little attention to the multitude of *other* adaptations of space. We prefer the later approach of Clawson and Stewart (to which Guttenberg contributed). They take a wider view, and distinguish between improvements embodied *in* the land as much as those which are *on* the land. Improvements to the land 'include levelling or smoothing . . . drainage . . . roadbeds and dams . . . even some kinds of farming practices, such as irrigation, desalinisation and liming. . . .'

The prime examples of improvements *on* the land are of course buildings ranging 'from the simplest and crudest of sheds to the tallest and most complex of city skyscrapers with numerous specialised intermediary types. But there are many other kinds of improvements essentially on the land–water and sewer lines, electric power lines, even cadastral survey lines which are reflected in rural fence lines and other structures. Some improvements may be below normal ground surface, as in the case of underground storage of natural gas.'

Information on improvements should be recorded for each parcel. For example, improvements to or in the land might be recorded as 'about 2 feet depth of imported high-quality topsoil covers the site' or 'area planted 1961–2 with mixture of silver birch, sessile oak and rowan'. More commonly, the record will be of the building or structural improvements thus: 'multi-storey framed building, sub-basement 1,000 square feet: floors 15, 16 and 17 are vacant: total floor area 17,270 square feet'. Or, another example: '20-bay single-storey load-bearing brick structure with internal steel columns, each bay 250 feet × 50 feet: total floor area = 250,000 square feet; tarmacked area on north side 1,000 feet × 220 feet = 220,000 square feet'. Notice that in these examples we have not referred to *activity*: in the first case we simply described the multi-storey building *not* that it was used as 'basement car park, stores, small shops and offices'; in the second example we record the details of the large single-storey building *not* that it is in use as a storage and distribution depot for a wholesale foodstuffs firm with lorry and car parking space attached. These details would of course have been recorded already under 'activities'.

Improvements which are associated with utility services – gas pipes, electricity lines and cables, water and sewer pipes, etc. – present a special problem because of their *linear* form. How are we to define the 'parcel' for a trunk sewer? Or for an overhead power line? The method we suggest is as follows. All activities which are essentially *transmissions* should be regarded as *communications* whilst interchanges and terminals should be regarded as *activities*; this is entirely in keeping with our whole approach in which we see the environment consisting of located activities (the elements of our system) and communication flows between them (the connections or links).

Thus, what goes on inside railway stations, bus stations, sewage treatment plants, car parks, generating stations, gas works and so on are *activities*; trains running along tracks, buses along roads, sewage along pipes, cars along streets, electricity along conducting wires and cables and gas along mains are all *communications* of one sort or another – the transmission of materials, persons, information and energy.

So, in considering such matters—we record the *fixed interchanges or terminals* in such systems, recording the nature of the activity (e.g. 'sewage purification', 'electrical transformer station', 'water pressure-reducing valvehouse') and the nature of the improvements (e.g. '2 × 36 feet diameter percolating filters, 20′ × 20′ sedimentation tank, 10 × 100′ × 25′ sludge-drying beds, remainder in grass and shrubs, total area 13·25 acres' and 'brick structure 50′ × 13′ with large access doors surrounded by 8′ high metal spiked safety fence topped with barbed wire and containing 6·6 kv/1·1 kv transformer').

One final word about the observation of improvements. We have stressed the difficulty of dissociating these from activities—the activity of oil-refining from the complex structure of the refinery, the activities of coal mining from the shafts, headstocks, galleries and all the ancillary developments. As always, the best advice is to remember the *uses* to which the information will be put. In the planner's case these are to describe his system in present and past terms seeing the relationships which exist between activities and the improvements which have been constructed and developed to 'house' them and also to be able to estimate what changes are likely or desirable by way of the *relocation* of activities. Could those cotton mills be used for other forms of manufacturing or for storage and distribution? Is it likely that those empty cinemas will come into some other use? Where is there land which could most easily be used for car parking, or for tennis courts, or for public parks? Which areas of building would most easily be redeveloped (considering the structural problems of demolition only)?

When the problem is approached this way we see that the more closely and intimately improvements are related to a specific activity, the less necessary is it to give a minute description since the likelihood of such a building or space being otherwise used is remote (e.g. steelworks, petrochemical plants, athletics stadia, telephone exchanges); conversely, the less intimate is the relationship between activity and improvement, the more useful is a full description since the succession of another quite different activity (with or without alterations to the present fabric) is more likely.

The Intensity of Activities

We also need to observe the *intensity* with which activities are carried out. This may be measured either by relating annual *inputs* of labour or capital, outlays on goods, etc., by annual *outputs* of crops, manufactured goods, retail sales, or by the *stock* of persons, structures per unit area. The main problem here, as Clawson and Stewart emphasise, is that the way we scale intensity 'will depend in large measure upon the kind of activity'—employees per square foot in office buildings, persons per net acre in housing, sales per square foot in retailing, etc. They go on to show how intensity is often related to improvements (as discussed above). Furthermore, redevelopment of low-density residential areas with blocks of flats and maisonettes will permit a higher intensity of activity; the changeover to supermarket methods has had this effect on the intensity of retailing though this is more a matter of changing management practice.

Most importantly, the choice of areal unit will affect the level of intensity recorded. Haggett (1965, pp. 200–10) has shown in general terms how data are distorted by the choice of the size and shape of area. A very familiar example is the population density map where a local government area will be shaded to represent a moderate population density overall but concealing the very high densities in some parts and the very low occupation of other sectors, which would be revealed by mapping the individual wards, census tracts or parishes.

Once again we can see the value of recording our data at the finest possible grain. Finely detailed information can always be summed to yield more general results, the reverse is seldom true but always difficult and expensive. Whilst at present it does not seem possible to have a single measure of density for all types of activity, we can nevertheless urge that an effort be made to keep the number of measures as small as possible. It may be found that the intensity of most activities may be measured in (or converted to) units of *persons* or *annual money flows* in relation to area.

The intensity of extractive, agricultural, processing and distributional activities may be measured in terms which are reducible to annual inputs or outputs of money; recreational, cultural and educational activities may be measured in terms of annual person-visits or by visitor-expenditure. In the important case of residential or domestic activities, we are accustomed to measures of persons per room, per dwelling, per acre or households per acre, or dwellings per acre but it is becoming clear that measures of family or *per capita* income and expenditure are invaluable for many planning purposes. For example, transportation studies estimate present and future trip-making patterns and car ownership rates by reference to family or *per capita* income whilst information on household expenditure on retail goods and services provides a starting point for studies of shopping centre sales (University of Manchester, 1964 and 1967). The usefulness of such measures derives from observations which show that if the income, occupation and educational attainment of the head of a household is known, then much of that household's behaviour (journey to work, recreational pursuits, shopping patterns, etc.) can be estimated within certain limits of probability.

Vacant or unused land
One of the most important kinds of information needed by the planner is concerned with land which is variously described as 'vacant', 'idle' or 'unused'. At first glance this is a simple concept but on closer inspection it presents the most thorny problems. Does 'vacant' mean the total absence of any kind of activity? Permanently or temporarily? If the latter, how long is 'temporary'? What about the temporary vacancies caused by movements of occupiers – what the estate agent calls 'voids' – and the agricultural land which one year is 'unused' but is actually lying fallow in a rotation scheme?

As Clawson and Stewart point out, the idea of intensity is involved too inasmuch as 'some land is used at such a low degree of intensity that one cannot say with any assurance that it is used at all, or cannot know for what purpose it is used.' But for obvious reasons this category of 'unused' or 'vacant' land (and buildings) is one of prime importance both in estimating the efficiency with which land is currently being used and in allocating land for new uses in a plan.

Anderson (1962) believes that 'the condition of idleness can best be stated in terms or an area's last, or most obvious productive use. A subsequent return to economic productivity may be within the present category of use, although frequently a state of idleness may merely represent a transition period during which a change from one major use to another is occurring'. Thus we could distinguish vacant *residential* building, vacant *storage* building, idle *grain* land, idle *forest* land awaiting replanting, and so on. But Clawson and Stewart admit that 'the probable future use of some idle land is so unclear that a general or miscellaneous idle category may be necessary'.

Chapin's approach is directed towards the framing of general urban plans. 'We must look at vacant and open land as something more than a residual category in the land use survey, something that is amenable to classification in some detail and the subject of special attention in land use planning. . . . The purpose of classifying vacant land is to determine its suitability for various forms of urban development' (Chapin, 1965, p. 300). He first identifies topographic characteristics, the presence of swampy ground, steep slopes, land liable to flooding or subsidence–and so classifies vacant land into *prime* for development (in the absence of such disadvantages as given above) and into *marginal*, the remainder. The application of different standards (e.g. of slope) would enable classes of prime land to be distinguished.

Next Chapin turns to the classification of vacant land according to the improvements present–water, sewerage, power, rail and road access–and uses these in various combinations to subdivide the prime land, 'obviously, a classification system which accommodates every possible combination can become unwieldy'.

His classification is developed by combining factors of activity (i.e. its absence), natural characteristics, improvements and communications. This results in a vacant land classification scheme which though very useful for a 'one-off' planning exercise would be too rigid and combined for an ongoing data system in a planning agency.

It would in our opinion be desirable to keep these characteristics separate to the greatest possible extent: physical characteristics noted as such, improvements as such, and so on, as for all other activities and parcels. The key aspect is activity itself, or rather its absence. It is suggested that Anderson's advice be followed–sub-distinguish the *absence of activity* by reference to the last known activity or most likely future activity. If all these aspects were recorded then Chapin's practical requirements would be satisfied also, and in a far more flexible manner.

Tenure and Ownership
We must also have information on the tenure of land and as before this will relate to parcels. Since tenure is not observable, details will be collected by questionnaire or interview. Ideally, the following would be distinguished: freehold, leasehold and sub-leasehold tenure; names of freeholder(s) leaseholder(s) and sub-leaseholder(s), the expiry date (month and year) of the current leases and sub-leases. In Great Britain it is presently very difficult to discover this information. This not only makes certain planning (especially development and re-development) operations difficult but also makes for lack of fluidity in the land and property market. A scheme for the registration of all titles of land has been in force for some time but at present only a small proportion of all freeholds are registered. There are other sources of information which we discuss later.

Land Values and Prices
The disposition and intensity of activities and the improvements made in and to land are inseparable from the questions of value and price. The historical development of the theory of planning and the development of the practice of planning is riddled with the thorny questions of the value of land, with taxation, with the payment of compensation, the recouping of betterment and the collection of taxes on capital gains. Development and relocation decisions, as many writers point out, can largely hang on questions of land price and credit based upon the expected or existing value of land and buildings. The existence of plans and planning controls can affect the values and prices of land very considerably.

It follows that planners must have ready access to information on these issues. Valuation is a complex business and it is quite outside our scope here to discuss what basis shall be used for this head of information. Again, an ideal data system would hold data on values at the parcel level but for reasons we shall give later it may be neither possible nor necessary to have such finely detailed information.

Communications and Channels

The counterparts of activities and spaces are the communications and channels which link the system's elements. We shall deal with these topics in similar fashion, outlining the principles which should guide the planner in seeking, classifying and recording the necessary information. Also we shall still be dealing with the finer levels of detail so that we can deal later with aggregation into broader formats.

Communications

With 'land uses' it was shown to be important to distinguish very clearly between activities as such, and other facets such as intensity, location, tenure, value and so on. Similarly with communications we must identify the various elements in the idea and record them clearly. The ruling principle once again is that detail can always be generalised and factors combined but the reverse is difficult, wasteful and costly.

We have seen in earlier chapters that communication occurs in order to transmit 'information' from the location of one activity to another. In other words, for the planner, the ideas of activity and communications are very closely linked. Activities can become spatially separated only by the existence of communication and most theories of urban growth accept this either explicitly or implicitly (Meier, 1962). We showed earlier the necessity for recording activities by *parcels*, that is by identifiable areas distinguished by a single activity, intensity, unit of tenure, etc., etc. It follows that the description of communications must be directly related.

Locations of origins and destinations

Since communication is essentially *transmission between located activities* we can describe them in part by the location of their *origins and destinations*. But it will be convenient to begin with a given parcel (previously identified in the survey of activities and spaces) and consider this as the origin of communications. For example, a parcel containing, say, residential activity is located at the reference point 889843 and has regular communication with related (work, social, recreational, educational, service, etc.) activities at

points 845965 – the principal wage-earner's work-place
891845 – the local 'convenience' goods shops
893904 – the medium-sized durable goods shopping centre

square 83 98 – the nearest regional city centre
892863 – a large suburban park

square 81 84 – the airport (as spectators)
757858 – a small musical group

–
–
– } home of relatives and friends
–
–

The content transmitted

Communication occurs primarily because of the spatial separation of activities. The transmissions take many forms – the raw materials brought to the factory, the component parts to the assembly plant, finished products from factory to wholesaler, wholesaler to retailer, telephone messages, letters, radio and television signals, personal journeys and so on. We also include *sensory data* i.e. impressions on the human senses arising from the environment as a whole and its constituent parts, for as we have seen in earlier chapters these flows of information are very important in creating impressions of desirability or undesirability and thus they influence location decisions. This is particularly obvious in certain kinds of decisions – e.g. it is clear that pleasant scenery and the likelihood of warmth and sunshine influence the choice of holiday and recreation areas, to a lesser extent questions of environmental quality influence the choice of home, factory and office location. Advice on planning 'survey' has usually dealt with such questions separately; we believe it is important to see sensory impressions as communications and to treat them as such.

Broadly there are four categories of transmission:

(1) Persons   – e.g. by walking, riding, driving a car, etc.

(2) Material goods – e.g. coal, iron ore, timber, manufactured goods, components, parcel post, water, oil, etc.

(3) Information   –e.g. telephone messages, radio, tele-
communication, etc. and sensory im-
pressions including sights, sounds,
smells, etc.

(4) Energy   –e.g. electrical transmission by overhead or underground conductors.

Modes of transmission

These include road vehicles, railway trains, aircraft, ships, pipelines, cables, electromagnetic radiation, the human senses, and
so on.

Volume, frequency and intensity

Finally we must know how often or how regularly transmissions are made. Chapin has said that we are particularly concerned with activities and communications that tend to regular
patterning and persistence. It is of little interest to record a
twice-yearly visit by a young man to his ageing aunt and uncle
in Bournemouth; vastly important to note the volume of the
regular pilgrimages made by faithful supporters of a popular
football team. Volume, frequency and intensity are inter-
related. For instance, most urban roads are quite capable of
carrying the *daily* volume of trips imposed upon them but in-
capable of coping with the *intensity* which results from the desire
of most of us to begin and end work at similar times. The *frequency* of this behaviour is usually five or six days out of seven–
hence the absence of a Sunday morning 'rush hour'. Special
events held at irregular times and places–agricultural shows,
fairs, ship-launches–can cause great volumes and intensities of
communication but may not be noteworthy because of their
relative infrequency. Special circumstances demand special
arrangements (e.g. a royal wedding)–the planner's main concern
is with the patterned, the regular, the frequent, the predictable. The foregoing notes may be brought together by considering a typical record of the communications made by a
single activity at a particular location–let us say it is a small
factory assembling watches.

Chronos Watches Ltd: grid ref. 809543

COMMUNICATIONS RECORD

From	To	What Transmitted	Means of Communication	Frequency	Time	Notes
London Airport	809543	Watch movements	Road vehicle	1/week	3–5 p.m. (Friday)	Not in August
Northampton	809543	Leather straps	Road vehicle	20/year	irregular	
965267	809543	Watch faces	Road vehicle	20/year	irregular	
842787	809543	J. Smith, worker	Bicycle	1/day	08.15–08.30	
843951	809543	T. Jones, worker	Motor car	1/day	08.15–08.30	
.	.	.	.	.	.	
etc.	etc.	etc.	etc.	etc.	etc.	
*809543	Glasgow	Watches in bulk	Aircraft	10/year	irregular	
809543	Manchester	Watches in bulk	Rail parcels	10/year	irregular	
809543	London, W.1	Watches in bulk	Road vehicle	10/year	irregular	
.	.	.	.	.	.	
etc.	etc.	etc.	etc.	etc.	etc.	
†809543	810156 (GPO)	Approx. 200 letters and packets	Road vehicle	1/day	16·30	Half volume in July and August
809543	Central London	Conversation	Telephone	20/day	irregular	Mostly before 11 a.m.
.	.	.	.	.	.	.
etc.	etc.	etc.	etc.	etc.	etc.	etc.

The schedule could obviously be extended to cover all the communications made by this particular activity. It could also be more finely detailed–for example at * and in the following

147

lines the shipment of the finished watches to Glasgow by air could be sub-divided to include the vehicular trip from the factory to the airport, and at † the movement of letters and packets could be expanded to show what percentage were destined for say, London and the South East, other parts of Great Britain, various countries overseas, and so on. Decisions as to the fineness of detail will depend, *inter alia,* on the scale of the planning exercise. In an urban or metropolitan plan, the movements of postal packets from premises to Post Office would be useful but in regional planning a grosser treatment showing only movement *between post offices* would probably be sufficient.

We stress that we are giving a highly detailed example in order to provide a firmer basis for subsequent generalisation. Also, whilst it is very unlikely that any planning agency would be able to hold information as detailed as we have illustrated, it may be that some classes of activity or of communication may need such treatment because of their special importance to that city or region. Our examples might be characteristic of such specially detailed parts of the information store.

Channels
Finally, we deal with information on the means by which communications are transmitted and accommodated–the channels. These include, on the widest possible view, the whole of the land and water surface of the globe, the stratosphere and space beyond. But as planners, we are principally interested in the idea of specially adapted channels devised (or inherently suitable) for frequent, patterned and regular use. Pathways, tracks, rivers, lakes, seaways, canals, roads of all kinds, pipelines, conduits, cables, tunnels, railways, air routes, 'corridors', flight-paths and airport approaches, in fact any physical means for carrying communication comes within the ambit of our concern.

Networks
Some communications, especially telecommunications, are diffused or broadcast and occupy fields or volumes. Planners are most concerned with communications which tend to a linear flow and use *networks of channels.* As we shall see later, the geography or geometry of the network is its most important

characteristic and for describing and recording this, maps are unsurpassed. Familiarity may partly blind us to the fact that maps contain a rich store of information on networks. They show with consistency and precision not only the shape and texture of road and railway networks but also intersections and interchanges, the relative importance of different kinds of links and nodes and in some cases distinguish ownership of channels. Obviously the smaller the scale of the map, the greater is the use of generalisation and conventional symbols. But even then, the British 1″ to 1 mile Ordnance Survey goes a very long way in providing information on channels and networks for *regional* planning purposes, as does the 6″ to 1 mile and 1:2500 scale plans for *urban and metropolitan* planning.

Not all the necessary information can be shown on maps, however, and the planner must augment it to give him the required scope and detail. The extra information which will almost always be needed can be grouped as follows:

Capacity

The record should show for each link or section in a network the maximum amount of communication throughput which it is capable of carrying *in its existing state*. The measures used will depend upon the nature of the channel and the communication. For example, road capacities are commonly stated in terms of passenger-car-units per hour per lane, railway capacities in terms of trains per hour or passengers per hour or goods trains per hour, telephone cables in terms of the number of (simultaneous) messages which can be accommodated, electrical cables in terms of the designed capacity in kilovolts or megavolts. Any special restriction on capacity should be noted—a 'bottle-neck' on a road caused by a narrow bridge (or, more importantly, the capacity of intersections which constrain capacity on the entering links); an operating restriction imposed administratively or by legal means limiting jet aircraft operation or the speed of trains over certain weak stretches of track; the use of one way or 'tidal flow' systems on roads at certain times of the day and days of the week—and so on. One very important aspect of capacity is that of *potential increase*. Here we are in a highly complex field; consider the case of urban roads where capacity may be increased by a great range of actions including parking and waiting restrictions, 'clearway' regulations, pavement (surface) marking, traffic-light systems, one-way or tidal-flow systems, human controllers, computer-aided traffic controls and so on. All these possibilities for increasing channel capacity do so *within the present physical limits of the road*; the planner will not then wish to record such information but rather to co-operate with highway and traffic engineers in testing wide ranges of possible action in the course of his normal work. Rather he will have to record the *possibility of enlarging the channel*. This information will come mostly from information already gathered under the headings of 'activities' and 'spaces' —e.g. the nature and intensity of activities alongside a congested road, the value and ownership of adjoining land, its physical (topographic, geological) nature and other relevant matters. There the matter may well rest except in the case of channels which are quite obviously critical to the future working of an area when it might be desirable to make a special collation of such information, even at the risk of duplications, which could be filed with the rest of the data on that particular channel.

Ideally information on potential enlargement of channels will show the extent of the possible increase. For example, a stretch of road might be labelled in the record as 'capable of being widened to dual 3-lane carriageways; but cutting 30 feet deep through sandstone near Ironmasters Arms (grid ref. 263451) needed'; a suburban railway line might be 'capable of carrying 30 passenger trains, say 15,000 passengers, per hour in each direction when new train control and signal system introduced; British Rail hope 1971–3'.

Information on capacity, its restriction and potential increases are vital, as we shall see, when we come to deal with the stages of devising, testing and evaluating alternative plans.

Vacancy, unused channels

As in the case of space, it is useful to know of the existence of vacant or unused communication channels. Again, we can distinguish between those channels whose usage is so light as to be virtually unused and those which carry no communication at all and are lying idle or derelict. It may be that they could usefully be reopened under future conditions of land development, or used for a new purpose (such as the recreational use of once-commercial waterways) or used for a different mode of transport (disused railways as footpaths or roads). Notes on the extent of needed co-operation and improvement and on the extent of dereliction are useful.

Tenure, ownership

It is important to record the owners or owners and operators of communication channels. We should note too that whereas the *means of transport* may be owned by one agency (an airline, a bus company), the channel itself is often owned or leased by someone else (a municipal or private airport authority, a private landlord, the Postmaster-General). In Britain at least, most roads are 'public highways' and any question of ownership is a complex problem! In practice however various agencies are responsible for their construction, upkeep, improvement and maintenance (the 'highway authorities') and it is they who should be recorded. Private roads, streets and bridges, being the exception, are simply recorded as are toll bridges and ferries.

Price, charges, costs

The actual usage made of various means of communication (and hence the flows in channels) and the choice between modes or routes is to a great extent a function of the cost of using each available mode and route in return for the resulting quality of service. This is a complex field to which we shall return; for the time being we mention it to show the relevance of recording information on fares, tariffs, tolls and similar charges.

A note on terminals and interchanges

Here we include railway stations, bus stations, docks and harbours, airports, parking places of all kinds, interchange complexes (e.g. combined road/rail stations, taxi rank and car hire facilities) in general *any* place of interchange between one mode of transport and other involving specially adapted space.

We regard these as *activities contained in spaces* and suggest that they be included under those heads of information and treated in precisely the same way as all other activities. Obviously they will loom as large entries when considered under the heading of 'communications' but the format we have given as an example (see above) is we believe useful and convenient. The reader should compare it with say a page in an ordinary railway or bus timetable; he will see that very little adaptation would be necessary to suit the planner's purpose and to co-ordinate it with all the rest of the information we have been considering.

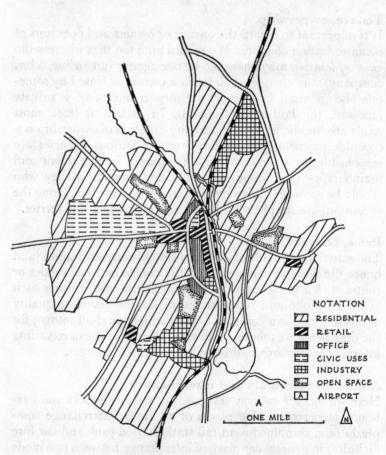

NOTATION

▨	RESIDENTIAL
▨	RETAIL
▥	OFFICE
▤	CIVIC USES
▦	INDUSTRY
▨	OPEN SPACE
Ⓐ	AIRPORT

ONE MILE

7.2 Traditional land use map

Integration and Simplification

We have now given an outline of the format of information on activities, spaces, communications and channels (see Figures 7.2, 7.3, 7.4, 7.5 and 7.6). This has been given in some detail for reasons which have been stated. It is extremely unlikely, even

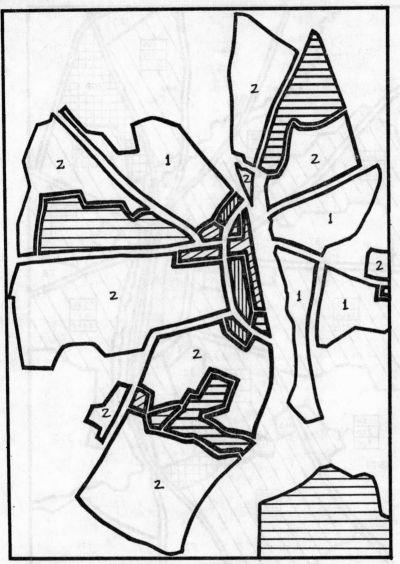

RESIDENTIAL AREAS:
EMPLOYMENT AREAS:

| 1 | "WHITE COLLAR" (E.G. S.E.G.'S 1-4, 13) |
| 2 | "BLUE COLLAR" (E.G. S.E.G.'S ......) |

 INDUSTRY (E.G. S.I.C'S I, II, III)

NON RETAIL SERVICES (S.I.C. ......)

RETAIL (S.I.C. ......)

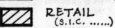 OTHER (S.I.C. ......)

7.3 Activities

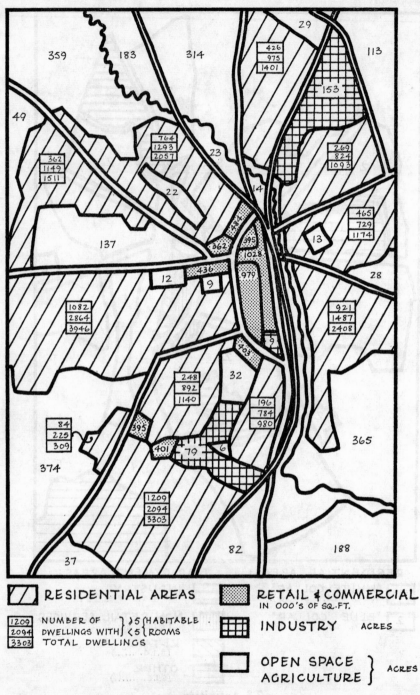

359   183   314

29   113

| 426 |
| 975 |
| 1401 |

153

49

| 764 |
| 1293 |
| 2057 |

23

22

| 362 |
| 1149 |
| 1511 |

| 269 |
| 824 |
| 1093 |

14

634

| 465 |
| 729 |
| 1174 |

137

362   395

13

1028

12   436

979

9

28

| 1082 |
| 2864 |
| 3946 |

| 921 |
| 1487 |
| 2408 |

9

403

| 248 |
| 892 |
| 1140 |

32

| 84 |
| 225 |
| 309 |

395

| 196 |
| 784 |
| 980 |

401   79   6

374

365

| 1209 |
| 2094 |
| 3303 |

37   82   188

▨ RESIDENTIAL AREAS   ▦ RETAIL & COMMERCIAL
IN 000's OF SQ.FT.

| 1209 | NUMBER OF   } ≥5 { HABITABLE
| 2094 | DWELLINGS WITH } <5 { ROOMS
| 3303 | TOTAL DWELLINGS

▦ INDUSTRY   ACRES

▢ OPEN SPACE
AGRICULTURE } ACRES

7.4 Spaces

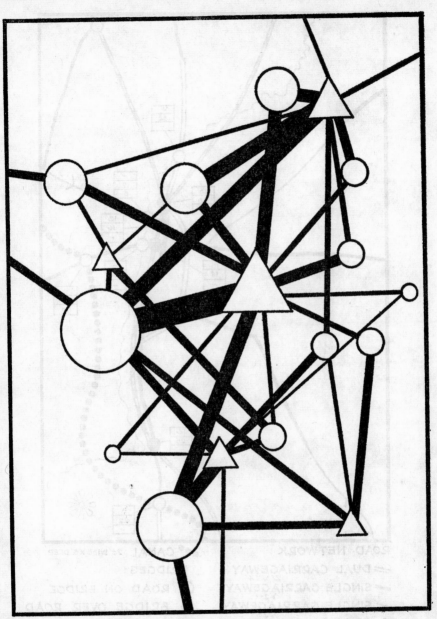

⬤ ORIGIN
(RESIDENTIAL AREAS)

△ DESTINATION
(EMPLOYMENT CENTRES)

AREAS PROPORTIONAL TO NUMBERS OF PERSONS.
AS ARE WIDTHS OF FLOWS

7.5 Communications

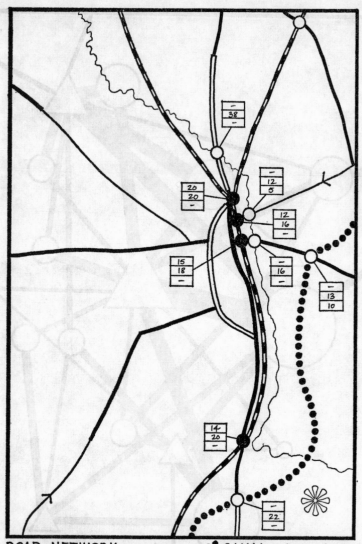

ROAD NETWORK:

⟹ DUAL CARRIAGEWAY

➤ SINGLE CARRIAGEWAY 2' X 24' > 25'

— SINGLE CARRIAGEWAY < 25'

❯ GRADIENT > 1 IN 8

⟹ RAILWAY
MAIN LINE DOUBLE TRACK
CAPACITY 25,000 PASSENGERS/DAY
IN EACH DIRECTION

●●● CANAL 25' WIDE X 5' DEEP

BRIDGES:

○ ROAD ON BRIDGE

● BRIDGE OVER ROAD

14
20
4

BRIDGE HEIGHT IN FEET
BRIDGE WIDTH IN FEET
WEIGHT RESTRICTION IN TONS

 AIRPORT
RUNWAYS : 3500' ; 2400'

7.6 Channels

given the enormous potential of modern data-handling equipment, that any planning agency could afford to collect, manage and regularly revise the volume of information which would result if all of it were in the form we have given. Even a very small community might consist of around 100,000 activities and spaces and *millions* of separate communications on that basis—in large cities the figures would be in astronomical range.

How detailed should the planner's information be? If some reduction of detail, i.e. some generalisation is to be made how should this be done? When must detail be maintained? How are these matters decided, and by what criteria?

The answers to some of these questions will be given later. Here we will confine ourselves to dealing with the questions of *how* to get more manageable volumes of information.

In addition, we have spoken of activities, spaces, communications and channels in somewhat separate terms—for the sake of greater clarity. But our approach to the environment has been to see it as a system—an integrated whole. Is it not important that information should also be sought, stored and managed in ways which respect the integrated nature of the environment? We shall discuss ways in which this can be done.

Activity Systems

Chapin (1965, Chapter 6; Chapin and Hightower, 1965) is the originator of this useful concept which he defines as 'behaviour patterns of individuals, families, institutions, and firms which occur in spatial patterns that have meaning in planning for land use'. He goes on to make it clear that 'the analysis of movement systems—the related component of interaction—has become the basis for transportation planning, the study of activity systems serves a corresponding purpose in land use planning'. Chapin maintains that hitherto planners, by concentrating on 'land use' (itself a vague and imprecise notion as Guttenburg showed) which is the *result* of recurrent behaviour patterns, have failed to study *spatial or location behaviour itself* (Foley, 1964). Such behaviour patterns lie at the very heart of the planner's concern; they give rise to the problems he is called upon to solve and he must manipulate those patterns for a solution.

Therefore, the survey of activity systems may be regarded as having a central place in the information needs of planning in two senses: first, because of its overriding relevance in dealing with the actual 'workings' of groups occupying the city and the region and second, in that it integrates and illuminates nearly all other forms of information (e.g. on population, industries, land, transport systems, etc.).

This view has important practical consequences and suggests that the survey of activity systems can be a key survey covering a great deal of the material we have outlined so far. In other words, by focussing on one particular *activity* at a time, on the *space* which it occupies, and by examining the *communications* made as it interacts with many other activities (and to some extent the *channels* which they use), the activity-system survey performs the integrating function we referred to above.

Chapin suggests a 'typology of activity systems' in which three broad groups emerge; firms, institutions and households (including individuals). Firms are typically associated with productive activities such as extraction, processing, manufacture, assembly and distribution; institutions perform such functions as education, police and fire services, social, political, religous, recreational and other 'special interest' activities whilst households and individuals engage in a rich variety of activities ranging from the winning of income, raising children, many forms of formal and informal personal contact to recreation, community service and the mundane business of shopping and visiting the dentist.

The behaviour patterns of the three main groups are sufficiently different to warrant slightly different forms of survey in detail which nevertheless conform to certain general principles. These are: the need to establish the precise nature of the *activity or activities* carried on by the unit; to describe the nature of the *space* it occupies (location, buildings, land, floor areas, services available, etc.); and to record the origin, destination, frequency, content, mode and volume of all forms of *communication* engaged in.

With these principles in mind, and guided by the details we have given earlier in this chapter, and by the formats suggested by Chapin, the reader will be able to devise activity-system surveys suitable for use in particular circumstances.

Simplification by Sampling
Once again the problems of the volume of work and the handling of the sheer mass of information are raised. The most

obvious and proven method of reducing the size of the task is by resort to *sampling* (Jay, 1966). It is a matter of common observation as well as rigorous analysis that whilst behaviour patterns of one retail tobacconist may differ greatly from those of another, or whilst the activities engaged in by two families may be grossly dissimilar it is nevertheless possible to identify certain underlying common features (inputs from wholesalers of cigarettes, daily trips to work, etc.). If classification of activities is done with sufficient care a good sample will be a reasonable and useful indication of the behaviour of all the activities in that class.

Simplification by the use of larger areal units

Simplification and economy may be gained by the acceptance of lower standards of detail than we have set out so far. We suggested earlier that the basis for the finest detail of recording activities was to identify 'parcels' which were the smallest spaces resulting from the superimposition of areas denoting physiography, soils, tenure, value and other patterns including activities and then to record the activity contained in each parcel. A great deal of simplification results if we begin by defining much larger spaces at the outset. These might be census Enumeration Districts or Divisions, Urban Wards and Civil Parishes, Employment Exchange Areas or some other type of space. Usually the choice will be with areas like these for which certain ranges of published information are available. Great disadvantages are apparent because whilst census data obviously fits E.D.'s perfectly, it is very difficult to convert other information (e.g. on employment, derived from the Employment Exchange records) to fit the E.D.'s. To make matters worse, government departments may change the boundaries for which they collect and publish information; they may do so regularly (as with the Census E.D.'s) or irregularly to suit their own convenience in relation to changing circumstances.

These are some of the reasons why it may be desirable to adopt an arbitrary areal unit and to convert all information to that basis. The initial labour will be considerable but many benefits could accrue. For example, the National Grid system used by the Ordnance Survey has many advantages. First, it is 'nested', i.e. any grid square itself comprises a number of

smaller constituent squares. For example, a square of one kilometre contains one hundred squares each with a 100-metre side.
This enables data to be built up easily into larger units, and
subsequently returned into smaller areas. Second, the squares
themselves are directly related to the sheet boundaries of O.S.
maps: for this reason rough field survey data obtained on, say,
a 1:2500 sheet can be totalled to produce the information required *for that square kilometre*. Third, areas may readily be
identified by the O.S. sheet number e.g. TF 6013. Fourth, a
number of agencies which collect information useful to planners
are beginning to use the National Grid as their areal units
system and, finally, grid systems are well suited to use with
electronic data-processing and retrieval methods, notably the
computer's line-printer (which, like a typewriter, works ortho-
gonally) as a quick means of producing 'maps' direct from,
say, a magnetic tape which is storing information by grid
squares.

Other methods may exist, or may be devised. What we wish to
reiterate is the need to bring all data to *a common system of areal
units*; unless this is done its utility is very considerably reduced,
indeed it may be valueless. This is because of our cardinal need
to understand *activities within spaces* from which it follows that
information on all aspects of activity (e.g. the familiar conventional measures of population, employment, land value,
ownership, etc.) as well as the spaces which support them must
be coincident and congruent; this principle must be maintained
strictly.

This does not necessarily mean that all the areal units in a
good system need be of common size; quite the reverse. It is
convenient if approximately the same amount or diversity of
activity and of origins of communication is contained in each
areal unit. Thus in densely-settled parts of a planning area the
areal unit should be smaller than in remoter parts of less intense activity. For example the centre of a large city might be
recorded on a 100-metre square basis, the remainder of the city
mostly on 500-metre squares and the rest of the study area on 1-
kilometre squares. The amount of information to be recorded in
each 'cell' might be roughly the same throughout but a large
range of flexibility would be inherent. The city centre itself could
be studied in some detail at 100-metre square level, but in area-

wide analysis it might be generalised as (say) four one-kilometre squares or up to sixteen squares with 500-metre sides.

It will be plain that attempts to simplify the detail and scope of the data by choosing a large areal unit or *space* will immediately have simplifying effects not only on *activities* (since these will have to be generalised to e.g. 550,000 square feet of retail shopping, 270,000 square feet of wholesale warehouse or 77 detached and semi-detached single-family homes and bungalows) but also on *communications*. We can no longer identify the single activity on its parcel and list all its interactions; we must make do with a cruder statement which is aggregated. Thus, a one-kilometre residential square would be recorded as generating 200 *outward* work trips, 50 shopping trips, 15 journeys to school . . . etc. and 12 *inward* work trips, 170 trips to school . . . etc., perhaps showing the breakdown of these into modes of transport. Of course the inward trips would be divided by zones (other grid cells) of origin and the outward trips by destination zones. Notice too a further simplification – all communications which begin and end in the same zone are 'lost'.*

Simplification by reducing the detail on communications
Another means by which the volume of information may be reduced is by the reduction of detail concerning communications. In our detailed account earlier we suggested a comprehensive approach covering all forms of *interaction* between a located activity and others – all forms that had spatial and temporal regular patterning of course. Even for a single activity this could amount to a formidable amount of information. This can be reduced by several means:

First of all, seasonal or weekly variation could be ignored in the records which would therefore be for a 'typical' or a 'peak' day, week, or month.

Secondly, sampling techniques can be applied to the framework of 'content transmitted' so that a representative cross-section would include *some* kind or kinds of person-movement, *some* kind of material goods-movement, *some* data transmission

---

* This is indeed a general point worth making and it will be obvious that the choice of areal unit must be made initially with great care since the compromise is between simplicity and economy on the one hand and some loss of information and understanding on the other.

and *some* energy flows. A more drastic measure would be to dispense entirely with, say, the collection of energy-transmission data in this fashion and to rely solely on information gathered in more general terms for the study area as a whole or for substantial sub-areas (Smethurst, 1967).

Thirdly, it is possible to sample from the framework of 'mode of transmission' and to select for survey only certain kinds of road-vehicle movement, rail, air and water transport shipments or, again more drastically to leave out entirely, say, pipeline and conduit transmissions (Starkie, 1968).

Whatever decisions are reached will be based on a reconnaissance level of knowledge about communications in the study area both at the time of survey, in the recent past and in the light of major trends which might continue into the future. For example, it would have been foolish some years ago to dispense with surveys of personal movement by private car (and yet . . . !). In 1970, it might be wise to pause and consider carefully before rejecting a survey of the transmission of data and sensory impressions.

It is particularly important that such decisions about the scope, content and detail of the communications survey are made 'across the board', i.e. that they should apply equally to every activity system considered. If decisions are taken individually for each activity-system survey the gross results will be valueless because they will not be representative and show the variation in the usage of communications and channels as between the various kinds of activities represented.

Simplification by reducing the detail on channels

Finally, of course, we can simplify our surveys of *channels*. There are two main ways of doing this:

First, to restrict the *kinds* of channels considered e.g. to omit pipelines, conduits and cables or the whole field of telecommunications and, second, to omit the finer levels of the networks themselves. This is usually done by setting a threshold, e.g. 'no sewers below 12″ diameter and water mains below 9″ diameter to be recorded' or (very familiarly), 'only motorways, trunk roads, class A and B roads to be considered'.

All the forms of simplification we have mentioned are commonplace in principle (we stress that the examples we have given are *illustrative only* and might when taken together be quite unsuitable in practice). Practising planners must bow to the needs of economy and convenience by being selective about the scope and detail of their surveys. But far too often the selections are made in an *ad hoc* fashion and result in anomalies: population data will be very fine grain but there will be a total absence of similar detail on occupations or employment; the distribution of holiday caravans will be recorded minutely but there will be a dearth of information on all other forms of holidaying and recreation; and so on.

The design of an information system is a critical step in the planning process, perhaps the most critical of all. It must be taken with great care because the considerable investment will be very difficult to write off if serious errors of judgement occur.

The remainder of what we must say about describing the state of our system at any time may be dealt with quite briefly because it is both familiar and well-documented. This is the description *in toto* of the study area. Gross statements can arrive in two ways; by aggregation of the sort of detailed coverage we have discussed at length (and by the 'grossing-up' of sample surveys) on the one hand, or by direct compilation of study area totals on the other. Preferably, both methods will be used so that the latter, often deriving from published official sources, can act as a check on the former.

The sort of headings to be covered are very familiar: population (numbers, age-and-sex groupings, households, etc.), economic activities and employment, land studies of all kinds, building development, transport and communication networks and flows, energy generation and transmission, generalised 'land uses' (more properly 'activities') and so on. The point to be stressed is that in general *the content and format of these study-area surveys should be identical with that of the detailed studies we have been discussing*.

It will also be very useful, often necessary, to express totals for the study area as proportions of those for wider areas such as the region and the nation or both. The special value of this will become clearer later when we deal with projection techniques. Beyond these brief statements, the reader is referred to the standard works on the subject (e.g. Jackson, 1962; Moser, 1960).

All that we have said so far concerns the descriptions of our system at a point in time. But we have shown already that our system is dynamic i.e. changing *through* time. We also showed how a changing system could be described by observing its state at intervals, preferably at regular intervals. It follows that our system can be described by carrying out the surveys we have outlined in this chapter at regular intervals. What ought these time intervals to be? Is it necessary to carry out the whole survey each time?

The question of intervals depends on a number of factors: the frequency of surveys made by other agencies, the results of which are used by the planners—for example the census of population; the rates at which certain conditions (of economic activity, car ownership, building and engineering investment, etc.) are changing, and as always, the resources which can be devoted to revisions of data.

The interval for comprehensive updating of the surveys could well be five years. In Britain there are at least two principal reasons for this choice. First, five years is the interval at which development plans have to be reviewed and this involves a 'fresh survey'. Second, the Census of Population which had been taken every ten years from 1801 to 1961 (with the exception of 1941) was supplemented by a sample census in 1966—a full census will be taken again in 1971 but the practice of taking partial or full censuses at *five*-year intervals is likely to continue.

So much of the planner's work depends upon a knowledge of people—how many, how old, how grouped into households, their educational levels, their housing conditions and so on—that is most convenient to tie in major revisions of information with the intervals of the national census.

But a great deal can happen in five years—sudden changes in local population and the local economy, a ready supply of loan money for house purchase may quickly stimulate private building, a new road opened can transform the traffic flows over an entire city. For many reasons (and especially those connected with *development control* which we deal with in Chapter 11) it will be necessary to carry out revisions at shorter intervals than five years. The obvious choice is an *annual* re-survey of certain sections of the information. A year is convenient from many points of view—children beginnning school, the annual cycle of human behaviour reflecting the cycles of weather and holidays, the need for annual reports and annual budgeting in public agencies are among the most important. There can be no hard-and-fast rules about what should be included in an annual up-dating but a bare minimum might be to note changed activities and changed 'improvements' to spaces in some degree of detail (much of this information being simply amassed from planning department, building inspectors, fire officers and other day-to-day records) and to note major changes in the communications networks (perhaps for the channels most likely to change, i.e. the road system) and to obtain an idea of changed flow volumes, which might be done on a sample basis (as in fact is done by the Ministry of Transport, though for a too-limited number of points for urban planning purposes).

Only experience and particular circumstances will give a clearer idea of the scope of such annual updating; some experience ought to be available soon since a few British planning authorities have begun to do it recently. But every five years the updating must be comprehensive and include all the investigations we have referred to throughout this chapter— both the 'grass roots' examination of activities, spaces, communications and channels, their integration in the activity-system surveys and their generalisation in the surveys of the study area as a whole for the same topics.

If all this is done we have satisfied the general requirements with which we set out, viz: to describe a dynamic system by the recording of certain characteristics at regular intervals. In this way we can understand its workings at *points in time*, how any factor (population, land in residential use in a small part of the area, person-trips by private car originating in a certain zone, etc., etc.) changes *through* time, i.e. we can establish *trends*, and finally we can observe the evolving *trajectory of the system as a whole* (Jay, 1967).

As we shall see, herein lie the keys to discovering what the future behaviour of the system might be, to what extent it can be directed and steered, some of the problems of choosing a desirable trajectory and of trying to keep the system on the chosen course. In other words, information lies at the very heart of the devising and choosing of plans and of their subsequent implementation.

8

System Simulation: Forecasting and Modelling

In the preceding chapter we considered the principles and touched on the practice of recording information which would describe the salient features of the system with which planners deal—one of interacting located activities. In this chapter our main concern is to explore ways in which we may anticipate the future with which plans are concerned. Many problems are involved—those of the time-scales to be used and the intervals at which projections are to be made; those of projecting single *aspects* of our system (e.g. population, employment, demand for sailing facilities, goods vehicle trips, etc.) and of projecting the system in more comprehensive fashion; the whole question of how far human behaviour is predictable; problems of projecting trends or 'natural' changes and identifying the effects on the system of different planning policies, be they stimuli or restraints. Additionally we must look forward to the ultimate use of projections, perhaps their most important use, that is, in helping to implement the plan itself by charting the course of change to be steered in appropriate detail; this requirement, we shall see, (as was foreshadowed in Chapter 5), will be critical in deciding what projections to undertake, how they shall be made, what degree of refinement and detail they shall contain and what time-intervals shall be used.

We divide this chapter into three main sections: first a discussion of the nature of projection and its difficulties, commenting on the role of theory in relation to practice and discussing certain practical points of general application in projection; we then go on to discuss various methods by which *aspects* of our system may be projected, drawing heavily on the best of current practice which seems specially suited to planning; and finally, the larger problem of projecting the system (of interacting activities) as a whole.

Scientific Method, Theories and Prediction

The problems of projection or prediction have long occupied civilised men; indeed the necessary skill to predict river floods in association with the development of astronomy and the calendar was a hallmark of the growth of civilisation in the Near East. At once we see that the problem of prediction is intimately bound up with scientific method in general and theory-building in particular. For it is hardly possible to predict in the absence of some general idea about the phenomena in question. How could the Sumerian priest predict the flooding of the Tigris or the Euphrates without a theory of the relationships between the rising and setting of celestial bodies and the behaviour of the rivers? (He may have quite simply assumed a causal relationship between the two kinds of events, but that, for the moment, is beside the point.) As Harris (1966) has said, 'In very simple terms, theory is a general statement about the real world.' He goes on to show how theory-construction fits in with the 'classic description of scientific method: First, induction: the collection of information and its organisation into patterns. Second, generalisation: a restatement of the cause-and-effect relations behind the patterns, or a redefinition of the patterns themselves in a more abstract form which includes the observations as a special case. Third, deduction: the search for new special cases previously unstudied, as suggested by the more general statement, or theory. And finally, testing: a check to see whether the new cases perform as predicted—if not, the theory must be revised.'

Notice that the step labelled 'deduction' does not necessarily imply prediction in the time sense—it can, and often does mean the derivation of new statements about a situation at a point in time. For example, Harvey's theory of the circulation of the blood enabled him to *deduce* the existence of the capillaries which were discovered by subsequent work in the dissecting room. But the extremely important special case of interest to us is that the theory which involves time or the behaviour of a phenomenon *as it changes through time* and the deductions of *how*

167

the phenomenon may occur at various future times. This process, prediction or projection, clearly cannot be done in the absence of a theory, or generalising statement about observations made presently or in the past, again in Harris' words, 'a precise statement regarding formal relationships, usually including relationships of cause and effect'.

An example might serve to clarify this point. The projection of population relies on observations of the population in the past and on some generalisation or theory concerning the causes of change. Long periods of study have revealed the importance of natural changes (births, deaths), the effects of migration and the ways in which the structure of population at any given time plays a large role in influencing future change.

When understanding is limited, powers of observation poor or resources limited, it may not be possible to have a detailed picture of the underlying structure of the population e.g. only *totals* for past periods may be known. In such cases a generalised idea or theory will of necessity be crude and the projection a simple extrapolation of the observed trend.

As understanding, information and resources improve not only does a more complex picture emerge, but more sophisticated theories which might better explain the phenomena become possible. When the age-and-sex structure of a population at various past times became available (in the nineteenth century) it was possible to formulate better theories of population change which in turn enabled better projections to be made. The rôles of the age of marriage, fertility, contraceptive practices as they influenced the birth rate; the effect of various diseases and environmental conditions on the death rate and the ways in which births, deaths and migratory changes altered both total population and its structure became far better understood. Notice that a theory is 'better' *by definition* when it puts up a better performance than its predecessors and that this is decided by the tests of deduction—in this case the ability to predict future population.

Another example concerns the ownership of private cars. If we have past data which simply record the total numbers of private cars in the country (or in an area) we can formulate only simple theories to explain the figures. We would obviously derive the more important figures of cars per head of population and cars per private household and study those series. We might try to find some relationship between these figures and the Gross Domestic Product or the total of personal incomes. Then, given future estimates, of population, GDP or personal incomes we could predict the likely numbers of private cars by standard statistical or graphical methods provided we had formulated some theory on the basis of study of the available data.

Alternatively, very detailed information might be available which recorded the ownership of private cars in relation to occupations of heads of households, to household size, to *per capita* income, to total household income, to the residential density of the area in which car owners lived ... and so on. Searching inquiry at a more sophisticated level might yield theories giving more complex explanations of rates of car ownership. Then provided that estimates of future occupations, incomes, residential density, etc., etc. were available, it could be possible to project car ownership and its incidence.

In these examples, the reader will notice that we have introduced a distinction between *simple projections* which operate on limited data directly and usually extrapolate a series of observations in a direct manner and *analytical projections* which depend on more detailed information and in which the projected value is often the dependent variable derived from projections of independent variables (e.g. as car ownership in our last example was derived from projected values of occupational classes, incomes, etc., etc.).

Generally speaking, analytical methods are to be preferred over simple ones since they allow us to account for or assume differing patterns of change in the components of a situation; this usually leads to more accurate results than is the case with simple projections where the internal structure of a phenomenon is ignored.

We mentioned above that generalisations or theories which would explain the observed data usually state or imply *cause-and-effect relationships*. If not, they will be statements about the *correlation* of different sets of observations.

Three levels of relationship between two (or more) sets of observations may be distinguished:

   deterministic causality in which whenever A occurs B also occurs i.e. A causes B;

probabilistic causality in which whenever A occurs there is a
probability *p*, that B will also occur, i.e. A has probability
p, of *causing* B;

correlation in which A occurs *in association with* B (which
association can be measured statistically) but there is no
observable cause-and-effect relationship between them.

Chapin (1965, p. 73) says that 'human behaviour is so com-
plexly affected by chance considerations, that we anticipate ...
that probabilistic causality is likely to be more prominent in our
theoretical research. ...' Not only there, but also in practice
must we keep this firmly in mind. Nearly all of the projections
the planner must make—for example, population, economic
activity, recreational behaviour, choice of transport modes—are
directly concerned with human behaviour. Plans must be
capable of sufficient flexibility—e.g. in land allocation, highway
capacities, etc. to cope with variations in taste, technology,
social and economic values which might occasionally be expected. It follows that the projections which form important foundations to the plan should indicate the limits of probability
within which important factors might vary. Seldom, if ever,
should a single figure be given for any projected factor; to do
this implies that deterministic causality is at work ('if we do
this, there *will* be 175,000 male employees in 10 years from
now'). Since the best we can hope for in predicting human behaviour is a high level of probability, and since planning must
accept this fact, it follows that *projections must always take the form
of ranges* lying between the limits of stated levels of probability.
(For example, '... given our assumptions about female fertility,
the rates of decline in mortality and the possible incidence of
migratory movements, the total population of the area is likely
to be between 983,000 and 1,105,000 in 15 years' time. ...')

Common experience as much as formal demonstration indicates that forecasts can be more certain in the short run than
when made for longer periods. If we know the total employment
in manufacturing now, we can give an extremely accurate prediction of the figure for next week, a reasonable estimate for
next year, for five years' hence we might give an estimate to
within ± 3 or 4 per cent but a projection over twenty years would
of necessity be rather hit and miss. This is of course because we
are dealing with *probabilities*. It is easy to show that the reliability

of such projections becomes increasingly doubtful as the period of projection is extended.

The reader is invited to draw on log-normal graph paper two straight lines which are inclined at a slight angle one to the other so as to represent a higher and a lower rate of change in a population. (The lines might slope gently upward from left to right to represent constant rates of growth.) The x-axis, i.e. the normal scale, may be calibrated to show equal time intervals whilst the logarithmic y-axis can be marked up to indicate the total population. It will now be possible to see how the range of estimating error, i.e. the difference between the 'high' and 'low' curves, diverges increasingly as the projection date is advanced.

How far should projection be carried? Is there any general rule? Are there different recommended periods for different factors (employment, car ownership, numbers of households)? To some extent the answers depend on the nature and purpose of the plan, deriving from given or assumed terms of reference. Sometimes a 25- or 30-year view is demanded, at others it is clear that the planner is being asked to fill out in more detail a previously prepared strategic plan by providing a 'middle-range' programme of suggested investments and developments for a period of 10 to 15 years ahead. In another way, the projection period chosen depends on what is being projected. Some fields (e.g. demography) have been the subject of more detailed and prolonged study than others (e.g. economic activity and employment) and thus the projection period which can be attempted bears a direct relationship to the 'state of the art'.

But in a sense the question of *the* projection period is a red herring. This is because of the nature of the planning process which is one of continuous control over the system (see Chapters 4 and 5). The projections are closely related to the goal formulation (Chapter 6) and plan formulation (Chapter 9, following) parts of the process in showing how activities and communications might alter with the passage of time. In particular, projections which are based on a number of varied assumptions about 'natural' (or uncontrolled) changes and about the effects of different kinds of policy intervention will result in a number of different 'trajectories' or paths which the system might follow (see Chapter 9). Plan formulation is in essence the selection of the path which *should* be followed. Since this will be chosen from the various trajectories (or will be some variant of one of them, or a combination of two or more) it is clear that *the plan itself will be precise for the early stages and increasingly 'fuzzy' as the period advances*. Put another way, the statements which the plan embodies can deal quite firmly with investment programmes, specific area policies, precise boundaries for action, etc., in relation to the first few years but for the middle and later period must be confined to dealing with broad principles and aims concerning the directions in which change should be steered if the longer-range goals are to be attained.

As we showed in Chapter 5, implementation (both by 'positive' action and by control in its usual sense) and periodic regular reviews leading to further projections and extensions of the plan period ensure that the immediate future is always being clarified and mapped in more detail whilst, at the other extreme, what was previously outside the range of projection is brought within the limits of the planning period.

Of much greater importance than the total span of the projection period are *the intervals or steps for which the projections are made*. How are these determined?

Once a rationale has been decided for any particular projection there is nothing which thereby determines the intervals. To take a simple example, if it is decided to use a graphical method to project national change in the population, this will usually be done on log-normal paper and the trend extrapolated by pencil-and-ruler, by curve-fitting or some other suitable means. Once the extrapolation has been drawn the projected population may be read off at any intervals of future time. If the cohort-survival method is used then the projection intervals will of course be those of the age groups chosen for the starting population, e.g. if that is in five-year intervals of age, 0–4, 5–9, 10–14 ... etc., then the projection intervals will be 5, 10, 15, 20, etc. years forward from the datum year. The method as such does not determine the interval – if a single-year interval was needed then clearly the datum population would have to be broken into single years of age, 1, 2, 3, 4 ... etc. Clearly, then, it is the nature of the existing data about the present and about past trends which might limit in some way the projection intervals. The point we made with some force in Chapter 7 about the need for updating information at regular intervals might now be better understood. This shows the close connections between the quality and nature of information and the ease or difficulty of projection.

But neither the projection methods chosen nor the quality of information should be the main factors in deciding on projection intervals; the principal element will be *the way in which the plan is to be devised and implemented*. It will be clear from much of the material of preceding chapters, especially 4 and 5, that the plan (or alternative possibilities) should be expressed in terms of a charted path or trajectory of change and that implementation will take the form of *controls* which seek to keep the system on the chosen course. Deviations must be noted in good time and the necessary corrective actions applied. It follows that all the projections of the many different possible paths of change, both 'natural' or 'trend' as well as a variety of 'planned' trajectories must be in such a form as to be adequate chartings of the course, suitable for measuring deviations at the necessary intervals of time. The best information about the 'state of the system' will be obtained at Census years. At the moment the British Census occurs at 10-year intervals but in 1966 a limited form of mid-decennium census was taken and it may well be that in future a full census will be taken quinquennially. Obviously there are innumerable advantages in tying major reviews of progress on the implementation of a plan to the same intervals. As we say elsewhere, detailed checks on the course of change will be occurring all the time, certain matters need annual review but major checks can well be made at five-yearly intervals, and this may be regarded as *the standard interval for most projection purposes*.

In the early sections of Chapter 7 we showed how a system could be described by means of a vector—in our case a check on the state of certain parts *made simultaneously*. Obviously then, the five-year intervals in our various projections must be coincident if they are to be combined to form vectors. It is no good projecting employment for 3, 8, 13, 18, etc. years and population 1, 6, 11, 16, etc. years and car ownership 5, 10, 15, 20 years from the datum year, since at no time in the future can the plan which these projections help to chart be used in a major comparison with the actual state of affairs. Clearly the several projections must be for coincident intervals of n, n+5, n+10, n+15, n+20, etc. years from the datum year. (We develop the theme of 'monitoring' progress on the plan in Chapter 11.)

Projecting aspects of the system

Our system is one of activities in spaces linked by communications in channels. It follows that projection of aspects of the system involves projection of these elements. Obviously 'projection' of spaces and channels is a distinct matter and will be considered separately. The bulk of the planner's task here, then, is to project activities and communications. If we consider the propensity or desire to communicate as an aspect of activities we can reduce the problem to one of activities-projection.

Activities

In Chapter 7 we suggested (following Chapin) a basic 3-fold division of activities–'productive', 'general welfare', and 'residential'. Clearly these divisions are breakdowns of the whole fabric of human life and are inter-related in complex ways. The main thread of connection however may be seen as a dependence of 'residential' activity (i.e. population) on 'productive' (i.e. economic) activity and similarly a dependence of the 'general welfare' activities on the size and nature of the population. But it can be argued that economic activities are dependent upon population (e.g. expansion is constrained by the rate at which the labour supply can be expanded in the short run and this is usually achieved by the migration of workers into the area). This *inter*dependence of economic activity and population is very strong indeed–stronger than that of the general welfare activities with either. Although migration may occur in response to the presence of excellent educational or health services or for religous reasons, these are exceptional cases and the urban analyst can recognise them and treat them accordingly; we are dealing with the general case here of the strong relationships between demographic and economic changes. We suggest that these differences be recognised in the way in which projections are carried out, namely in this sequence:

1. Inter-related population and economic projections
2. Derivation of general welfare activities from 1.

The requirement that population and economic projections be inter-related does not demand that they be carried out simultaneously; nor does it mean that each cannot be the subject of a distinct set of operations. Techniques for performing the projections separately are better developed than those for simultaneous projection but, for a number of reasons, the latter are likely to receive more study in future. What we are urging is that if the two sets of projections are performed (largely for practical convenience) as distinct operations, *each must take full account of the implications of the other and affect the other*. This may well result in an iterative or 'see-saw' process which is continued until some reasonable and acceptable relationship between the population and economic forecasts is obtained.

We now briefly review a number of methods for projecting population and economic activities separately as well as methods which take their relationship more or less directly into account.

Population projection

This is as Chapin (1965, p. 196) says, 'perhaps the single most important population study for planning purposes'. Very many important factors of the future situation facing the community on which the planner must advise are derived directly from the population projection. It forms a framework for a great deal of the subsequent work in devising, testing, evaluating and implementing the plan. Most of the important decisions about major land uses and services are derived from population estimates: the demand for water, power and waste disposal facilities; housing, open spaces and schools; the supply of labour; spending power available for the retail trade, the numbers of private cars to be expected, possible recreational demands – all may be estimated from the projected population.

Demographers are extremely chary of forecasts for 'small areas' (i.e. of the sizes that planners use as 'study area' and sub-areas). This is understandable as they are whole-time experts in this field and are acutely conscious of the nature of the assumptions on which even the best techniques are based. To some demographers, accurate projection is an end in itself – to the planner it is simply a means. Of necessity we *must* produce small-area projections.

Whilst we must respect the demographer's expertise and his professional attitudes we must also realise that even a projection of great sophistication will eventually be used to derive land areas by the application of a *standard*, (for example 100,000 persons require, at a *standard* of 10 acres per 1,000 persons of urban recreational land, 100 acres) and that the accuracy or relevance of the standard may be far more important to us than great refinement in the population projection. Finally, we should recall that the cyclical nature of planning, involving regular reviews, gives us the opportunity to revise and improve the population projection as part and parcel of that process.

We shall now very briefly describe six methods of population projection. They are arranged roughly in ascending order of accuracy and sophistication: mathematical and graphical methods, the 'employment' method, ratio and apportionment methods, the migration and natural increase method, the cohort-survival method and matrix methods. For a full treatment of the more complex methods the reader should consult the works cited but we give here sufficient guidance to enable these methods to be carried out in the office.

(a) *mathematical and graphical methods* (Isard, 1960, pp. 7–15) These are simple or direct methods since they operate with past population records and take no account of the components of change. Where past data suggest that the population has been changing by constant *absolute* amount an *arithmetic* progression is involved; the figures may be plotted on plain paper (conventionally with y = population and x = time) and the resulting straight line extrapolated to give the projection. More usually population change approximates to a *geometric* progression, i.e. the change in unit time is a constant *proportion* of the preceding figure; in this case semi-logarithmic paper should be used to yield a straight line for extrapolation (see Figure 8.1).

If the past data does not seem to lie in a straight line or an exponential curve, a 'best fit' straight-line equation can be derived by the method of least squares and extended to provide the projection.

In certain cases, an analytical approach can be adopted using, e.g. births, deaths and net migration data as independent variables in a linear multiple regression equation which has population as the dependent variable.

With the exception of the latter method all the preceding techniques are simple and relatively crude. They are of very limited value since they cannot be used for long-range projection and in any event should not be trusted for more than 10 years in stable situations or 5 years where population change is more volatile.

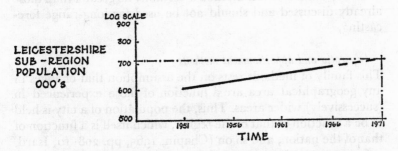

8.1 Simple graphical population projection

(b) *the 'employment' method*
Given a series of past values of the activity rate, i. e.

$$\frac{\text{economically active population}}{\text{persons in working age groups}} = \frac{E}{W} \text{ and the ratio}$$

$$\frac{\text{persons in working age groups}}{\text{total population}} = \frac{W}{P} \text{ it is possible by using}$$

graphical or mathematical methods such as those just described to produce future values for these ratios. Then, given forecasts of total employment, population may be estimated, since

$$\frac{E}{W} \times \frac{W}{P} = \frac{E}{P}$$

A range of employment forecasts (made for different assumptions about the economic 'climate') will yield a range of population forecasts. If regression techniques are used to project

$$\frac{E}{W} \text{ and } \frac{W}{P}$$

then the application of calculated estimating errors will of itself produce ranges of values for

$$\frac{E}{P}$$

The reliability of this method is certainly no greater than those already discussed and should not be used for long-range fore-casting.

(c) *ratio and apportionment methods*
This family of methods rests on the assumption that changes in any geographical area are a function of those experienced in (successively) wider areas. Thus, the population of a city is held to be a function of that of the region, which itself is a function of that of the nation, and so on (Chapin, 1965, pp. 208–10; Isard, 1960, pp. 15–27).

The requirements for such projections are time-series of populations for the areas to be used in the analysis and a fore-cast or set of forecasts for the largest area. In *ratio* methods the population of the second largest area (e.g. the region) is plotted against that of the parent area (the nation), thus:

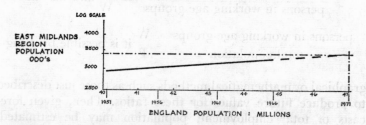

8.2 Ratio method (graphical): Step from nation to region

A curve is fitted to the points thus obtained and, by least squares, correlation, graphical or other method is extrapolated to inter-sect the projected value for the parent area at a given forecast date. Clearly, if a range had been given for the parent-area forecast this would have resulted in a range for the region.

In the second step down the process is repeated using data for the study area and the region:

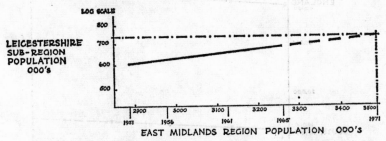

8.3 Ratio method (graphical): Step from region to sub-region

Again the curve is fitted and extrapolated to intersect the (derived) forecast for the parent area.

In apportionment methods the technique is broadly similar, but the incidence of changes in *all sub-areas* of each parent area is considered at each step-down and the resulting forecasts for each sub-area totalled and adjusted *pro rata* so that their total is equal to the forecast for the parent area. Repeating the previous example, we now use data for all of the Standard Regions of England at the first step-down and adjust them before proceeding to the second step-down in which all sub-areas of the East Midland Region are used in order to derive a forecast for the Leicester sub-region. In this case, curves are fitted for each region and extrapolated to intersect the national forecast. The resulting regional forecasts are tabulated, totalled and adjusted *pro rata* so that they add up to 47 million.

	unadjusted forecasts (000)	adjusted forecasts (000)
Northern	3,500	3,488
Yorkshire and Humberside	4,800	4,783
North Western	6,890	6,864
East Midland	3,490	3,478
West Midland	5,210	5,191
East Anglia	1,680	1,674
South East	17,800	17,735
South West	3,800	3,787
ENGLAND	47,170	47,000

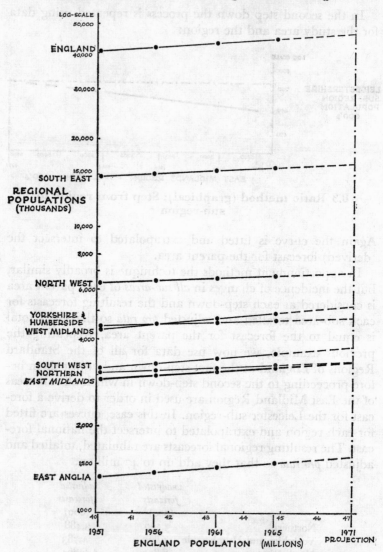

8.4 Apportionment method (graphical): Step from nation to region

In similar manner, using the derived forecast of 3·478 million for the region and data for all the constituent sub-areas, the study-area population may be estimated.

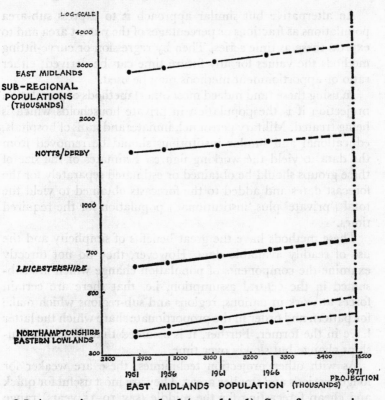

8.5 Apportionment method (graphical): Step from region to sub-region

Proceeding as before we total the sub-area forecasts and adjust them *pro rata* until they total 3·478 million.

	unadjusted forecasts (000)	adjusted forecasts (000)
Nottingham-Derby Sub-Region	1,700	1,783
Leicester Sub-Region	735	773
Eastern Lowlands Sub-Region	409	431
Northamptonshire Sub-Region	465	491
EAST MIDLAND REGION	3,309	3,478

We should emphasise that the above methods do not explictly use time-series data; rather, the methods plot relationships between sub-areas and parent areas irrespective of time.

An alternative but similar approach is to express sub-area populations as fractions or percentages of the parent area and to express these as time series. Then by regression or curve-fitting methods the values for any future time can be derived; either ratio or apportionment methods may be used.

In using these (and indeed most other) methods of population projection it is the population in private households which is being treated. Military personnel, inmates and staffs of hospitals, educational and similar institutions should be removed from the data to yield the working figures. Estimates of the size of these groups should be obtained or estimated separately for the forecast dates and added to the forecasts obtained to yield the total ('private' plus 'institutional') population for the required times.

These methods have the great benefits of simplicity and the use of readily available data. However, they do not directly examine the components of population change which are subsumed in the central assumption, i.e. that there are certain forces at work in nations, regions and sub-regions which make for pattern and order in the proportionate share which the latter have in the former. Further, it is assumed that these relationships change but slowly over time.

As with other projection techniques, these are weaker for longer periods and smaller areas. They are most useful for quick and cheap forecasting for the middle (say 10–15 years) range and for areas not less than a whole metropolitan area or 'city region'.

(d) *the migration and natural increase method*
This is the first method we have discussed in which an element of analysis occurs and as its name implies, the method enables natural and migratory changes to be handled separately (Isard, 1960, Chapter 3).

By examining past data on nett migration rates and by attempting to relate these to economic conditions, particularly to the demand for employment in the study area, it will be possible to adopt varying assumptions about the patterns of future migration. These might simply be 'high' and 'low' e.g. +5,000 persons per annum and +1,000 respectively; they may be expressed as different *programmes* e.g. +1,000 per annum in the first 5 years, +2,000 per annum in the following three years and +3,000 per annum in the final 12 years (of a 20-year projection) would be Programme I. Other programmes would be developed which reflected as far as possible different assumptions about the size and timing of new job opportunities, housing land capacities, the output of the construction industry, the expansion of utilities and so on.

Next a set of programmes of future natural change would be developed either by subjective projection of past maximum and minimum rates or by 'stepping down' from projections produced nationally or regionally. Of course, in some cases, projected natural changes might be available for the study area itself (e.g. as provided to British local planning authorities, though these do not usually state *rates* of natural change but rather present the finished results for certain time-periods in terms of absolute numbers).

The essence of the method is to begin with the starting-date population, add the nett migratory element to produce the next figures to which is then added the natural change thus completing one cycle of the projection. The cycle may be for 1 year, 2 years, 5 years or other convenient period. The process is then repeated until the end of the projection period. Separate exercises are carried out for each set of natural change and migration assumptions.

Several points must be noted. Whilst this method is likely to be more accurate than the crude and simple methods so far discussed there are nevertheless a number of imperfections which limit its usefulness. First, the method uses total populations; age/sex structure is not accounted for. This means that changes in birth and death rates (the elements of natural change) which might result from changing age/sex structure cannot be seen and acted upon. Nor, of course, does the planner have the direct benefit of knowing this information for future times when estimating school-age population, numbers of women of working age, etc., etc.

Second, the effect of the age and sex composition and the (possibly) different biological characteristics of the migrant elements are not accounted for thus introducing further possibility of error. It should also be stressed that we are dealing with a *nett* migration figure and recent work shows that nett migrations are the result of far larger in-and-out migrations. Unfortunately, in Britain at least, no regular direct measurement of migratory changes is attempted though a limited exercise was included in the 1961 census on a sample basis. We shall say more about the purposes for treating actual migratory movements in population projection later in this chapter.

Whilst recognising its great shortcomings, the migration and natural increase method does reveal the possible sequence and the main elements of change far better than the methods previously outlined. At the same time it is scarcely more time-consuming or expensive.

(e) *the cohort-survival method* (Chapin, 1965, pp. 203–5)
This is the standard method of population projection used by official (government) agencies in most advanced countries. It is not a rigid method, and can be adapted in a great variety of ways to suit the data available or the needs of the analyst whilst at the same time retaining its underlying logic. It is an analytical method which allows births, deaths and migration to be handled separately, it gives results for any pattern of age-groups, it can handle male and female elements separately or together and it can be disaggregated into ethnic or racial groups (with different biological characteristics) if necessary to attempt greater accuracy.

The general form of the cohort-survival method is as follows. Males and females by single-year age-groups are tabulated separately, the figures being extracted from the latest available census. Next the nett migratory change for the first year is allowed for by the addition (or subtraction) of the assumed change for each age-group of males and females. Then the appropriate age-specific birth rates are applied successively to each group of women in the child-bearing range (usually 15–49 last birthday); the resultant births are divided into males and females, adjusted for mortality in the first year and entered in the next column, first row of the male and female tables. Finally, age-specific mortality rates or survival rates are applied to each age-group of males and females to estimate the numbers who will survive to the next year (i.e. of their life and of the projection).

This sequence is repeated until the projection date is reached.

It can be noted here that the analyst has complete control over the projection at all stages and can introduce special adjustments to births, deaths and migratory changes at any point in the process.

A very common simplification is to work with five-year (quinary) age groups 0–4, 5–9, 10–14, ... etc. and to project by quinquennial periods. Whilst possibly reducing the accuracy of the method and the degree of control which can be exercised over the process, the gains in time and the reduction of tedium (if manual calculation is used) may be felt to outweigh the losses. Slightly different data are needed–e.g. five-year fertility ratios to estimate births and, of course, the pattern of migration assumed must be expressed by five-year periods.

Before discussing the sources of these data and some of the problems associated with deriving future values for use in the projection we show diagrammatically overleaf the procedure using five-year cohorts.

The MALES table is identical except that of course there is no 'births' element. At each cycle of the projection the new baby boys are transferred from the female table to the appropriate '0–4' row in the next time period in the males table. The figures entered in both tables will have been adjusted to take account of mortality rates up to the fifth birthday.

The projection is started with a population structure derived from the latest census. If quinquennial steps are to be used then obviously the projection will yield results for 5, 10, 15, etc. years from the census date. If for some reason the projection is needed for 5-year periods *not* in phase with the census then the starting data will have to be run forward 1, 2, 3 or 4 years as the case may be. The easiest way is perhaps to obtain the census population by *single* years of age and to survive the cohorts 1, 2, 3 or 4 times then to form into quinary groups as a start for the quinquennial projection.

The simplest part of the remainder of the data concerns deaths. Death rates are relatively stable and have long-run trends which can be predicted with reasonable accuracy. Age-specific mortality rates or survival ratios may be used; the particular need is for values of these for each year (or five years as the case may be) of the projection period. The analyst should seek actuarial advice on these (in Great Britain the Government

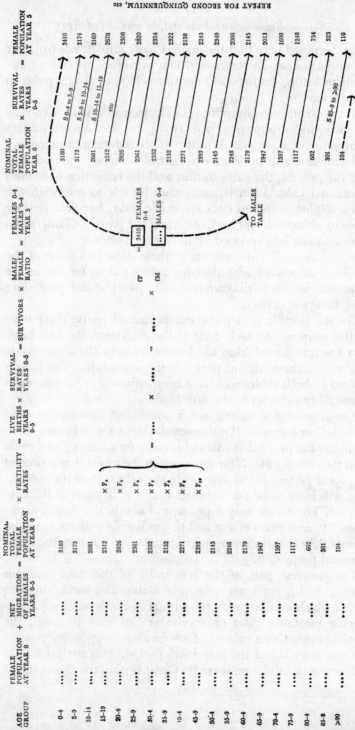

8.6 Cohort-survival: Female table, first quinquennium

Actuary's Department may provide information on expected future mortality rates).

Much more difficult is the question of birth rates which are very hard to predict being dependent upon so many factors which are likewise subject to rapid change – contraceptive practices and attitudes, the age of marriage, preferences concerning the size of families, perhaps even Government influence via family allowances and tax reliefs for dependent children – and so forth.

There are many ways in which the births element of the projection may be introduced and the reader is referred to the standard texts and the examples which we cite. What we do advise most strongly is the general principle of the examination of past trends in birth rates and their intelligent extrapolation, taking into account the most recent past, in the form of high and low estimates (or a range of possibilities between two extremes).

Still we have dealt only with natural changes – there remains the question of migration, the thorniest problem facing the analyst. In advanced societies (and in their characteristic settlement, the metropolitan region) this is likely to form a major element of total change. Indeed nett change alone may loom large but is itself merely the result of inward and outward movements which may be of considerably greater magnitude. When this is the case the age, sex, socio-economic, racial and other important *characteristics* of the population may be drastically altered without necessarily altering its *size* greatly.

The problem is compounded by the serious lack of information about migration. In this country we probably know as much about the migratory patterns of wading birds as of humans. Apart from special studies (e.g. by social surveys, universities and planning authorities on an *ad hoc* basis) information about migration must be inferred by comparison of natural changes (records of births and deaths) with total changes (census returns and mid-year estimates). Note that this yields estimates of *nett* migration, not about the gross in-and-out-movements with respect to an area. Until good data are available, *faute de mieux* the analyst must have recourse to the best estimates he can get of nett changes. Total nett change is easily estimated from published figures. But in cohort-survival projection it is better to try to obtain the nett changes in terms of the same age and sex groups being used for the analysis of natural change.

One obvious way to do this is to go back to the penultimate census and by using the appropriate birth and death rates to 'age' that population by the cohort-survival method up to the date of the most recent census–a period of ten years. A comparison, age-group by age-group, males and females, of the resulting figures with the actual census figures will yield an approximation to the 'profile' of the nett migratory element. This is obviously an approximation since the method does not take account of the possible effects of the migratory changes on birth and death rates themselves. The greater the volume of the migratory changes, the more serious will the inaccuracies be. In any event, what we are after is a 'profile' to use for the *projection* and no amount of refinement concerning the *past* data will have a significant effect on the reliability of the migration assumptions in the projection, particularly in the period beyond say, the first ten years.

Another way of tackling the problem is to assume that the net migrant element to be added in the projection period will approximate in its age and sex structure to some particular kind of community. For example it is often argued that migrants (on a considerable scale into definable areas) are typically youthful or young-middle-aged skilled persons together with a sizeable proportion of children and adolescents and that therefore communities with these characteristics (the New Town, big overspill areas around the conurbations, etc.) may provide the age/sex profile needed by the analyst. This is obviously an acceptable approach where the projection is being made for an area in which industrial and services expansion is foreseen or is to be stimulated deliberately; clearly it would not apply in a seaside or inland resort notable for its attraction for retired persons.

In addition to questions of the profile of migrant elements we finally must settle our assumptions concerning the size and timing of the future migratory changes. Many factors are observed to affect migration, principally economic (job) opportunities, educational opportunities, social characteristics, qualities of natural and man-made environment, local or regional climates as each factor differs between the areas of origin and destination. It is probable that economic opportunities (the demand for labour) is the single largest element; it may outweigh all the others. If this is so, it follows that *assumptions about migration cannot be dissociated from questions of the future of the local economy.* This is a most important point to which we have already referred and to which we return in our discussion of economic projections later on in this chapter. In fact the link between the population and economic projections will be the numbers of workers 'supplied' by the projected population compared with those 'demanded' by the projected economy. If the population projection is being carried out *before* the economic projection or if the latter has not reached the stage at which future labour demands can be estimated, what is to be done? Questions of land availability, the capacity of the construction industry, investment in schools, hospitals and utility services should receive preliminary attention in drawing up these programmes. Obviously they will receive detailed attention at a later stage when it might be necessary to repeat all or part of the projection. The answer must be to apply a variety of different programmes of migration within the projection (cp. the treatment of births). These could vary not only in terms of the total *size* of the assumed nett migration but also in terms of its sequence and timing. For example a high forecast might be 20,000 and a low forecast 10,000 nett migratory change in all over a 25-year period. These might be varied as follows:

1966–71	71–76	76–81	81–86	86–91		
+4000	+4000	+4000	+4000	+4000	Migration programme	1
+2000	+2000	+3000	+3000	+4000	,,	2
+4000	+3000	+3000	+2000	+2000	,,	3
+2000	+2000	+2000	+2000	+2000	,,	4
+1000	+2000	+3000	+4000	+5000	,,	5
+4000	+4000	+2000	+1000	0	,,	6

Each of these might be combined in various ways with high, medium and low birth-rate assumptions to give a number of different *trajectories* each generated by a particular combination (Buchanan, 1966, Supplementary volume 1).

Having assembled all the necessary input data and checked it carefully the cohort-survival projections may be carried out.

Obviously, whilst one projection is not an undue burden (a five-year age-group projection with say, five or six cycles may be accomplished in as many man-hours using a simple desk calculator) the carrying out of a large number of variants is a considerable task and resort may be had to a computer. Computers perform the projections very quickly, the programming is elementary, and there is also the luxury of neatly printed results, perhaps captioned and including notes on the assumptions made for each run. All planning offices should have access to such a facility for this fundamental part of their work.

(f) *matrix methods*

One of the latest and potentially most fruitful methods of population projection is to apply matrix algebra following the lines indicated by Keyfitz, Rogers (1966 and 1968) and others. Essentially, these methods follow the logic of the cohort-survival technique. The initial age-and-sex distribution is similarly represented as a column vector but the incidence of births and deaths is handled by means of a 'survivorship matrix' which operates on the original population (column vector) to age the population through successive time periods, simultaneously performing the calculations of births and deaths. As Rodgers shows, this matrix operator is of the form shown in Fig. 8.7: The example given here is for the *female* population grouped into quinary ranges of age (0–4, 5–9, 10–14 . . . 85 and over). b_4, b_5 . . . b_{10} are the age-specific birth rates and the sub-diagonal terms, s_1, s_2, s_3 . . . s_{17} the probabilities of survival from the nth to the $n+1$th quinary age-range.

Rodgers goes on to show how the effects of migration may be introduced by replacing the initial population *vector* by a *matrix* in which columns are regions or areas and where the rows, as before, are the age groups. Similarly the survivorship *matrix* is replaced by a *set of matrices*, one for each region.

Migration is then introduced by means of a set of transition matrices (one for each age group) in which the elements represent the probability that an individual of that age group and in region i at any time will move to region j in the next time period.

The population projection is then carried out by multiplying the initial population matrix (columns are regions, rows are age-groups) by the survivorship matrix and then adding the

0	0	0	b_4	b_5	b_6	b_7	b_8	b_9	0	0	0	0	0	0	0	0	0
S_1	0	0	0	0	0	0	0	0	0	0	0	0	0	0	0	0	0
0	S_2	0	0	0	0	0	0	0	0	0	0	0	0	0	0	0	0
0	0	S_3	0	0	0	0	0	0	0	0	0	0	0	0	0	0	0
0	0	0	S_4	0	0	0	0	0	0	0	0	0	0	0	0	0	0
0	0	0	0	S_5	0	0	0	0	0	0	0	0	0	0	0	0	0
0	0	0	0	0	S_6	0	0	0	0	0	0	0	0	0	0	0	0
0	0	0	0	0	0	S_7	0	0	0	0	0	0	0	0	0	0	0
0	0	0	0	0	0	0	S_8	0	0	0	0	0	0	0	0	0	0
0	0	0	0	0	0	0	0	S_9	0	0	0	0	0	0	0	0	0
0	0	0	0	0	0	0	0	0	S_{10}	0	0	0	0	0	0	0	0
0	0	0	0	0	0	0	0	0	0	S_{11}	0	0	0	0	0	0	0
0	0	0	0	0	0	0	0	0	0	0	S_{12}	0	0	0	0	0	0
0	0	0	0	0	0	0	0	0	0	0	0	S_{13}	0	0	0	0	0
0	0	0	0	0	0	0	0	0	0	0	0	0	S_{14}	0	0	0	0
0	0	0	0	0	0	0	0	0	0	0	0	0	0	S_{15}	0	0	0
0	0	0	0	0	0	0	0	0	0	0	0	0	0	0	S_{16}	0	0
0	0	0	0	0	0	0	0	0	0	0	0	0	0	0	0	S_{17}	0

8.7 A survivorship matrix

nett migration matrix (whose rows are age groups and whose columns are regions).

As presented by Rogers (1966) the method is appealing in its elegance and yet leaves certain questions unanswered; for example survival- and birth-rates are assumed constant over time and over each age group. None of these assumptions could easily be defended in the majority of practical applications.

Nevertheless, the method appears to have enormous potential, especially as it seems capable of handling interregional migrations, both inward and outward, and specific to age-group and sex. It also seems capable of doing so with economy and elegance of operation in a manner ideally suited to simple computer operations. It should be possible to overcome the objections raised above fairly easily and thus to gain a neat and effective method of performing interregional projections which handle the *four** elements of change separately–births, deaths, inward and outward migration. This indeed would be an enormous boon to the planner. The potential offered here makes even more obvious the woeful lack (in Britain) of data on migration.

It will usually be insufficient for the planner to know simply how *many* men and women of various ages are likely to be in the area at particular times. At least of equal importance is knowledge of their likely composition into *households* so as to derive housing demands (Cullingworth, 1960; Walkden, 1961; Beckerman *et. al.*, 1965, Appendix 6); to know their likely *incomes* (per capita, per household, etc.) so as to estimate expenditure on durable goods, on transport (Isard, 1960, Chapter 4; Beckerman *et. al.*, 1965, Appendix 6), on recreation and so forth and the probable rates of *car ownership* as estimators of one aspect of travel behaviour (Tanner, 1961; Beesley and Kain, 1965).

Again, one may wish to estimate the proportions of the future population to be found in each of several *socio-economic groups* since many important aspects of behaviour (housing choice, demand for higher and further education, recreational preferences, tendency to migrate) have been shown to be associated with income and occupation (Herbert, 1967).

The reader is referred to the works cited for details of the methods currently available and which are capable of being applied in almost all planning offices. Also, we give references to methods for and examples of national projections (e.g. of car ownership in Britain), which could serve as a guide for obtaining estimates for local areas or regions.

Economic Projection

We remarked at the outset of this chapter that all projections which, directly or indirectly, involve assumptions about future human behaviour are hazardous and fraught with difficulties.

***

* N.B. we said *three* earlier (births, deaths, migration).

This is perhaps especially true of economic projection. There are a number of reasons why this should be so. In the first place, accurate projection depends as we have seen on the interrelationship of theory, i.e. satisfactory exploration of a phenomenon and reliable data about it. Economic theory may appear to have a longish history going back at least to the 'classical' writers, Smith and Ricardo. But many economists would argue that until more recently, perhaps the last thirty years, the economic theory was largely 'literary' and conceptual, that it contained statements which were for the most part untestable in practice either because their concepts had no 'real-world' equivalents, or because the variables could not be identified or measured. It is only in recent decades that economics (or perhaps as some would claim, so as to force the point home, *econometrics*) has begun to be founded on a growing body of theory which itself is subject to the acid tests of empirical verification.

In turn, verification and therefore theory have been retarded in their growth by the absence of comprehensive and useful series of statistics collected and published at regular intervals. This is true even of the most advanced societies of western Europe and north America; economic data on the less advanced countries and regions is woefully weak or totally absent.

Again, by comparison with demographic theory and statistics, economic analysis suffers not only from being 'younger' but also because it is dealing with inherently more complex issues. The demographer's unit–the human being–whilst of infinite variety, nevertheless exhibits certain broad similarities of behaviour in the biological sense. Mortality is no respecter of persons and its incidence may be predicted with a certain confidence (as every life insurance man will testify). Birth rates are less certain, being involved with the social institution of marriage and even fashions in family size. Significantly it is migration which is most difficult to forecast being closely related to *economic* factors.

The units of economic analysis are many and diverse: money, rents, salaries, profits, wages, taxes; the firm or corporation, national and local government activities; the household, the individual person and the institutional group; the industrial 'sector' or classes and sub-classes of economic activities. Unlike the demographer he has also to contend with a variety of units of measurement: monetary units (which alter in value in subtle and complex ways all the time), jobs of all descriptions either in terms of occupations or of industrial sectors, value added by manufacture, value of production, productivity, *per capita* income, disposable income, gross national product. Yet again, whilst *biologically* the human being changes but slowly (even the 'dramatic' reductions in mortality rates have been going on steadily for well over a century) the economist is struggling to develop theories of economic behaviour and structure against a background of the most rapid and far-reaching change in the structure of national and international economies which the world has ever seen.

It is small wonder that with these Herculean difficulties, economists are not eager to make projections: the remarkable thing is that they attempt to do so at all (Beckerman and associates, 1965, introduction). The principal reason they do arises from the very point we have just mentioned—that the rapid evolution of the economies of post-industrial societies as Galbraith (1962) has pointed out, forces both businesses and governments inexorably towards planning which must be based upon projection exercises however crude these may be.

But in stressing the difficulties facing those who attempt economic projection we do not suggest that it is crying for the moon, less still do we wish to ignore the considerable progress which has been made in techniques. We shall go on to review those that are most useful to the planner very shortly. Before we do, let us again draw attention to the fact that we are here concerned with such techniques *as used in the physical planning context*. Our methods of treatment, choice of techniques, the degrees of refinement (or lack of it) with respect to methods, assumptions and data might be disastrous if applied to say, analyses of market potential for a particular product or the estimation of the wage-bargaining strength of a local occupational group. As we stressed in the case of population projection, the particular needs of projection in the *planning* context must be borne in mind. Fundamentally we are concerned with the likely demands on land development, on the demands for movement of goods and raw materials, on the possible locations of these within the city or region, on the scale and impact of extractive activities, and on the broad relationships between likely rates of change of labour demand, the possible scale and timing of migration into and out of the area and the relationships of these with the supply of housing, hospitals, schools and other social facilities.

In short, we are concerned with economic activity in the round, in the relationships between its various sectors and between sectors and the population of the area; especially we are concerned with the possible *locations* of broad classes of activity within the area in future, the demands they are likely to place on land development, utility services and communications and the effects they are likely to have on the character and quality of the environment (Sonenblum and Stern, 1964).

Finally, the remarks we made earlier about *continuous monitoring and review* apply with at least equal force to economic activities.

Let us then go on to review a number of methods of economic projection, arranged as before roughly in ascending order of sophistication. We begin with simple extrapolation of total employment, total output, throughput or value or other measures of economic activity; next we deal with analytical methods involving both output, employment and productivity as variables before we continue with methods which project by sectors of the economy (e.g. extractive, manufacturing, services, etc.). Finally, we discuss a number of methods specially suited to the needs of physical planning since they involve the spatial or areal dimension within themselves—the economic base method, ratio and apportionment methods, input-output methods and social or regional accounts methods.

(a) *simple extrapolation* (Isard, 1960, pp. 7–15)

Measures of economic activity—employment, volume or value of production, value added by manufacture, etc.—may be ordered in time series from published or other sources and extrapolated in a variety of ways. The methods used will be broadly similar to those defined earlier in the sections on simple population projection—graphical, correlation or least squares, curve-fitting and so on. These methods have the advantage of simplicity, they can rely on readily-available data (especially on employment) and they do not require any high level of skill. But since they do not attempt to look behind the phenomenon

(e.g. employment) to reveal the possible causes or influences upon it, they are likely to be unreliable as anything more than a
very general guide. Again, the smaller the area considered and
the longer the projection period, the more unreliable the projections may be.

(b) *forecasts including the study of productivity* (Beckerman *et al.*,
1965, p. 530)
The variables of 'production' or 'output' on the one hand and
'employment' on the other are linked by the variable 'productivity'. This is simply measured as *output per worker* but may take
more refined forms such as 'output per man-shift'. The simplest
form is suitable for planners to whom employment is the most
useful measure. The projection is accomplished by obtaining
from some reliable source an estimate of future production or
output and a projection of productivity. Hence

$$\text{Output} \div \frac{\text{output}}{\text{workers}} = \text{workers}$$

or, in other words, output divided by productivity yields an
estimate of employment.

Clearly this method has advantages over the simple manipulation of employment data since it enables us to examine
separately and therefore more clearly the future trends in output or production and those in the productivity of labour.
'High' and 'low' forecasts for both variables would yield a
range of four possible levels of future employment, conditional
upon the assumptions made in each case.

Now obviously it will be more desirable to treat *sectors of the
economy* separately in this way for two reasons. First, estimates
of output are necessarily made in different terms or units for
different kinds of economic activities (e.g. agriculture, shipbuilding and professional services) and expected changes in
productivity are likely to be quite different in, say, school-
teaching as compared with electronic engineering. Thus, we
might derive the estimate of future schoolteacher employment
by dividing 'throughput of children' by the future estimate of
the productivity measure

$$\frac{\text{throughput of children}}{\text{teachers}}$$

whilst to estimate the employment in electrical engineering we might divide 'value of total production' by

$$\frac{\text{value of production}}{\text{man-shifts}}$$

yielding an estimate of man-shifts which would then (via a sub-assumption about the numbers of shifts to be worked in the estimate year) be converted to terms of employment.

Summarising the separate results will yield an estimate of total employment. This discussion leads us directly into

(c) *Projection by sectors of the economy*

It is more valuable to have estimates of the future levels of output or employment in the various sectors of the economy – for example to estimate the possible amount of extractive activity (mining and quarrying), the land requirements for different kinds of manufacturing, the floorspace needed by wholesaling and retailing and office-type employment.

All the methods discussed below yield estimates in this form with greater or lesser refinement; obviously then, they will also yield employment or output *totals* as well.

In the simplest (and crudest) case the forecaster simply extrapolates, by a means of his choosing, the past trend in each sector of the economy. He may do so by using output or employment figures on their own or with greater hope of reliability, convert from output to employment by means of separate forecasts of productivity for each sector of activity. The degree of improvement to be gained by doing so here is likely to be greater than when using the total employment methods described earlier since estimates of productivity trends for individual sectors of the economy are usually more refined than a generalised figure.

The estimates which result from the separate forecasts will be summed and should be compared with a forecast of total employment derived from some other source or calculation. They may also be compared with forecasts obtained from management or labour in each sector for which these are available. For example in Britain the 'little Neddies' or Economic Development Councils for specific industrial groupings prepare estimates which derive in the main from such 'grass roots' sources (Beckerman *et al.*, 1965). At the regional or local level, the forecaster will be well advised to have had contacts with at least the biggest and most significant of the area's industries (Leeds School of Town Planning, 1966). In these ways the statistical exercise may be refined and qualified by comparison of its results with national or regional trends in the various sectors and also with the forecasts of firms and other organisations actually at work in the area of study.

(d) *Economic base methods*

Perhaps no method of economic analysis and projection has seen such widespread use in planning offices, certainly, no method has been the subject of such widespread discussion and has attracted so much comment as the economic base method. We should say 'economic base *methods*' since there are possibly as many variations both subtle and substantial as there are analysts. We discuss here only the essentials of the theory and the technique, referring the reader to the voluminous literature for the fullest critiques and expositions (e.g. Tiebout, 1962 and Pfouts, 1960).

In essence, the economic base method of urban analysis applies the theory of international trade (this *country* with the rest of the world) to the region or city (this *area* with the rest of the country and the rest of the world). It postulates that growth in an area's economy comes from expansion of the *economic base* which is defined as all those '*basic*' activities which produce for *export* beyond the boundaries of the local area and this increases its wealth and its ability to pay for imports. The remaining activities which do not produce for 'export' but which exist to satisfy local needs are referred to as the 'service' or '*non-basic*' activities.

The chief practical problems associated with the method are the definition of the 'local area' and the identification of the basic sector of the economy itself. It will be obvious that the actual line chosen to delimit the study area will have a considerable effect on the economic base study; for example if a manufacturing plant on the outskirts of a city is included within the study area its activities will comprise part of the economic base of the city, whilst if it is excluded it forms part of the 'rest of the world', to which the city sells its goods and services. This is a somewhat obvious example chosen to stress the point; not all cases will be as simple as this. In general, the area chosen should approximate to the primary trading area of the principal urban centre, defined by reference to public transport routes and frequencies, patterns of journeys to work, the area served by local press and advertising media, and so on. In this way, an area is defined in which the 'non-basic' or service activities are in balance, that is, the area is self-sufficient in service functions; it follows that all *other* economic activity must exist in order to supply the 'rest of the world' beyond the defined area, that thus, by definition, it forms the economic base.

Having delineated the area for analysis, there remains the problem of identifying the basic activities themselves. There are several methods. Ideally, a complete survey is made of all firms and other agencies to discover what proportions of local output or total value of output or total employment (depending on the unit chosen for purposes of measurement) are attributable to local sales and to 'rest of the world' sales respectively. The difficulties are obvious: firms may not have records in suitable form and the exercise is very time-consuming, even if sampling methods are used. Alternatively, a list of all activities (whether as individual firms and establishments or as aggregates of each economic sector) is worked through systematically and each activity or establishment is allocated so far as possible to 'base' or 'non-base'; in cases where it seems likely that output will be divided between local and non-local sales these are apportioned in a variety of ways. For example, one approach is to assume that areas use quantities of goods and services in proportion to their share of the national population and that therefore any excess of output or employment (over the same proportion of national output in that line) must be attributable to sales beyond the local economic area boundary. By using this method (or other methods quoted in the literature) the analyst is enabled to apportion the employment of each 'difficult' case, or indeed of the whole range of economic activity into basic and non-basic categories.

The projection can then be made in a number of slightly different ways which have the following common features: first, the basic activities are projected, a sector at a time, by the use of ratios of local to national trends; then, by way of an extrapolation of the past trend in the basic/non-basic ratio the forecasts of basic employment are expanded to a total employment estimate.

The shortcomings of the economic base method of analysis have received considerable attention in the literature. There are at least equally strong objections to the use of this method as a means of projection. The most important are first, that the reliance on employment as a measure ignores the possible effects of changes in productivity; second, that the basic/non-basic ratio is a suspect measure even at a point in time, and has been shown to be highly unstable over time.

The many criticisms that have been made of this method by no means rule it out—if used with discretion and with certain refinements, and if its results are interpreted with caution it can provide a useful first approximation, *faute de mieux*. For beyond this level of sophistication the very real problem of lack of the right kind of data looms very large indeed, at least to British planners.

An interesting example of careful use of the economic base method in projection, and its refinement in a number of important ways is to be found in the work of Buchanan and Economic Consultants Limited (1966, Supplementary volume 1) in South Hampshire. In projecting the local economy the economic base was defined by a combination of common-sense interpretation of Ministry of Labour data, supplemented by a survey of local industry by direct interview and postal methods, which also yielded individual forecasts of possible growth in output and labour demand. Basic (or 'nationally-dependent') activity was projected by a refined ratio method which derived local from national forecasts and moderated these by reference to the local industrial surveys. The remaining non-basic (or 'locally dependent') activity was then forecast by the use of ratios relating it to both the *size* of the local population and to *increases* in it (e.g. in the case of the construction sector). Thus the use of the discredited basic/non-basic ratio was avoided. Other interesting aspects of this particular exercise were the use as 'givens' of three different national forecasts which provided ranges of basic activity from high to low and the derivation of a range of non-basic forecasts from a range of population estimates for the area of study.

(e) *Ratio and apportionment methods*

Generally speaking these methods make use of a similar *rationale* to those described earlier in population studies: that is, local levels of economic activity (either in total or sector by sector) bear proportional relationships to levels of economic activity in successively larger geographical areas; that these relationships may be studied as they change over time and extrapolated so that, given a set of forecasts for the largest geographical unit (e.g. the nation), estimates for the local area may be derived (Chapin, 1965, pp. 169–80). As before, the ratio method considers only *one* parent area at each step-down, whereas the apportionment method studies *all* component areas of each successively larger unit and adjusts these shares *pro rata* before proceeding to the next step. In its simplest forms direct measures are used (e.g. employment data) and totals derived for the whole of the economy. Refinements which may be introduced are the division of the economy into sectors at each step-down and the use of output figures which are then connected to employment estimates via estimates of future productivity in each sector.

A number of benefits follow the introduction of such refinements. First, in theory the derivation of employment estimates analytically by way of output and productivity is more accurate then the use of employment data directly. Second, if the projection is carried out by sectors of the economy, the resultant local forecasts may be compared directly with local employers, managers and trade associations' own estimates which have been derived from the local survey.

Short of the use of input/output and regional accounts methods (which carry us into a realm of data availability and technical refinement which is still some years' distant in local planning studies) the use of the apportionment method in a sectoral projection combined with a local economic survey is likely to provide the planner with the best practicable economic projection for a moderate expenditure.

(f) *Input/output methods*

As Abe Gottlieb (1956) has so succintly put it, 'perhaps the most important contribution of an input-output analysis to area planning is the element of forecasting that it brings to bear on the process. For if the total output of a particular industry is distributed among all the other sectors of the economy (including consumers and export) in a known proportion, it should be possible to calculate a "table of co-efficiency" which would show the effects of a given increase of output of one industry on the purchases of all others ... this kind of definable relationship or "chain reaction" spelled out in an input-output grid can be exceedingly useful to the city planner.' Originating in the work of Leontief (1953) input-output analysis studies how the output from each industry (or sector) is distributed to each of the other industries or sectors and also the distribution of inputs per unit of output from all others (Isard *et al.*, 1960, Chapter 8). These relationships or coefficients are most conveniently expressed in the form of a square table or matrix in which columns arc outputs and the rows inputs; furthermore, it is usual to express each row figure as a percentage or fraction of its column total so that each figure records the proportion of *input* needed from each sector (rows) to produce unit *output* in each particular sector (columns).

Having set up the matrix and given a forecast of demand in any particular sector, study of the appropriate column will yield the extra inputs needed from all sectors which contribute to that sector's output. But of course these extra inputs to the sector in question *are themselves outputs* of the 'contributory' sectors and so the first process must be repeated to find out the 'second-round' effects, this time sector by sector. These will branch out into further 'third-round' input requirements ... and so on.

An example may make things clearer. The first table following represents the actual transactions in thousands of pounds between three sectors of the economy with households as a fourth (payments of wages, salaries, rents, dividends, etc. and receipts of taxes, purchases, private investment and so forth).

	Sector 1	*Sector 2*	*Sector 3*	*Households*
Sector 1	50	30	20	40
Sector 2	70	40	100	30
Sector 3	95	50	70	20
Households	15	60	10	10

We then convert to coefficient form by expressing each row figure as a (rounded) percentage of its column total:

	Sector 1	*Sector 2*	*Sector 3*	*Households*
Sector 1	22	17	10	40
Sector 2	30	22	50	30
Sector 3	41	28	35	20
Households	7	33	5	10

This latter table tells us that £100 worth of output in sector 3 needs £10 worth of input from sector 1, £50 worth from sector 2, £35 worth from sector 3 and £5 from households (i.e. mostly in labour). It also tells us that household income is derived mostly from sector 1 and that sector 2 is very 'labour-intensive'.

Now, supposing a considerable expansion is planned in sector 1—and that this will increase the value of its output by one million pounds. What will be the effects on the other sectors—i.e. what additional output will they have to provide in order to make possible the increase in sector 1? First consider the column headed sector 1 and the coefficients in it. These state that £1 million of output from sector 1 requires £220,000 worth of input from sector 1 itself, £300,000 worth of inputs from sector 2, £410,000 worth from sector 3 and £70,000 worth from the household sector. We can record these in tabular form for convenience as shown below; these are the 'first round' input requirements. But the £220,000 extra input is extra *output* as far as sector 1 is concerned and must itself be produced by increased inputs from all sectors, as must the £300,000 worth of output from sector 2 . . . and so on. As round succeeds round the total extra output required will decrease; in other words the series is convergent and so the results can be summed after a number of rounds (usually between six and twelve).

It will be seen that the input/output method is a powerful analytical tool for studying the interrelationships within an economy and for observing the effects of any particular change which might be introduced (Artle, 1959). The results however are valid for *the short term only* since it cannot be assumed that the relationships between sectors (implicit in the coefficients in the matrix) will be stable through time; in fact, everyday experience tells us that they are not.

There are a number of problems associated with the use of the input/output method as a tool for projection (Pfouts, 1960, pp. 396–407). First we must derive by some means or other (expert advice or informed estimate or assumption) the relationships which are likely to obtain between the sectors at the forecast date or dates. Next we must obtain estimates of the effective demand for the output of each sector of the local economy for those dates and this may be extremely difficult to do. In Britain for example, it is only recently that concerted attempts have been made to arrive at estimates of demand for the output of key sectors of the *national* economy for future dates, to do this new and unfamiliar techniques and consultations have had to be developed; it is far too early to expect such forecasts of demand for regions, let alone for smaller areas (Stone, 1962a, 1962b and 1963). But even if these were available and could be applied to the input/output matrix so as to project the local economy it would still be necessary to convert the value of output figures so obtained into estimates of employment and this would require figures of expected productivity in each sector for the forecast date expressed as value of output per worker.

Having said all this the reader may despair of ever using input/output methods or may wonder why they are referred to here at all. They are briefly mentioned because of their con- conceptual elegance and great practical potentiality in urban and regional economic analysis and projection; but as Chapin (1965, p. 164) says, 'these factors and the problem of technical know-how in the execution of input-output analysis thus represent deterrents in the use of this method at the present time'.

(g) *'Social' or 'Regional' accounts methods*

We mention these only briefly since of all the methods noted, these are the most recently-developed, indeed they are still in an embryonic stage (Isard, 1960, Chapter 4; Hochwald, 1961; Hirsch, 1964). At the same time their potential value to all those involved in matters of public policy (and to private investors and others) is sufficiently great to warrant at least a mention here. Generally speaking, these methods employ a similar logic to input/output but are more comprehensive in that by using money (rather than production or employment) as the measure they can be more fully comprehensive in their analysis of the interrelations within an economic system by the inclusion of capital formation, investment, and trade as well as industrial production. In this way the matrix is really a record of the income-and-expenditure relationships between all sectors of the economy which, as before, may be used to obtain projections of the income each sector may be expected to enjoy at future dates; provided of course that the coefficients expressing the inter- sector relationships (each cell in the matrix) can be adjusted to express those relationships as they may be at the forecast dates required. Then, given estimates of productivity in the form of projected figures of (sectoral) income per worker the levels of employment may be estimated.

Relationship between population and economic projection

So far we have treated these two types of exercises separately. This has been done for the sake of convenience but in no way implies that population, economic activities and employment can be considered in isolation one from the other. To do so would be to violate a very important principle that we shall be developing a little later – that projection which is one aspect of *simulation* should, as that word implies, attempt to mirror the real world as closely as possible. Since common sense and experience, as well as deeper analysis, tells us that there are close links between population changes and changes in economic activities it follows that we must try to reflect this in the way we carry out our projections.

A wealth of evidence suggests that human migration occurs very largely in response to differential levels in economic activity between the 'exporting' and 'importing' areas. In other words people tend to leave areas of low, declining or uncongenial job opportunities and tend to move to areas where opportunities exist for more, better paid and more pleasant employment.*

This suggests that the relationship between employment and migration should form a link between the projections of population and employment; there are many practical ways in which

* Of course the issues posed here are extremely complex. For instance net migratory changes are often shown to be the resultants of considerably greater inward and outward movements but current data do not reveal these with the necessary detail and accuracy. The relationships between these movements and the changes in employment is also complex and poorly understood. But it is not simply a matter of 'employment growth attracting the migrants'. People are very diverse in their skills, tastes, preferences, desire for different ways of life, social contacts, climate and landscape and their motivations for moving are just as complex. Moreover the relationship is to a great extent *reciprocal*, i.e. economic activities may grow in an area in response to growing population (Clark, 1967). This is especially true of 'labour-intensive' industries, industries requiring a large market close at hand, those requiring a large pool of very diverse skills and those which provide ancillary services to the former. All we can hope to do at present is to recognise and understand these complexities as we strive to simulate them in our analyses and projections.

this can be done and we discuss a few of these (see for example Berman, Chinitz and Hoover, 1959).

The simplest connection which may be established has already been discussed and that is between total population and and total employment using the idea that employment growth will support additional population *pro rata*. Again, the South Hampshire Study example we quoted in discussing economic base methods estimated future 'non-basic' employment as a function of population growth (Buchanan, 1966). Further refinement may be introduced by comparing the *demand* for employment deriving from the economic projections with the *supply* of workers deriving from the population projections. The latter estimates may be obtained by applying projected activity rates (i.e. the proportions of the population who will be 'economically active' or in 'gainful employment') to the projected population. The degree of sophistication here will of course be controlled by the form of the population projection: if this is a simple one of total population then a crude activity rate will be applied: if in terms of males and females then separate male and female activity rates can be used; if cohort-survival methods have been used the projected population will be in terms of age and sex groupings and age-sex-specific activity rates can be applied in order to estimate the numbers of people who will be available for employment.

As explained in the sections on population projection, it may be that different 'programmes' of migration have been assumed which (together, perhaps, with different birth-and-death-rate assumptions) will have yielded a number of different projected populations. These in turn, by the methods just described, will have yielded a range of estimates of the probable workforce.

Again, it may be that the economic projections will have been devised so as to give a range of different possibilities in terms of total employment estimates.

From all we have said, the relationship between these should be clear: the various alternative population and economic projections should as far as possible be grouped into mutually consistent pairs. This is done by examining them for the most close matching of supply of, and demand for, labour so that it is possible to say that for each pair of projections the natural and migratory changes assumed in the population projection, together with the activity rates, yield a supply of workers which is broadly consistent with the demand suggested by its 'paired' employment projection.

Of course, the projections should have been made in the form of trajectories as we suggested in the first section of this chapter rather than for a single date and therefore this process of 'pairing-off' the population and economic projections is a matter not of fitting two sets of figures but of *matching two trajectories*. The question remains if the range of population suggested is wider or narrower than that suggested by the economic projection, which is 'correct'? For obviously, to be consistent with each other the numbers of jobs implied by the numbers of workers in the population projections should be of about the same magnitude and vice versa. If parts of the range of projected population lie well outside anything implied by the employment forecast what does this mean and what should be done?

Assuming that all data, assumptions and methods have been fully checked, the forecaster should take a long look at the study area as a whole, its past, its present and possible future. He should consider not only the prospects implied by trends (which of course reflect current policies of national and local government) but also consider the possible effects of significant changes in policy. By so doing it should be possible to say whether, and under what circumstances, population growth rates will restrain the advancement of a very buoyant economy–i.e. the fastest net inward migration rates which could be assumed will not provide sufficient workers to expand the economy as fast as it is capable of being expanded, *or*, that the sluggish local economy will fail to provide sufficient jobs for the expected labour force and people will tend to migrate *out* of the area. Thus in many of the older industrial regions of Britain the problem of decline due to the structure of the local or regional economy (typically based on coal, 'heavy' engineering, shipbuilding and extensive agriculture) has been exacerbated by the net outflow of the younger skilled workers whose scarcity then acts as a deterrent to the introduction of new industrial investment. Projections taking no account of the possible influence of policy here would spell out slower or quicker relative declines in employment and population. Since central intervention is clearly necessary to shift the system's trajectory by creating jobs or halting a decline in employment, it follows that the employment projection will act as a constraint.

The relationship is of course a complex one involving other factors besides assumed activity rates and simply-derived labour demands. A prolonged labour shortage may cause managements to experiment with all possible ways of increasing productivity. In this way the area's output may eventually reach a level beyond the most optimistic forecast which could not have seen some of the spectacular advances in productivity which in fact occurred. Again, forecasting may be confounded by unique decisions such as the establishment of an exceptionally large new industrial (or governmental) employer in an area, by a technological advance which renders usable areas of land which had hitherto been left out of consideration. To say this is in no way to suggest that careful projection is of no value—quite the reverse. All plans must occasionally face the unexpected and the random occurrence; the plans and policies must be sufficiently flexible to cope with such situations and thereafter be based on revised projections which now allow for the fact that the unexpected has occurred and chart a fresh course. Major changes act as 'shocks' to the system and the chain of possible repercussions (on economic activity, population, housing demands, traffic flows, etc.) needs to be estimated to see to what extent current plans and programmes are affected and what revisions are necessary.

It will be clear that in developed 'mixed' economies, that is, advanced industrial and post-industrial societies with a large measure of governmental control, in general it is the rate of change in economic activity which acts as a regulator of population change. In less developed economies or those with little or no central control there is a more evenly balanced relationship and it is therefore more difficult to determine for projection purposes whether population growth rates are constraining economic growth or vice versa.

Other factors are extremely important in any case: the rate of development of social and political organisations, particularly as instruments of control over the evolving situation; the availability of land and the rate at which it can be brought into a condition for use, patterns of tenure (which may hinder development)—all are important. We must return to a more comprehensive view of these problems later at the close of this chapter when we consider projecting the system as a whole.

In the meantime we briefly consider some of the important aspects of the system which can be derived from the population and economic projections.

Projection of other activities

Most writings on projection focus attention on what is called 'economic activity' or even more narrowly 'industry'. But there is more to life than earning a living—education, cultural and social activities, recreation of all kinds—and with the development of society these aspects of advancement or affluence occupy a larger share of people's time and resources. Since they too have spatial and recurrent characteristics they fall within the province of the physical planner.

Education

The numbers of children and young people who will be of school age at various times in the future may be simply derived from the population projection (Beckerman *et al.*, 1965, Chapter 14). The more disaggregated (into age and sex groupings) the projection the easier is the task; it is simplest of all if the cohort-survival method has been used with single-year age groups since this makes the extraction of age-ranges such as 5–11, 11–16 easy. If the more common quinary groupings have been employed some pro-rata apportionment will yield the necessary figures from the 5–9, 10–14 and 15–19 age-group forecasts.

The problem of estimating the numbers who might be involved in higher education (beyond 18 years of age) is rather more difficult since this is voluntary and since such institutions usually cater for very wide areas (the region or the nation, even the world community in the case of famous universities) there is no simple areal relationship of the local community to the institutions concerned (Committee on higher education, 1963). Some are, however, organised on a more local basis (e.g. Colleges of Art and Technology run by the local authorities) and the population projection will serve as a useful guide to possible demands in the future.

Cultural and 'social welfare' activities

The population projection has a very wide range of applications. Among these are the estimation of the demands that can be expected of the health, police, fire and library services of the public authorities, commercial (indoor) recreational facilities, churches and institutes. It can be used to estimate the demand for domestic water supplies, the numbers of beds in hospitals of different kinds (e.g. maternity and geriatric units) and the required strength of the police and fire services. Private investors in many kinds of enterprises which depend upon the total size of the population or of certain age groups will find much they can usefully derive from the projections. If the projection was disaggregated by racial or religious groups those who cater for the special needs of Catholics, Pakistanis or other socially significant minorities (e.g. by providing places of worship or special schools) will turn to the population projection. Since these facilities eventually need land the population projection serves as a guide to the planner and as a basis for discussion between him and various groups in the community.

Outdoor recreation

It is almost superfluous to say that the rise in demand for all kinds of outdoor recreation is one of the most remarkable phenomena of our times, bringing with it a host of new problems for the planner. It is equally true to say that our ignorance of recreational behaviour, its motivations and its relationships to the economic, social and geographical conditions of the population is as profound as the problems thrown up by the recreational demands themselves.

Since recreation is obviously associated with economic advance it is not surprising that both recreational activity and its study are most highly developed in North America (O.R.R.R.C.). The research so far suggests that the principal factors which 'explain' the total demand for outdoor recreation are the age structure of the population, income, educational levels, and car ownership. These demands are also influenced by the ease with which outdoor activities can be enjoyed and this is a function of topography (especially scenery and water), climate and the accessibility of favoured areas. The fact that the *supply* of recreational facilities, whether organised or otherwise, appears to influence the expressed demand makes forecasting a very difficult problem. At the present stage it seems that whatever facilities are provided will be fully used but clearly amounts of leisure time and disposable income must set certain limits. In most parts of Britain these limits seem far from being reached.

The most reliable tool of analysis may be multiple regression in which the dependent variable is some function of the demand for a certain kind of outdoor recreation and the independent variables are derived from the analysis–typically population (perhaps in a certain age-range) income, educational level and car ownership.

The numbers who might be attracted to various recreational areas can then be approached by way of some spatial model of the gravity, potential or intervening-opportunity type, calibrated by reference to actual survey data.

But the real need is for information derived from surveys of actual recreational behaviour and until such information builds up it will be necessary to make large assumptions and possibly to use 'borrowed' estimating methods gleaned from closely comparable studies (Palmer, 1967; National Parks Commission, 1968). Some would argue that since it needs no sophisticated analysis to demonstrate current shortages it is best at the present time for planning policy to concentrate on short-term and medium-term measures to improve the present facilities in an area so as to maximise the number of people they can accommodate at certain standards.

Spaces
The second aspect of the system which requires projection is 'spaces', the measuring of which was fully described in Chapter 7. There, we took it to mean the whole of the land area including water surfaces, buildings and structures forming 'adapted' spaces of all kinds. We stressed the importance of distinguishing clearly these from the idea of activities no matter how closely they may be associated in specific cases.

In general the 'projection' of spaces must be closely related to the activities projections in two ways: first, there must be spatial conformity; as we discussed at length in Chapter 7 the information on activity and spaces should be related to the *same areal units* and this is equally true in projection; second, the time intervals between steps of the projection should be the same. Generally we have suggested this should be a five-year interval but this may be an aggregation of one-year intervals for particular aspects or for highly complex ones, especially where rapid change is experienced.

The notion of 'projecting' space may seem somewhat strange at first and needs a little explanation. It will be helpful to bear in mind that the object of the exercise is to see what stocks of land and buildings are likely to be available in the future for the accommodation of activities (e.g. see Little, 1963). This means that we wish to project at five-year intervals the nature and condition of all the identifiable parcels of land which make up the study area.

In Chapter 7 we identified those characteristics of space which are important to the planner: activity, location, parcel definition, ownership and tenure, value, physical characteristics, adaptation (by structures, buildings or otherwise), facilities, sensory qualities and so on. Generally speaking it is these factors of space which we wish to 'project'. The objective of the exercise is to have the best possible knowledge of the kinds and conditions of space which are likely to exist throughout the study area at specified times in the future. But it will not be possible to know all of the characteristics observed in the survey; also, some factors will be unchanging, notably location and physical characteristics (except perhaps for changes to the latter which will usually be insignificant).

The projection of activities can be distinguished into two parts: first, the changes which will be introduced by the plan itself by the allocation of land to various uses; second, the 'commitments' which exist either by way of the continuation of an activity into the foreseeable future (e.g. worship at a cathedral, professional football at a football stadium), or by allocations in an existing plan or by permissions granted for the use of land under the provisions of the existing plan, or by virtue of the expressed intentions of agencies outside the sphere of planning control to use land for particular purposes at certain times in the future. We deal with the changes introduced by the planner himself in Chapter 9.

The 'committed' activities arising from existing plans and permissions will usually apply to a period of up to twenty years ahead at most; most parts of the plan's intentions will be precise for a shorter period only, perhaps five or ten years. Commitments by way of permissions will usually relate to the immediate future, that is, they relate to the establishment of activities or to 'changes of use' which have not yet occurred on the ground. If we now consider a series of maps which are dated 5, 10, 15, 20, etc. years from the datum year we will be able to plot on those maps the extent of the 'commitments'; we would expect that these would be extensive and detailed for the first map, less so for the second and third, sketchy for the fourth and almost non-existent for any subsequent (25 year, 30 year, etc.) maps. The only exceptions would be those activities which are expected to persist as far ahead as can be foreseen; these would be 'carried forward' in the account through all the stages of the mapped projection. We should emphasise here that changes in activity include the future *removal* of activity which exists at the datum year. Common examples are the removal of residential activities through housing clearance, the discontinuance of mineral workings, the felling of forests (without replanting) and the termination of a refuse-tipping operation and the restoration of the land. In all these cases the space may be regarded as available for other activities at the appropriate time in the projection.

As far as possible the pattern of ownership and tenure should be projected systematically and mapped at five-year intervals. It will not be practicable in most cases to do this in detail since changes in the large number of small ownerships are to a great extent unpredictable. But in the case of the largest ownerships some degree of projection will be possible. It may be the intention of various public authorities (the departments of central government, public corporations, nationalised industries, local authorities) to acquire areas or to dispose of them. Also, it may be known that a freehold area is to be divided into a number of leaseholds, and that a number of long leases are to 'fall in' at certain times in the future. Since these changes in ownership or tenure can significantly affect the way in which activities are likely to change and the degree to which it will be possible to *plan* those changes, such information is of considerable interest and importance and should be mapped for the same intervals as before.

The amount of space available in the form of land and buildings must be projected also. In exceptional circumstances actual land areas may change in the future; for example, severe coastal erosion can reduce the area available whilst the Dutch polder projects provide dramatic evidence of the possibilities of creating new land areas for potential use. All the changes in the stock of buildings and the floor-space available which can be foreseen should be allocated to the various future projection intervals.

The planner will have sought information from the agencies responsible for major utility services (gas, water, electricity, sewerage, etc.). This information will enable him to record the changing incidence of the presence or absence of those facilities in all parts of the study area in the future. The smaller-scale elements of the utility services at domestic or local service level will follow the development of areas for residential use. We are therefore referring here to decisions already taken or in mind concerning major facilities such as high voltage lines, trunk sewers and treatment plant, principal water mains and gas storage depots. In the long run and in later stages of the planning process such decisions are taken in consultation with the planner: for our present purpose we are concerned with decisions affecting the short and medium term (say 5–15 years) which have already been taken when the planner is beginning his work. These decisions about important utilities clearly affect the suitability of land for many kinds of activity (e.g. manufacturing, large-scale housing) and as before changes should be recorded in 5-year periods of the projection.

In summary, all relevant aspects of space should be projected as far as possible and expressed at five-year intervals. The aim should be to show the relative availability and potential of land (and buildings) in all parts of the study area to accommodate activities at future times. It may be convenient to construct some sort of 'index of land potential' by a weighted combination of the various factors (of activity, tenure, physical characteristics, utilities, etc.).

Communications

In Chapter 7 we distinguish between *communications*, that is, the flows of persons, goods, energy and information between located activities and the *channels* which serve to carry these flows—for example, roads, railways, pipelines, cables and rivers. We shall deal with the problems of 'projecting' channels in the next section of this chapter; here we are concerned with trying to estimate the patterns and volumes of future interactions.

In general, what is needed is a projection of the origins and destinations of all the various forms of interactions which have been noted in the survey (see Chapter 7); these will have to be identified by the mode of communication (telephone, roads, private motor car, goods train, etc.) and in some cases further subdivided according to purpose (shopping, school, social visiting, raw-materials movement, etc.) and frequency (day, week, month, etc.). In addition, the possibility that new forms of communication may come into use at significant levels in the projection period may be considered in this part of the work.

How is it possible to forecast such a complex situation many years ahead? This is a difficult problem but not insuperable; the solution lies in a return to our central notion of the system. Communications are the connections which link the various activities; in other words, specialised and differentiated activities can exist remotely from one another by virtue of the existence of communications. A great deal of the reshaping and growth of the physical environment in this century can be expressed in terms of the development of new forms of communications and changing relative costs. It follows that the whole pattern of communication observed at any moment can be (at least in large part) accounted for by the nature of the activities which are exchanging communications and their spatial disposition. The 'explanation' will be imperfect to the extent that it leaves out, for the moment, the question of the existence of channels. Obviously telephone messages will not be transmitted in the absence of a line, nor does one travel to work by boat if there is no watercourse conveniently available. This is almost a restatement of the ideas we developed in Chapter 7 when discussing communications and Chapin's 'activity systems'.

It also follows then, that we can associate or correlate particular frequencies, modes and volumes of communication with particular activities and their relationships with others. This being so, if we know future spatial distributions of identifiable activities, and if these activities can be described in appropriate ways (e.g. numbers of people in a residential area, median *per capita* income, rate of car ownership; type of manufacturing activity, size of payroll, net workshop floor area, etc., etc.) it should be possible to estimate the pattern of communications that each activity will generate.

This technique is well established in transport planning and there are a host of documented examples of such studies covering the last fifteen years (Zettel and Carll, 1962). It has been found in this work that the observed trips made, for example, by private cars from home (residential activity) to work (say, commercial activity 'x') were strongly associated with observable characteristics such as the occupational group and income of the head of the household, the possession of a car, the net residential density of the area ... and so forth. Multiple regression analysis yields equations in which the dependent variable is the number of trips 'generated' by an activity (typically a zone which obviously must be as homogeneous with respect to the activity characteristics as possible) and the independent variables are the other observed characteristics of the persons or households in the zone. These equations have the general form

$$Y = A + B_1 X_1 + B_2 X_2 + \ldots B_n X_n$$

where Y is the number of trips, X_1, X_2, ... X_n are the activity characteristics (median income, percentage of heads of households in socio-economic groups 1, 2 and 13, percentage of households with at least one private car ... etc.) and $A_1 B_1$, B_2, ... B_n are coefficients derived in the course of the statistical analysis. More strictly, Y is the number of trips made *with a certain frequency*, usually on a 'typical weekday'. Y, then, the quantity 'explained' by the variance of the activity characteristics is specified by mode (private motor car), by purpose (trip from home to work–i.e. another *specified activity*), and by frequency (each 'typical weekday'). In the great majority of transport studies these equations, derived from surveys of *existing* conditions are then used to estimate the trips that would be expected to be generated in future; this is done by supplying the equations with assumed future values of the appropriate variables X_1, X_2 ... X_n. In other words, given the series of equations and a future pattern of the town, expressed in terms of activities, densities, incomes, car ownership and so forth, the engineer will produce forecasts of the numbers of trips of each kind which might be generated by each zone of activity (for example, Leicester City Planning Department, 1964, pp. 105–8). The problem of 'assigning' the trips to a network of *channels* will be dealt with later.

As we have seen already, transport, and especially road transport is only one kind of communication. Our problem is to forecast in similar terms the propensity for each of the activities we are considering to undertake all the forms of communication with which we are concerned. We suggest that the principles on which the forecasting of vehicular trips are based may also be used to forecast the levels of many other forms of communication. For example, the numbers of telephone calls made by private (residential) subscribers per week might be related to such characteristics as socio-economic group, size of household, distance from a major city centre, gross residential density . . . etc. Multiple regression analysis could yield equations similar to those derived for estimating vehicular trips. Rail travel, air travel, usage of public road transport, taxis, the parcel service—all may be to some degree 'explained' statistically if the appropriate studies and measurements are made.

One final (and very thorny) problem remains; this concerns the relative costs of the various means of communication for to some extent these are substitutable and are thus in direct competition for the consumer's patronage. It is a matter of everyday experience (and currently a matter of great public debate) that private-car trips are increasingly substituted for trips to work by other forms of transport—bus and train especially (Foster, 1963). Or consider the journey between Manchester and London in the early 1960's where the choice lay between a bus journey of some six or seven hours (centre to centre) but with only one or two services each day, a private car journey of about five or six hours before M6 was completed and four or five hours when the motorway extended through Staffordshire and Cheshire, a rail journey of between three-and-a-quarter and four-and-a-half hours depending on the time of day and whether or not the excess first-class Pullman fare could be afforded and finally, an air journey of thirty to forty minutes which in fact was about two and a half or sometimes three hours centre to centre. The choices of mode made by a representative thousand Mancunians travelling to London ('modal split' in transport jargon) would depend upon a number of factors: costs both direct and indirect, comfort, convenience, frequency of service, time taken for the whole journey and personal taste or whim.

The extent to which one mode may be substituted for another is dramatically illustrated by this example. In April 1966 British Rail inaugurated the Manchester-London electrically-hauled service with a frequent service of well-equipped, comfortable and fast trains taking only 2 hours 40 minutes centre to centre. Passenger traffic increased by 40 per cent almost immediately and is still rising. Airline operators conceded defeat almost immediately and withdrew many domestic services between Manchester and London.

Clearly the forecasting of communication is no simple matter; certainly the issue extends far beyond characteristics of the activity and includes questions of *relative costs and degrees of convenience, comfort, speed, etc.* (Roth, 1967). Very little is known at present about the relationship of these factors to the demand for and choice of the various modes of communication and transport (Meyer, Kain and Wohl, 1966). Some research is now being carried out and the first results are beginning to appear. But it will be a long time before these can be brought into the form of operational tools which can be combined with the well-tried multiple regression methods to give even better and more reliable forecasts. We must therefore confine ourselves to mentioning this very large gap in our knowledge and lend our plea to the growing clamour for more research into the problems of communication costs and convenience as factors in the choice of mode.

Our general solution must therefore be careful analysis of our survey information on activities, communications and especially of activity systems (Chapter 7) in order to derive relationships between them. The best method which will enable us to explain the frequency of a particular unit of a mode of communication in terms of the characteristics of each 'activity-couple'. Then these estimating equations can be used to forecast future communications by employing values of the characteristics of activities derived from the projection of activities (see earlier in this chapter). Since those are expressed at five-year intervals it follows that the results for communications will take on similar form.

Channels

We can deal quite briefly with the question of 'projecting' channels since in general there is a close resemblance to the approach used in the case of spaces which we outlined a little earlier in this chapter. Once again the channels we have in mind were listed in Chapter 7; each particular planning service will have chosen certain types of channel for study (e.g. in the case of the American and British 'land use and transportation' studies the channels emphasised are roads and to a lesser extent railways; sometimes new channels such as monorails or underground railway systems are envisaged in the projection), the choice will depend on the locale and objectives of the exercise.

The projection of channels will be done as before at five-year intervals and will in essence consist of a description of the likely state of each network for each step of the projection. The networks will be described by type (dual 3-lane carriageway limited access road, quadruple-track railway, sewers, waterpipes, etc., etc.), ownership (public highways, private roads, British Rail, XYZ Urban District Council, Central Electricity Generating Board, etc., etc.), conditions (e.g. maintenance), special restrictions on use or capacity, and network *geometry*. This latter characteristic is the most important for the planner since it is the 'shape' and 'connectivity' of each network which, in relation to the disposition of activities and their needs for interaction largely determines the flows that can be expected to arise on the 'links' and through the 'nodes'. So, whilst we will need to describe the state of all types of channels in terms of ownership, etc. etc. in the network, *geometry* is the essential and indispensible factor on which we must obtain information.

Following the argument of the preceding section on 'spaces' we see a similar need for a series of maps showing for each type of channel the network geometry and other important characteristics at 5, 10, 15, . . . etc. years from the datum year. Much of this information will be derived from the authorities responsible for the channels—in Britain the Ministry of Transport, the local highway authorities, British Rail, sewerage and water supply undertakings, the national and regional electricity and gas undertakings.

Once again, there will be for each type of channel a limited period of firm commitment (perhaps already embodied in current plans, e.g. road proposals are shown on the Local Planning Authorities' Development Plans), a further period of 'semi-commitment' where the agencies' thoughts are well-advanced but the statutory and other formal processes have not reached the stage of full commitment, and finally the period beyond that for which no ideas have yet been formulated. We deal with the question of variations or extensions of these programmes which are introduced *by the plan itself* in Chapter 9.

Projecting the system as a whole

We have now completed separate treatment of the projection of activities, spaces, communications and channels i.e. of the elements and connections of our system and the physical frameworks which accommodate them. We emphasise once again, that whilst this course has been followed for the sake of clarity and convenience we are dealing with systems which, by definition, are 'interconnected wholes'. We must now consider the question: is it possible to project the behaviour of a system as a whole? To estimate how it might change from state to state in the future? To foresee future states of the system as a whole and in terms of the states of the elements and connections? Answers to these questions require assistance from two fields which we have explored earlier in this book, especially in Chapter 3: general systems theory and theories of urban and regional growth. The recent signs of possible combinations and fusions of these fields is holding out the possibility of comprehensive projection of the urban and regional systems which planners seek to control. Because the field is in such a recent stage of development of both theory and practice, because so much is in its early stages both conceptually and experimentally and because the literature reporting this work is already so scattered and extensive we can do no more than sketch in an outline of the accomplishments and the potentiality. We do so because we believe that the war of attrition on the huge problems of human locational behaviour is slowly but surely being won and that the most significant advances (both in theory and practice which are often combined within the same exercise) have been made by way of a systems approach and that it is in this direction that the greatest future progress is likely to be made.

One very common form of description of a system and one which permits investigation of its behaviour under varying conditions is the use of *models*. This enables the experimenter to explore under controlled conditions a range of possible responses of the system he is studying without having to construct the 'real thing'—often a difficult and costly business (as with large-scale engineering works or intricate machines) or dangerous (certain chemical reactions or electrical processes) or in practice impossible. Ethical objections to experiment on living humans may force the researcher to use animals as 'models' of the human system. It is true to say that most scientific advance would be impossible without recourse to models for one or more reasons. Models are such a familiar feature of our lives that we often forget the many different forms they can take. We are familiar with the physical models of buildings, machines, vehicles and harbours which architects and engineers use in order to communicate their proposals to clients or to investigate the results of a design or modification. A new breakwater, pier or dredging programme can thus be tested for its effects on silting, river and tidal flow by the civil and hydraulic engineer in a model of this kind. Similarly the aeronautical engineer uses physical models of aircraft in a wind tunnel which simulates the behaviour of the actual aircraft under various conditions.

Sometimes different kinds of materials and forces are used in the construction of an *analogue model*, that is, one which is not a direct representation of the system under study but provides a reliable 'analogy' of it; for example electrical circuits are used as analogues of nerve structures and hydraulic systems. Direct physical or analogue simulation of these kinds is of proven value where the system being studied is (by definition) relatively simple, that is where the numbers of components and connections is of manageable proportions and the number of states the system can assume is not too large and its behaviour is more or less deterministic.

But when considering systems which are highly complex and

probabilistic (such as ecological systems, social and economic systems, urban and regional systems) such direct or analogue methods are unsatisfactory for a variety of reasons. In order to maintain acceptable simulation at reasonable costs a further degree of abstraction must be introduced in which the behaviour of the system is described *in mathematical terms*, the resulting equation or set of equations being referred to as a *mathematical model*.

Mathematical models themselves are very familiar and can take extremely simple forms. For example the general linear equation

$$y = mx + c$$

is a mathematical model relating the 'behaviour' or association of y with that of x by way of the constants m and c. A specific example is the equation of uniform motion

$$s = vt + c$$

that is, the distance travelled s is given by the velocity v multiplied by the time t plus the distance travelled c at the beginning of the observation (o in the simplest case).

Thus there is nothing inherently complex in mathematical models as such; models of urban and regional phenomena may be complicated because the systems which they represent are themselves highly complicated and *because* they are, the power and universality of the language of mathematics offers hope of their description and study.

Models have a very wide range of types, reflecting both the logic of their design and their intended application. They can be

descriptive of a situation at a point in time (for example, in expressing the relationship between shopping centre sales, localised spending power, the content and attractiveness of shopping centres and the means of transport from residential areas to the shops);

predictive of future states either in continuous or discontinuous terms, that is, given relationships of the form mentioned above *plus* measures of time 'built into' the form of the model it can be used to make conditional statements about future values of the variables whose relationships it attempts to explain and *prescriptive* (or planning), that is the model cast in such form as to generate a number of alternative future states of the system and to evaluate these in relation to a set of built-in criteria and thus to indicate a best solution to a problem. These models are sometimes referred to as 'decision-making' or 'evaluative' models.

We shall discuss all these forms of models in due course but in this chapter we are concerned almost entirely with the second category, predictive models—though we shall also mention descriptive models which can be adapted for use in projection.

We have spoken at length earlier in this chapter of the close relationship between theory and prediction in the context of scientific method; nowhere in planning is this more apparent than in the design and construction of mathematical models (Harris, 1966). The model-builder is seeking to make statements about the environment (the location of activities and the pattern of flows in urban and regional systems) which enable him to understand and cope with it. Inevitably these statements must be simplifications and seek a more generalised level of order in a highly complex situation. So the first steps are the recognition of order and pattern in a multitude of observations and the advance of a hypothesis. As Lowry (1965) has put it, the designer of a model must be able 'to perceive repetitive temporal patterns in the processes of urban life, fixed spatial relationships in the kaleidoscope of urban form'.

And he goes on to say that 'for the prediction of the future, an understanding of the relationship between form and process becomes crucial. In a descriptive model it may suffice to note that X and Y are co-variant . . . but when the aim is to predict the value of Y at some future time, the model must specify a causal sequence (e.g. that a one-unit change in the value of X will *cause* the value of Y to change by 5 units). If one is able to postulate the direction of causation, knowledge of the future value of the "cause" enables one to predict the future value of the "effect".' A necessary rider to these remarks is that some function of *time* is an essential element in predictive models. For example,

$$Y_t = Y_0 + ar^t$$

states that the value of Y at time t (Y_t) is found by adding the value at time o (Y_o) to the product of a and r raised to the power t; t might be measured in seconds, hours, years or any other unit of time.

Cities and regions are capable of being viewed with such complexity that the first problem the analyst faces is where to start. Clearly an almost infinite number of possible models exist which could make predictive statements concerning the variation of each factor of interest in relation to each of the others. A sense of purpose and prime objectives is indispensable at this stage. Let us pause for a moment and suggest what these prime objectives are; it will once more be helpful to consider the nature of our system.

We are concerned to guide and control the spatial patterning of change in activities and spaces, communications and channels. It follows that our line of attack in model design must be to make conditional predictions about future states of the system in such terms. Given that such-and-such policies will be in operation, that these major decisions have already been taken; that these are our assumptions about a and b and c (aspects of locational or communication behaviour) what changes in the location of activities, p, q and r and movements x, y and z can be expected at times t_3, t_4 and t_5? As Lowry has said 'the model literally consists of "named" variables embedded in mathematical formulae ..., numerical constants ... and a computational method ... the pattern generated is typically a set of values of interest to the planner or decision-maker, each value tagged by geographical location and/or calendar date of occurrence' (Lowry, 1965).

In Chapter 7 we indicated the kinds of information the planner needs to describe current and past states of the system and how this information related to relevant aspects of activities, spaces, communications and channels, 'each value tagged by geographical location and/or calendar date of occurrence'.

It therefore follows that predictive models must in essence be (i) attempts to 'explain' the pattern and sequence of changes in the past and (ii) attempts to derive thereby future states – on the basis of assumptions that future structural relations and co-efficients can be derived, at least in part, by a study of past situations. The construction of models which will perform such tasks will necessitate the adoption of some hypothesis or general-ising framework which satisfactorily fits the past data; the more satisfactory this fit, the greater the confidence that can be placed in the model's predictive performance. At this stage we can see the paramount importance in model-building of

(i) adequate data describing past and current states and
(ii) a hypothesis which would 'explain' the changes observed.

The type of hypothesis chosen (or derived afresh) will depend upon a number of factors: whether the model being constructed is of a small sub-system such as total population distribution or shopping centre sales or is more comprehensive in its approach; the particular nature of the town or region, its geography and history; the skill of the model-builder and the quality of his data. Earlier in this chapter we dealt with methods of pro-jection (i.e. predictive models) for *aspects* of the system (or sub-systems); now we will confine the discussion to models which aim to be more comprehensive. Data we dealt with in Chapter 7 and the other requirement (hypotheses to explain the changes observed) were considered in Chapter 3; the reader is advised to refresh his memory concerning the main theories of urban and regional growth at this stage.

Detailed discussions of theoretical approaches to aspects of the urban system – residential building, manufacturing locations, choice between transport modes, social ecology – are outside the scope of this book and are extensively treated elsewhere. Con-centrating on the strategic aspects of model design we turn to one of the most crucial questions of predictive modelling – the treatment of *time*. 'At first glance the problem seems to hinge merely on the question, how often need results be read out? But the issues go deeper, involving the model -builder's percep-tion of the self-equilibrating forces of the world represented by his model, the empirical evaluation of response-lags among his variables, and his interest in impact analysis as distinguished from other types of conditional or unconditional prediction' (Lowry, 1965).

Just how deep these issues do go, and how great their prac-tical significance is can be judged from the history of 'land use and transportation' studies in the U.S.A. Some fifteen years ago Carroll and Creighton attempted to predict vehicular movements given a future land use pattern – an unprecedented approach in highway engineering. The theoretical foundations for such methods were laid by Mitchell and Rapkin (1954), Ranells (1956) and others. The treatment of time in those early highway planning exercises was thus: the activities (land uses) were specified for some distant future in one step; next, given 'generation factors' (i.e. trips originating per day per unit of residential, industrial, commercial, etc. land or floor space) the pattern of flows required ('desire lines') was derived and a highway system for that future date could be designed to accommodate the demand (or as much as was feasible and acceptable). No account was taken of the *changing relationships through time* of land uses and movements. This omission came under serious attack as the years progressed, technique became more widespread and the political commitment to huge highway programmes greater. An outstanding example is the critique of the Washington, D.C. transportation plans; the principle point being that both changes in the locations of activities throughout the city (or region) *and* changes in the transportation systems (not merely *roads*) occur incrementally *through* time and each affects the other in a reciprocal fashion (Wingo and Perloff, 1961). In other words, changes in, say, the road network stimulate changes in land use, which alters the flows on the roads (and other transport media) which alters land values which sets up relocations which result in different flows which call forth demands for alterations to the road systems. . . .

The argument and the view of cities as dynamic systems is by now familiar to the reader. The points made by the American critics of their own fellow-professional and government agencies were met to a very large extent in a number of ways. Two of the most notable are Professor Robert Mitchell's forceful and cogent report to the U.S. Government (Mitchell, 1959) and the setting up of the Penn-Jersey Transportation Study at the beginning of the 1960's (Fagin, 1963). In these two developments (which represent landmarks in the evolution of planning theory and practice) several crucial points were explicitly recognised:

the mutual inter-dependence of activity locations and communication opportunities;

the reciprocal nature of changes in these and how they occur incrementally through time;

the need to approach the planning of cities and regions comprehensively because, as Harris said in a memorable paper at the time, 'the entire system of metropolitan function is the environment of the decision-making that shapes metropolitan growth' (Harris, 1961).

Thus, whilst a very large range of many different kinds of models will be of use in the treatment of sub-systems or facets, the system as a whole is best modelled in a way which simulates changes to the two central features (activity/spaces and communications/channels) as they occur through time and simulates the reaction of each to changes in the other.

For theoretical and practical reasons the most promising form of model to satisfy these conditions is that in which the system's evolution is handled *recursively*. A recursive model simulates the evolution of a system in a series of steps (usually representing the passage of equal units of time); the output of each stage is the input to the next. This essential characteristic of recursive models is an attempt on the part of the model-builder to replicate the processes we discussed first in Chapter 1, then in Chapter 3 and in Chapter 5 whereby actions to modify the environment can be seen to derive from responses to the perceived state of the environment immediately before the action is taken.

There are three particular advantages which accrue from the use of recursive models. In the first place it is possible to output the state of the system at each step in the process of change and observe how the system is evolving; second, it is possible to treat non-linear trends (e.g. in rates of growth of car ownership, in migratory changes between sub-areas, etc.) as if they were linear if the period of time covered in each step is short enough – in most cases five years is an adequate basis for such an assumption; third, the planner or analyst can intervene directly into the simulation in order to alter some of the main assumptions behind a particular run with respect to various time periods. For example in a recursive model with a five-year cycle it may be found on examining the results at, say, 10 years that the growth of the city of region is failing to respond in the way which was hoped for. It may be suggested that the value of certain parameters which express, for example, shopping-trip generation or land availability according to a particular policy assumption should be altered; these adjustments made, the model can be 'switched on' again and left to complete its run. The results would then be examined to see if the growth of the city had responded in 15, 20, 25 years in a more acceptable way.

Attempts at comprehensive mathematical modelling may be inappropriate, or unattainable in many situations: unattainable because of the lack of even minimally adequate information for present and past times or because of the lack of suitably trained staff (*and* employers!), time, money and computing facilities; inappropriate because a planning exercise may be of a reconnaissance nature where 'first approximation' investigations are the order of the day; or it may be for a small area whereas mathematical methods are more appropriate to large aggregations of population, land and so on, or where the planner has been asked to concentrate on a study of a particular subsystem or sub-area or to report on the 'impact' of a single large proposal such as a major shopping centre, a steelworks or chemical plant.

But whatever the difficulties may be which stand in the way of comprehensive mathematical modelling, whether of smallness of area or lack of money, etc., this should on no account deter us from an attempt to simulate the processes of change in our system to the best of our ability. One very promising approach is the use of 'gaming' (Meier and Duke, 1966; Taylor and Carter, 1967). As the name implies, these methods compare the development of and the competition for spaces and channels (by activities and communication-flows) as akin to the competitive moves made by players in certain kinds of games; we discuss gaming simulation in Chapter 9.

Whatever methods are chosen the paramount requirement is for the projection to provide, for stated policy and other assumptions, *a trajectory (or set of trajectories) showing the way the system is expected to evolve through time.*

In Chapter 7 we saw how a great deal of the essential information describing any state of our system was reducible to two forms—matrices and maps. The matrices show the activities in their various locations, spaces and their locations, communications by type in the form of interaction (origin/destination) matrices, and networks on a map or a set of maps. We also showed that the networks could be described in matrix form (e.g. a dual two-lane road connects locations 1 and 2, 2 and 17, 17 and 27, 27 and 36, etc.) although for many practical purposes the map is a more useful tool.

In this chapter we have seen that future trajectories of the system can be described by similar *sets* of matrices and maps, one set for each of the chosen time-intervals (Figure 8.8). For example, a typical projection might consist of a set of matrices and maps (activities, spaces, communications, channels) for each of the years 1971, 1976, 1981 ... etc. (Jay, 1967).

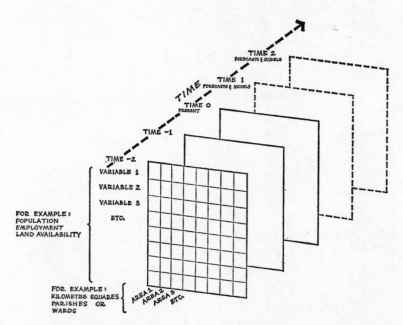

8.8 Diagrammatic representation of planners' information system

This conclusion reflects the point made in Chapter 7 that a dynamic system (one subject to ceaseless change) can be described by describing the *states through which it passes* – usually at constant intervals; similarly then, the future trajectory of a dynamic system can conveniently be projected in terms of *states through which it might pass* on the basis of various assumptions about its internal behaviour and external influences.

Such trajectories provide a starting-point for the formulation of plans.

9

Plan Formulation:
Charting Possible Courses of the System

'Plan formulation, in essence, is the choice of those projected or simulated future states of the system which yield optimum conditions. These optimum conditions are described by reference to the performance criteria derived from the goals.'*

When dealing with complex systems it is very difficult to derive at 'one shot' the optimum (or near-optimum) condition, although methods which attempt to do this are under development and will be discussed later. It is much easier to build a range of alternatives which might straddle the optimum and to test and evaluate them. A process of successive re-formulation and re-testing will then enable us to discover the best possible solution.

The alternatives referred to are of course various 'trajectories' of the urban or regional system—sequences of states through which it might pass. The variation among alternatives may be induced in the simulation in a number of ways. Essentially these derive from variation in two sets of assumptions—those concerning public policies (e.g. about economic growth, housing subsidies, centralised or dispersed forms of development, land conservation, public transport, etc., etc.) and those relating to private (household, corporate and institutional) responses or initiatives. Variations in one or the other or of both in different combinations will yield a number of different trajectories of the system as its evolution is simulated (Figure 9.1).

* I am indebted to Dr. G. F. Chadwick for this form of words.

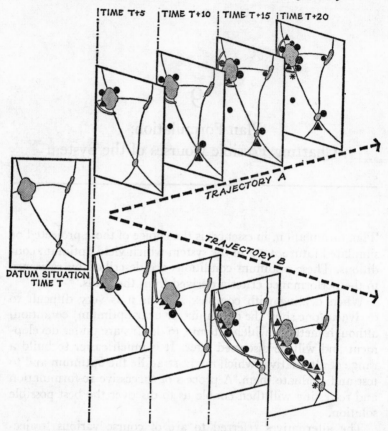

9.1 System trajectories

The numbers of alternatives produced will depend upon a number of considerations, but the resources of time, money, manpower and data-processing equipment will be the main ones. These factors affect not only the ability to produce the different trajectories, but also to accomplish adequate testing, evaluation and re-design.

More difficult to decide is the question of what *sorts* of alternatives to produce. Should simulation vary the future size of population and employment in the area? Or of policies for land conservation? Or particular types of activity in more detail such as extractive or recreational industries? Or of some, or all of these in combination?

Clearly the opening sentences of the chapter provide the clue. The basis of the variations should derive from the goals and objectives which have been agreed upon as the starting point for the planning programme. For example, if the question of maximising economic growth is so important that it overshadows all other goals, or indeed is the *only* goal, then obviously the basis of developing alternative trajectories will be first, different assumed rates of growth (to enable examination of what rates are feasible), different ways of achieving faster growth (e.g. by way of stimulating existing economic activity, introducing new industries, improving infrastructure together with different spatial configurations of employment centres, housing areas and so forth). Or, again, if the main goal is to maximise population growth, the variations should consist of different assumed rates of inward migration combined with diverse ways of settling the population in existing and new residential areas. In both these examples, it is not only a *constant* rate which may be varied, but also the rate at *different periods in the future*.

But if the size of the population and/or economy of the study area is not a matter of public concern and therefore does not appear in the goals statement then the variations must reflect other issues. Since we are talking about physical planning, it is variation in the spatial patterning of growth, the various 'anatomies and physiologies' which the city or region could assume in the future which will enable us to derive alternatives. The same principle applies: that the variations induced should be a reflection of important goals and objectives.

If it is clear that the question of the degree of centralisation or dispersal (or jobs or people, or both) which a city should have is an urgent issue, then the alternatives must reflect this. If one of the goals is to discover the optimum 'mix' of public and private transport facilities these 'mixes' must vary between alternatives. Similarly with other issues: conservation of agricultural land or particular areas of scientific or scenic interest, the exploitation of a major new transport facility, the location of a large centre of higher education—whatever the question may be, the alternatives must be devised so as to give the best opportunity of seeking the optimum.

If alternatives are not carefully related to goals and objectives there is the real danger that they will either fail to reflect certain important issues which the planning process is being used to study, or worse still, be almost irrelevant. To spend the clients' time and money on studying variations on a theme which is of little or no concern is irresponsible and may be worse than a misguided (but honest) attempt at a one-shot solution. Far too many plans have derived from the study of physical-form alternatives – e.g. 'satellite towns', 'linear growth', 'suburban sprawl', 'circuit linear', 'polynucleated' (National Capitol Planning Commission, 1962). Of course, it is true that in so doing, different dispositions of jobs, population, shopping and recreational areas have been studied, together with different transport systems. But it does not necessarily follow that they will have been studied in the best way since there may be little or no variation in one or more of these as between a number of physical forms. To study different physical forms *as such* is justified only where physical form *as such* is a principal issue embodied in the goal statement (as it may well be in areas of great architectural, historic or scenic attraction). Alternatives must reflect the goals sought; the means must reflect the ends.

Having established the basis on which alternative trajectories are to be generated it is necessary to decide on the form of simulation to be used. This was referred to in the closing section of the previous chapter when dealing with the projection of the system as a whole. The type of simulation chosen will depend on a number of factors: the size of the planning area, the availability of data, the data-processing resources at hand, the skills and size of staff and, of course, the time and money which can be devoted to this part of the task.

The size of the area for which plans are being prepared will influence the kind of simulation chosen. Although larger regions and towns are not *inherently* more complex as systems (complexity being governed by how the system is defined), nevertheless, for a given size-range of component – say an employment concentration of about 1,000 jobs and a residential unit of around 2,000–3,000 persons it is obvious that greater complexity is encountered in larger settlements, if only because the number of possible states of the system increases drastically with the number of its components. Thus, relatively simple simulation methods might suffice for small-to-medium sized planning areas but more sophisticated methods will be needed in those of bigger population unless of course a very coarse-zone approach is being made, perhaps as a prelude to more intensive analysis.

Very often the quality of data will strongly influence the choice of simulation method. For example, if full demographic economic and 'land' data are available at a fine-zone level for two or more dates including a datum year, it is possible to choose a sophisticated simulation method which might model the growth patterns of the area in terms of a large number of small zones. However, if consistent data is lacking for such fine zones, being available for say twenty local authority areas only in a large conurbation, then this may limit the choice initially to a twenty-zone simulation model of fairly modest design.

Obviously the choice will be influenced by data-processing resources. If one has only an electric calculating machine and the very occasional use of a small computer it is no good trying to devise and operate a simulation process involving hundreds or thousands of calculations to achieve one step. Equally, the trap of attempting 'big' simulations merely because one happens to have access to a large computer should be avoided.

If the planning exercise is working to a strict deadline this will inevitably encourage the use of simple methods of proven effectiveness. Last, and by no means least, the director of the operation will of course, choose a simulation method which he knows can be understood and operated with confidence by his staff, although a certain amount of learning on the job may be admitted as a calculated risk.

Four broad types of simulation process will now be described in outline. For the sake of simplicity and to enable comparisons to be made between them, certain basic assumptions are common to all: first, they handle the passage of time in five-year steps; second, they are all to some extent recursive–i.e. the output of each step is in part the input to the next succeeding step and may influence its operation in other ways, and third, in all of them the changes in population, employment and so forth are assumed to be determined separately *outside* the simulation process (exogenously) i.e. they are spatial simulations in essence.

The four types of simulation may be termed:
Informal/manual

Formal/manual
Partly mechanical
Fully mechanical

Informal/manual simulations

Informal/manual simulations are carried out by locating the various activities (i.e. the 'components' of the system) which have been separately projected by reference to the known state of the system and respecting various constraints—e.g. those imposed by policy assumptions. The first step will be to introduce the changes from the datum year to the date five years ahead, $t+5$ making sure that the several changes total those in the projections and that the locations selected, the densities assumed, etc., are reflections of the particular policy variant being operated; and that the resulting overall land use pattern is sensible in terms of broad relationships. Supposing that the main 'activities' components of the system are gross residential, industrial, commercial and recreational and that the 'communications' considered are home-to-work trips by private vehicles and by public transport. The system is therefore described by four activities and two communications. The structure of the system may simply be defined in terms of acres of land (developed or vacant) for the 'spaces' and the primary road network for the 'channels'.

Each step in the simulation, representing the passage of five years, will be effected by altering broad zonal figures of population (residential activity), workers (in two types—industrial and commercial), some measure of recreational activity, and the corresponding areas of land used for residential, industrial, commercial and recreational purposes. At the same time, any alterations in the 'channels' can be introduced graphically, including the addition or deletion of bus routes.

It would be desirable to examine the pattern of activities at each five-year interval and to estimate the likely volumes of traffic and the usage of the bus services on all the arms of the network. In order to do this some simple means of estimating the trips generated and of assigning them to the network will be necessary. By manual means this is quite feasible, though laborious, for up to 20 or 25 zones of origin and destination.

The examination of these travel patterns and traffic densities may suggest some adjustments to the location of activities and re-testing to obtain better traffic patterns. When a satisfactory outcome has been obtained the simulation of the next five years of change can proceed.

As the simulation progresses, it may be desirable to introduce assumptions about changing human values and attitudes as they affect choices of location, movement, densities and so forth. For example, one might allow for the influence of rising car-ownership (which should have been projected together with population, employment, etc., before simulation begins). This could affect the choice between travel modes and thus the calculations of traffic flows. Additionally it might be held to be a contributory factor in requiring larger amounts of dwelling space and thus lower residential densities. Many kinds of reasonable assumption may be introduced in this way to lend accuracy to the simulations.

The process continues through successive 'rounds' each representing the passage of five years until the 'horizon year'–i.e. latest date to which all trajectories have been carried–is reached. Then the whole process is repeated beginning again at the datum year for each of the alternative strategic policy assumptions, thus completing the generation of a set of trajectories through which the area could pass–a sequence of states which it could assume if each of the specific policy bundles were applied (Figure 9.1).

Such 'informal' manual simulations make use of many of the customary procedures and existing skills of the planning profession–e.g. the use of projections to scale the future demands for land and the application of common sense and professional know-how to the problems of location, development and movement (compare Chapin, 1965, pp. 457–66). The important innovation as presented here is the treatment of the town or region as an evolving system, and simulating its growth as such in a recursive manner at the same time studying directly the influence of different public policies on the patterns of evolution. The main weakness of the method is its lack of analysis of locational and movement behaviour and its chief advantages are ease and economy in operation.

Formal/manual simulations

Formal/manual simulations are similar to the preceding ones in broad outline, but attempt to overcome their weakness by the introduction of much more firmly-based models of critical elements in the processes of change. Typical examples are the relationships between changes in population distribution and in employment, the effects on location behaviour of the main transport facilities and the relationships between trip-making, modal choice and socio-economic characteristics of the population. Often such relationships will have been studied at the datum year and for past times, and certain hypotheses advanced and tested so as to try and formulate some simple mathematical models. The models, when successfully calibrated are then built in to the simulation process at appropriate points where they will be linked to other mathematical or 'manual' operations which precede and succeed them. The complete sequence of procedures comprises one 'round' of the simulation process.

But the level of simulation we are describing here is still relatively simple. The mathematical models and the degree of spatial disaggregation do not require very powerful machinery – nothing more than a number of semi-automatic desk calculators and a medium-sized computer.

An example of such a simulation is shown in flow-diagram form in Figure 9.3 (see pages 248–9).

The (previously tested) major assumptions here are: first, that the change in population in each broad zone (say 15 for the whole area) in any five-year period is strongly correlated with the zonal changes in jobs and population in the immediately preceding five years; second, that *within* each of these coarse zones population change is strongly related to the proximity and number of jobs, to the presence of 'primary network' roads and public transport services and to the allocations of residential land made by the planning authorities; and third, that certain types of employment are located irrespective of population distribution whilst others are markedly 'labour-oriented'.

The input (left-hand) side consists of policy assumptions about 'strategic' job distribution, land conservation, redevelopment densities, etc., etc. stated with as much precision as necessary. The process begins with the deployment of the increments of two main types of employment – 'site-oriented basic' and 'centralised service' – e.g. large office and shopping concentrations. At the same time major public housing developments and the aggregated effects of many smaller-scale 'infillings' and conversion of houses into flats are simulated. Housing areas estimated as unfit are cleared and the decisions taken (consistent with the policy assumed) to develop or otherwise whilst other areas are examined for the possibility of improvements to housing and environment.

As these operations are simulated, accounting operations are performed to alter data on population distribution, socio-economic groups, housing condition scores, land availability and so on. The recorded changes at broad-zone level in jobs and population in the preceding period are used to predict zonal changes in the current period in a simple model, e.g.:

$$\delta P_i^{t5-t10} = a + b\delta E_i^{t0-t5} + c\delta P_i^{t0-t5}$$

where δP_i^{t5-t10} = share of total population change in zone i between t5 and t10.

δE_i^{t0-t5} = share of total employment change in zone i between t0 and t5 (etc.).

and a, b and c are constants.

These broad shares are then distributed more finely within each zone by reference to the road network, land availability and accessibility to employment. This latter function again might be the subject of a simple calculation whereby the pattern of jobs at point locations is used to generate an 'accessibility surface' e.g.:

$$AE_i = \sum_{all\ j} \frac{E_j}{d_{ij}^x}$$

where AE_i = the 'accessibility-to-jobs' index for zone i
E_j = the number of jobs at location j
d_{ij} = some measure of the distance between i and j
x   = an exponent applied to distance.

(N.B. in the actual example quoted here, this calculation was performed by computer, the output on the line-printer being set out cartographically.) The primary road network is updated five years. The population distribution has now been advanced by five years and certain assumptions are employed to divide each small cell into 'white collar' and 'blue collar' residents.

The increments of the remaining two categories of employment may now be distributed: 'labour-oriented' manufacturing disproportionately to blue-collar residential areas and 'other service' jobs directly in proportion to the new population distribution.

One round of the simulation is completed by converting all operations into terms of land development (via density assumptions), updating all land-availability records, and finally checking that all numerical operations total the projected figures for the study area as a whole. If any discrepancies are noted the process must be checked and errors distributed.

Although it is not shown in Figure 9.3 the resulting states of the system (activities, spaces and channels) can be filled out to include the missing *communications* at each round by using the distribution of people, jobs and road network as input to an appropriate trip-generation/distribution/assignment model. The output of this–e.g. total person- or vehicle-miles, approximate flows on each link of the network–may indicate the need for adjustments in the distribution of activities, or the network or both. Additionally, this may provide useful pointers to likely shifts in demand for housing and industrial locations or road improvements in the next round.

Gaming

An alternative form of 'formal/manual' simulation is provided by gaming which has already been mentioned in Chapter 8 (Meier and Duke, 1966; Taylor and Carter, 1967). The heart of any gaming simulation, as with nearly all others, is some sort of model. In fact, the example used immediately above could readily be adapted to become a gaming simulation. The critical differences are first, that some or all of the mathematical sub-routines may be substituted by a succession of 'plays' or 'moves' in the game; and, second, that the human operators of the simulation become directly and personally involved in the process by playing *rôles* assigned to them. Some of the rules of the game are provided by the real-world constraints–e.g. activities cannot be located if no land is available, the growth in population within a coarse zone is determined by the mathematical model (which now appears as a 'rule'–'a player cannot begin until he has thrown a six'). Other rules govern the way in which competitive disputes must be resolved, e.g. in the location of new employment and population at the fine-zone level, conflicts will arise between the 'industrialist' and 'house-developer' players in the game. Alternatively, mathematical sub-routines may be dispensed with almost entirely and major locational decisions made by players in the game. But this approach has its dangers–for example, the 'house developer' in the game may build far more houses in an area than would be justified in the real world by the level of job opportunities within reach; some form of constraint rule is obviously necessary though it need not take the stricter mathematical forms associated with non-gaming type simulations.

If the example we have used were adapted as a gaming simulation, the types of players might include the following:

Local politicians (goal-setting, strategic policy decisions, resolution of conflicting plays or moves).

Manufacturers (location of basic employment).

Chamber of trade/commerce (central shopping, and office employment).

Planning officials (allocate land for various developments; permit or refuse each 'move').

(Public) housing officials (developments, slum clearance, etc.).

Private house-builders (private residential developments).

Transport operators.

In addition, there would be 'neutrals'–non-playing personnel who would maintain the flow of information on which decisions would be based and carry out all the necessary calculations and accounting. It may be felt desirable to have someone in the rôle of central government or other agency who could arbitrate in cases of appeal by a developer against refusal of permission by the politicians and their planning officials.

Gaming simulation offers a number of advantages. Some of these are found in the more conventional simulations already described–cheapness, quickness, ease of operation. But there are advantages unique to gaming and these are chiefly the potential of gaming in enabling the participants to *learn* more directly the nature of the processes and the rôles of the protagonists in the real world and the ways in which the system's outcomes respond to the interactions of both. They introduce the effects of personal and corporate power and aspirations directly into the simulation and thus involve less abstraction from the world of public affairs than do other forms of modelling. Where a fuller understanding of these influences on the urban or regional system is of particular importance, and where an open-ended experimental approach to plan design is indicated – especially when the clarification of goals has proved difficult – gaming offers a number of advantages over other simple methods of simulation.

Partly mechanical simulations

Partly mechanical simulations are those in which more complex modelling of the system has been attempted and where the scale of the calculations required to accomplish the process warrants considerable use of automatic data-processing equipment including computers.

In the largely manual simulations, the random or probabilistic elements of human behaviour were reflected by allowing the human operators of the process to exercise discretions and options in their choice of say, locations, densities and land allocation details. The more mechanised a simulation becomes, the more these random outcomes are reflected 'inside the machine', for example by the incorporation of a 'Monte Carlo' routine perhaps achieved by reference to a set of random numbers to indicate the probabilities of a number of successive steps.*

Obviously in a *partly* mechanised process the human operator retains a considerable degree of control during each run. Very often this takes the form of programming the machine to output the state of the system after one cycle and, as the result of inspection to vary some of the key parameters (e.g. densities of development, the 'friction factor' of distance in a gravity model) or, less frequently, policy assumptions (e.g. concerning slum housing clearance rates or land conservation). The next cycle is then allowed to run in the machine with these varied inputs, the output is inspected again, and so on.

* Where 'Monte Carlo' routines are employed it is necessary to carry out a large number of runs consecutively and to obtain the mean outcome (Donnelly, Chapin and Weiss, 1964).

More commonly, each cycle itself will be a composite of manual and machine operations. For example, the distribution of what Chapin calls 'priming factors'—e.g. major public and private development decisions in manufacturing, distribution, transport and the like may be simulated by manual operations whilst the 'secondary' repercussions which follow—e.g. residential developments and the re-distribution of population may be simulated by a computer calculation of a previously constructed mathematical model (Chapin and Weiss, 1962a).

For these reasons, the more mechanical simulations are not only associated with the availability of the 'hardware' but also with bigger groundwork effort on the analysis of the urban or regional processes to develop the necessary models.

Fully mechanical simulations
Fully mechanical simulations are those in which all or nearly all of the simulated urban growth processes occur inside the computer. The actual simulation runs must clearly be preceded by a very considerable effort in the analysis of urban growth over past times, the setting-up, testing, modification and reformulation of hypotheses leading to successful calibration of models. Typically the complete model consists of a large 'family' of sub-models in a nested hierarchy. The opportunity will exist to stop a run at any point (say after two or three cycles, representing ten or fifteen years respectively) for the interim states to be inspected. But more usually the computer will be programmed to produce a complete trajectory of say 20, 25 or 30 years' urban growth in one set of operations.

This represents the fullest development of the recursive model whereby the state of the system at the end of each cycle is input *automatically* to the next and, moreover, where certain parameters may be generated endogenously (i.e. 'inside') and calculated afresh during each cycle.

At the present time such exercises require very considerable resources of skill, money, time and hardware. This is likely to be the case for many years to come; for even though computing power has recently been increasing by several orders of magnitude, our understanding of urban systems and the data with which to test hypotheses has not kept pace.

A good example of such an exercise is provided by the Penn-Jersey Transportation Study which was set up in the greater Philadelphia area in 1959–60. The underlying logic of the simulation was one of varying major policy assumptions, including the rate of regional growth in terms of population and economic activity, the basic form of the transportation systems and their networks and certain major public and private locational decisions–e.g. airports, oil refineries and steel mills. Assumptions governing these and other big issues were derived outside the model and supplied as some of its main inputs. Inside the model a complex array of sub-models simulated the myriad smaller-scale repercussions resulting from the effects of accessibility, land prices and rents, etc., and taking the form of location and relocation decisions and trip-making behaviour. Each cycle (of five years, beginning at 1960 as datum) of operations resulted in the generation of a new state of the system which was then automatically input to the next cycle.

One sub-model calculates least-time paths through transport networks and passes the results to another which relates these to the distribution of people and economic activities and scores accessibility measures between all pairs of sub-areas in the region. These results in turn are used on one of the most important sub-models–that concerned with 'activity distribution'. This involves assessing land availability (including the effects of public policies), locating all types of households and 'ageing' them, calculating their budgets for housing and transportation etc., etc. The outcome of this enables 'consumer-oriented activities' to be located followed by simulation of the relocation of light and medium industries and warehousing. The industrial and commercial 'population' of firms in each sub-area is also aged at this step.

The nett result of all these operations is an updated geographical pattern of human activities, of people, firms and institutions of varying kinds, occupying space and buildings with different prices and having various operating budgets related principally to the costs of using the space and of making the necessary journeys.

Clearly this can be related to the transport networks (supplied to the model from 'outside') and the whole movement pattern of the region simulated. This pattern in turn will affect the location and relocation of activities at the start of the next cycle.

At the end of a complete run, the computer output would indicate the trajectory of the urban system (given a set of policy and other assumptions).

The Penn-Jersey exercise involved prodigious effort, manpower and money, even by north American standards. Severe philosophical, professional, political, technical and operational problems were encountered. As the original director Henry Fagin proudly said, the team 'attempted to reach the moon'. It is likely to be some considerable time before many such enterprises are tried in Britain (but see Cripps and Foot (1968) for a notable British effort). Penn-Jersey (and certain other similar ventures) have shown that fully mechanical urban simulations are coming within reach though at considerable cost.

'Equilibrium' Plans

Throughout this book the over-riding necessity of approaching planning as the guidance of change in an evolving system has been stressed. The cyclic nature of the planning process, the emphasis on projection of data in equal time-periods to chart the main dimensions of change, the use of recursive models which show the step-wise sequences through which the *spatial form* of the urban system could pass–all these are derived from the same basic approach to the problem.

Nevertheless, there are occasions when it may be useful and necessary to develop fairly quickly an impression of the future form of a city or region *assuming it could reach an equilibrium condition*–albeit an unstable equilibrium.

A slight variation on this approach is to ask what form the city would take up if a number of stated conditions (e.g. about distances between land uses, densities of development, etc., etc.) are to be satisfied.

These approaches are quite different from the recursive models for simulating processes of change which we have been discussing. Their logic is to regard the city at the present time as a system in unstable equilibrium which is then 'disturbed' by the addition of a number of elements of change. For example, the disturbances might include a 10 per cent increase in basic employment and/or a 25 per cent in total population. The addition of an important new transportation facility such as a network of express buses or a number of limited-access highways might be the disturbance which is to be studied.

The variant approach already mentioned is sometimes applied to the 'generation' of land use patterns for completely new towns or parts of a town by deriving the equilibrium condition when certain locational and interaction constraints are fully satisfied simultaneously.

Two examples are now outlined briefly: Ira Lowry's 'Model of Metropolis' based on a study of the Pittsburgh region and Kenneth Schlager's 'Land Use Plan Design Model'.

Lowry's 'Model of Metropolis'

Initiated with the Economic Study of the Pittsburgh Region in 1962 and developed within the RAND Corporation in 1963 and onwards, Ira Lowry's model has become a classic demonstration of the potentialities of the equilibrium approach to urban metropolitan form (Lowry, 1964). His object was 'the development of an analytical model capable of assigning urban activities to sub-areas of a bounded region in accordance with those principles of locational interdependence that could be reduced to quantitative form', regional totals of population, employment, etc., having already been projected 'outside' the model.

Three broad groups of human activities are dealt with:

(a) A *basic* sector of industrial, business and administrative activities whose locations are assumed to be unconstrained by local circumstances of population distribution, market areas, etc., and whose locations and employment levels may therefore be taken as 'given'.

(b) A *retail* sector including all those activities dependent directly on local resident population and whose locations are powerfully influenced by population distribution. Their employment levels and locations are therefore determined inside the model.

(c) A *household* sector on which the retail sector depends and which itself depends on the total number of jobs (both basic and retail) available. It is assumed that the locations of households is powerfully influenced by the distribution of jobs. Therefore both population size and distribution is determined within the model.

The model generates (as output) distributions of retail employment, of households and of land development for these activities when given the distribution of basic jobs (as input). Geographic space is identified by one-mile-square cells in grid formation and land available within each cell is constrained by physical characteristics and public policy assumptions.

The model generates distributions by means of algebraic functions which express e.g. the 'potential' for workers and their families created by the distribution of jobs and in similar fashion the 'potential' for retail and similar activities created by the presence of these consumers. The parameters of these distribution functions were derived from previously completed traffic studies for the area in question (work and shopping trips).

Beginning, then, with a distribution of 'basic' jobs by one-mile-square cells, the computer allocates around each cluster of jobs the appropriate populations to provide the labour force needed. But these residents call forth the retail activities to serve them, which are thus located so as to take maximum advantage of the market potentials offered. These retail activities of course represent employment opportunities in themselves and so in the next round or iteration, further residents are distributed in order to provide the retail labour force. But this step 'disturbs' the market potentials so that the pattern of retail activities has to be modified, which in turn will disturb the residential distribution ... and so on *until an equilibrium position is reached* (Figure 9.2).

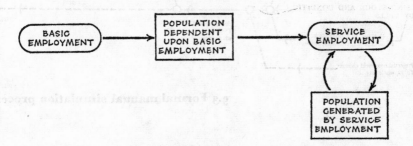

9.2 The essential argument of Lowry's 'Model of a Metropolis'

STATE OF SYSTEM: T5

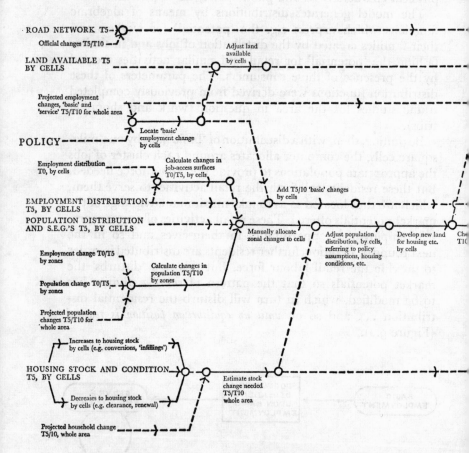

ROAD NETWORK T5
  Official changes T5/T10

LAND AVAILABLE T5
BY CELLS

Projected employment
changes, 'basic' and
'service' T5/T10 for whole area

POLICY

Employment distribution
T0, by cells

EMPLOYMENT DISTRIBUTION
T5, BY CELLS

POPULATION DISTRIBUTION
AND S.E.G.'S T5, BY CELLS

Employment change T0/T5
by zones

Population change T0/T5,
by zones

Projected population
changes T5/T10 for
whole area

Increases to housing stock
by cells (e.g. conversions, 'infillings')

HOUSING STOCK AND CONDITION
T5, BY CELLS

Decreases to housing stock
by cells (e.g. clearance, renewal)

Projected household change
T5/10, whole area

Adjust land
available
by cells

Locate 'basic'
employment change
by cells

Calculate changes in
job-access surfaces
T0/T5, by cells

Add T5/10 'basic' changes
by cells

Manually allocate
zonal changes to cells

Calculate changes in
population T5/T10
by zones

Adjust population
distribution, by cells,
referring to policy
assumptions, housing
conditions, etc.

Develop new land
for housing etc.
by cells

Ch
T1

Estimate stock
change needed
T5/T10
whole area

9.3 Formal/manual simulation process

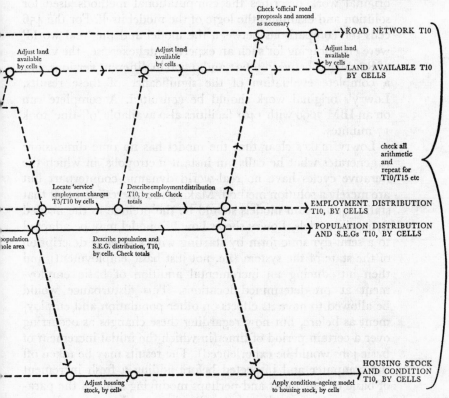

Check 'official' road
proposals and amend
as necessary

ROAD NETWORK T10

Adjust land
available
by cells

Adjust land
available
by cells

Adjust land
available
by cells

LAND AVAILABLE T10
BY CELLS

check all
arithmetic
and
repeat for
T10/T15 etc

Locate 'service'
employment changes
T5/T10 by cells

Describe employment distribution
T10, by cells. Check
totals

EMPLOYMENT DISTRIBUTION
T10, BY CELLS

population
hole area

POPULATION DISTRIBUTION
AND S.E.Gs T10, BY CELLS

Describe population and
S.E.G. distribution, T10,
by cells. Check totals

HOUSING STOCK
AND CONDITION
T10, BY CELLS

Adjust housing
stock, by cells

Apply condition-ageing model
to housing stock, by cells

s applied to a sub-region

Certain sensible constraints are specified–on densities of residential development, on amounts of land available in each cell, and on the minimum size of a 'cluster' of retail activities.

In mathematical terms the model is expressed as a set of nine equations and three linear inequalities as constraints. Lowry's original work describes the computational methods used for solution and examines the logic of the model itself. For the 456 cells the comparisons between the model and the 'real world' were encouraging for such an experimental exercise–the values of R^2 ranged between 0·621 and 0·676 in different versions. For a complete evaluation of the significance of these results, Lowry's original work should be consulted. A complete run on an IBM 7090 with 1401 facilities also available 'off-line' took 17 minutes.

Lowry makes clear that the model has no time dimension; it generates what he calls 'an instant metropolis' in which the iterative cycles have no real-world dynamic counterpart but are merely a solution method. Making the interesting point that static equilibrium models should be the prelude to the needed dynamic models, Lowry shows how his model may be adapted to a semi-dynamic form by starting with a *complete* description of the state of the system (i.e. not just basic employment) and then introducing an incremental addition of basic employment at pre-determined locations. This disturbance would be allowed to have its effects on other population and employment as before, but now regarding these changes as occurring over a certain period of time (in which the initial increment of basic jobs would be experienced). The results may be taken off the computer and inspected before adding a fresh increment of basic employment and perhaps modifying some of the parameters and constraints (e.g. allowing development of steep slopes on the assumption that above certain densities, market forces and prices will have made it worthwhile for builders to do so).

Finally, he does not consider the model to be a finished product but 'at best a prototype with a promising future'. Suitable adaptations of this would seem well within the competence of most of the larger British planning authorities and might handsomely repay the effort involved (Cripps and Foot, 1968).

Schlager's 'Land Use Plan Design Model'

Schlager (1965) makes it clear that his viewpoint 'conceives of the urban complex as a subject for design . . . the plan is a conscious synthesis of urban form to meet human needs . . . design, and not explanation and prediction, becomes the primary problem for solution'. Nevertheless, he shows how his land use plan design model fits into the wider framework of the plan-making process (following inputs of inventories, objectives and standards; preceding the transportation plan design which itself is followed by the final land-use-and-transportation plan).

Technically, his method represents a fusion of the analytical studies of Christopher Alexander (1964) on rational design methods, the specific algorithms of either linear or dynamic programming and the use of powerful data-processing machinery.

Then, given design requirements in terms of restrictions on possible land-use relationships (both within and between small zones) and a set of total needs or demands (based on previously prepared forecasts for the planning area) the problem is to 'synthesize a land use plan design that satisfies both the land use demands and design standards considering the current state of both natural and man-made land characteristics, at a minimal combination of public and private costs'.

The sort of restraints Schlager has in mind are limitations on density, the types of land uses that can exist simultaneously within a zone and the need to provide, say, schools and shopping areas within certain travel distances of all residential areas. The state of land is related to design standards and is associated with costs of development or renewal.

The form of linear programme is then as follows. The objective function is to:

$$\text{Minimise } C_t = c_1 x_1 + c_2 x_2 + \ldots c_n x_n$$

where $x_1, x_2, \ldots x_n$ are land uses and $c_1, c_2, \ldots c_n$ the respective costs of developing land for those uses.

The constraint functions are first, an equality constraint:

$$d_1 x_1 + d_2 x_2 + \ldots d_n x_n = E_k$$

where E_k is the total demand for land use k in the planning area and $x_1, x_2, \ldots x_n$ are as before

and $d_1, d_2, \ldots d_n$ are 'service ratio coefficients which provide for supporting service land requirements, such as streets, which

251

are necessary for primary land use development'. This constraint ensures that the allocations add up to the forecast total. Only major land uses (e.g. agriculture, industry, residential, open space) are handled in this model.

Secondly, there are constraints on the maximum (or minimum) of each land use within any zone:

$$x_1 + x_2 + \ldots x_n \leqslant F_m$$

Where x_1, x_2, etc., are as before and F_m is the upper limit of land use n in zone m.

Thirdly, there are constraints on land use relationships within and between zones:

$$x_n \leqslant Gx_m$$

Where G is the rate of land use n allowed relative to land use m where the land uses are in the same or different zones.

Four main classes of input data are required:

(1) Costs of unimproved land and land development by land use and type of soil.

(2) Forecast total demand for each land use.

(3) Design standards (e.g. densities) and inter- and intra-zonal limitations on land use relationships.

(4) The current land inventory including land uses and soil types.

As originally formulated the model needed about 1 minute per zone for solution on an IBM 7090 installation. The main disadvantages of this land use plan design model are inherent in linear programming–the need to assume linearity in the objective (costs) function; the fact that land use quantities are represented by continuous functions in the model, whereas in the real world development occurs in 'clumps' and finally that the constraint functions must be linear also.

All these objections and difficulties may be overcome by adopting a dynamic programming form of model but solutions will often be rendered impossible or extremely difficult because of computer hardware and software limitations.

The plan-making process in general

We have discussed the relationship of possible alternative system trajectories to varied goals and objectives, looked at a number of technical procedures for generating these trajectories via simulation, and finally pointed out that on occasions 'one-shot' equilibrium states can be studied in appropriate circumstances. We must now attempt a summary description of the sequence of operations by which the recommended land use and transportation plan is designed. This will of necessity include a number of *evaluative and testing* operations which are mentioned for the sake of completeness here, although their detailed treatment is deferred to the next chapter.

No better outline description of the plan-making process has been given than that by Mitchell (1959) to a Presidential Committee. He begins by listing the pre-requisites: inventories (survey information) of present transportation facilities and services; movements of persons, goods and vehicles; population, employment and land use; the economics and financing of developments in land and transport; the various powers and responsibilities of central and local governments and other public bodies concerned with urban and regional development; the best possible projections of population, employment, income and economic growth for the area as a whole.

Next, and drawing in part from these previous studies, a dynamic metropolitan growth model needs to be constructed, expressing the relationships among the components and influences on the future area distribution of population, jobs and land uses. The model must include variables which describe the 'amount, nature and location of transportation facilities and services'.

Parallel with this a traffic model is necessary which will generate, distribute and assign (to networks) the movements which will be demanded between sub-areas. This model will have been derived from origin/destination data related to land uses and 'other commonly found generative factors'.* Also, a model or sub-routine is needed to assign the expected movements to the networks and to divide such movements into those which would be made by private and public means.

---

* It is now becoming possible to build simple traffic models suitable for this stage of the plan-making process which do not derive from special detailed surveys of movement or from 'home interviews' of a sample of households, firms etc., but in contrast are derived from 'land use' data (e.g. zonal residents, workers, floorspace) and calibrated against simple volumetric traffic data, or even use assumed or 'borrowed' parameters. Clearly such models are intended for use in plan-making and could not be used for the detailed design of roads, junctions etc. (Jamieson, MacKay and Latchford, 1967; Farbey and Murchland, 1967).

With these major tools at hand, the goal-and-objectives part of the process must be carried to the stage at which clear principles emerge for the generation of alternative land use and movement plans.

Now, using the metropolitan growth model and holding transportation considerations constant (i.e. assuming past trends to continue and commitments to be binding in road building, public transport and parking policy) a first spatial distribution of population and major employment types is made. On this 'land use' basis, alternative transportation (i.e. networks and public transport systems) schemes which vary the emphasis given to public and private means are tried out.

The metropolitan growth model is again used, this time allowing the different access-opportunities embodied in the alternative transportation schemes to influence the spatial distributions of population and employment. At this point therefore we have a set of internally consistent land use and transportation plans.

But the public transport and road networks have not been tested to see in more detail what sizes and levels of service would be required to cope with the expected volumes. The traffic assignment model must now be called upon to produce this information. Study of the results may show that certain of the alternatives are not feasible. For example, one may depend upon a high degree of private vehicle usage and call for very large expenditures on new road construction. Another may demand levels of service in certain parts of the public transport system which are likely to be unattainable within the bounds of reasonable investments.

The remainder should now be subjected to first-level cost/benefit analysis to help determine the most efficient 'mix' of public and private transportation.

At this stage a near-optimal land use and transportation plan should have emerged 'which is both desired and apparently attainable'. Further refinements in land use dispositions and transportation systems should be attempted until the best balance is attained (see also Chapin, 1965, p. 458).

The remainder of the process of plan-making comprises an assessment of the capital and operating costs involved, the public powers available or desirable for accomplishing the plan, and the 'long-range programming of stages of development . . .

studies should be made to assure that at obvious stages the transportation system will function effectively'. Arrangements should be made for further study and revision as necessary, for the preparation of more detailed development plans'—e.g. for roads, public transport, recreation and schools and 'comprehensively for smaller areas within the metropolitan region in the spirit of the general plan'.

If this book were to follow strictly the ideal sequence of the planning process set out in Chapter 5, description of the form and content of general plans would follow discussion of the evaluation of alternatives. By now it is obvious that such a sequential treatment is not possible down to the last detail. Furthermore, this is a convenient point at which to deal with plan content.

Form and content of plans

In Chapters 7 and 8 we discussed the description and the projection and simulation of our system and foreshadowed the manner in which plans may be expressed and the material they should contain. We said then that the essence of describing an urban system is to indicate the locations and sizes of various types of activities and spaces, and the patterns and volumes of communications and channels. Such a description indicates the state of the system at a point in time; a sequence of these will describe a sequence of states, that is, a trajectory. We have now seen how projection and simulation produce such system trajectories; we shall deal in the next chapter with the selection of one of these to be recommended as a plan.

The form of the plan is therefore that of a trajectory of states at suitable time-intervals (say five years). The manner of presentation in general should be designed to be as lucid and informative as possible and at the same time to serve as a satisfactory tool for day-to-day implementation and control. It must be comprehensible to the general public and their elected representatives, and suitable for use by the planner and his fellow-professionals in the public service. Obviously, the principal documents must make the fullest use of all appropriate means of communication—the written word, maps and diagrams, charts and tables. But let us begin in the middle, so to speak, and work outwards.

The central core of the plan's content will be the trajectory of system states produced in the technical office. Each of these will consist of a map or other cartographic device which indicates the amount of each activity type located in a fairly large number of small areas. These areas will be the basic spatial units used in all the technical work or larger groupings of these. For example, if the basic unit has been the 1-kilometre square of the national grid, or the wards and parishes, then a system-state description will be provided by indicating the amount of each activity in all of these 'cells' or some aggregation of them. If the activity classification comprised two types of population, a socio-economic 'indicator' and four types of economic activity, then seven figures in each cell would describe the *activity* element in the system-state. And if 'spaces' were described by, say, area of land in non-agricultural uses, area in agricultural use, area not used, numbers of dwellings, shopping floor space and manufacturing floorspace, then six numbers per cell would describe the *spaces* element in the state of the system.

The *communications* element may be described either by an inter-zonal flow matrix, or by a diagrammatic representation, or both, for each main type of communication being considered (e.g. morning peak, home-work, private cars; 16-hour day commercial vehicle trips). If the technical procedures used have included the assignment of these flows to the networks, then a separate description of these may be unnecessary; if not, a map or maps showing the main *networks* being considered must be produced.

A series of such documents, one for each state or time period in the trajectory could serve as an irreducible minimum for professional planners to understand and operate. But even they would probably feel the need for something more communicative for many purposes. An obvious development is to produce from these core statements a series of simple maps, preferably in colour notation, which indicate the general form of the city or region showing its main land uses and transportation networks at each stage of its evolution. Each one could be annotated to show totals of population, employment, areas of land devoted to each major activity, and any other matters of interest and importance (Figure 9.4). It is a great help if significant areas of change and the preceding state are distinguished and annotated.

Certain activities of particular significance could be the subject of a special series of abstracts; for example, 'new' land to be used for residential purposes at each stage, and residential area improvements and redevelopments could form such a special series. The road and public transport systems could be given similar treatment. In an area where recreational activities are of prime importance, as at the coast and in certain inland areas, these could be picked out and highlighted by a special series of maps and diagrams (see overleaf).

But these numerical and cartographic descriptions must be fully explained by an adequate written document. The outline which follows is illustrative only and should not be regarded as a model of form, sequence or emphasis; instead it indicates the necessary content in broad terms.

Obviously the first requirement is to tell the general reader, and especially members of the lay public, what statutory force (if any) the documents have, and where appropriate the opportunities that exist for the making of representations, who has commissioned the plan, by whom it was prepared, whether it is produced for reaction and comment as an interim statement or is presented as a final view. There should be a clear statement of the goals and objectives which the plan seeks to achieve; where necessary and possible 'operational' measures can be given—e.g. to accommodate a population of 950,000 by about the year 1990, to raise the average *per capita* income of the area to £X by the same date . . . and so on.

Reference should be made to the processes of discussion and consultation which enabled these objectives to be defined, and the authority with which they are vested (e.g. are they the professional planners' assumptions based on the best available information, or were they adopted by resolution of a public body).

The ways in which these planning objectives are related to those set for larger and smaller administrative areas should be clarified as far as possible. For example, a county will refer to objectives defined at the national and regional levels and also to those of its 'second-tier' local government units and other local agencies (e.g. major industrial groups and social welfare bodies).

It will not always be possible to clarify all such issues. Perhaps

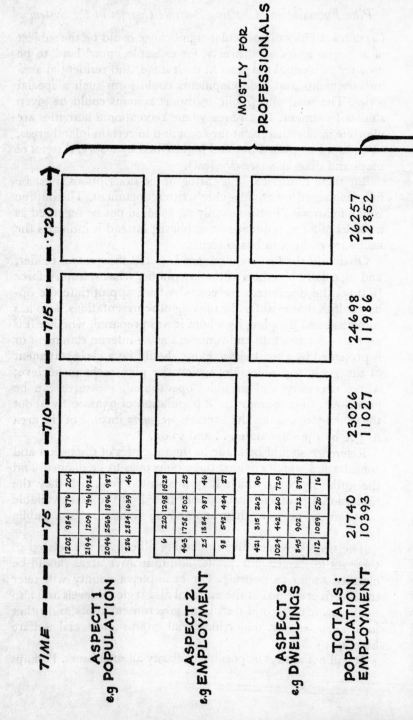

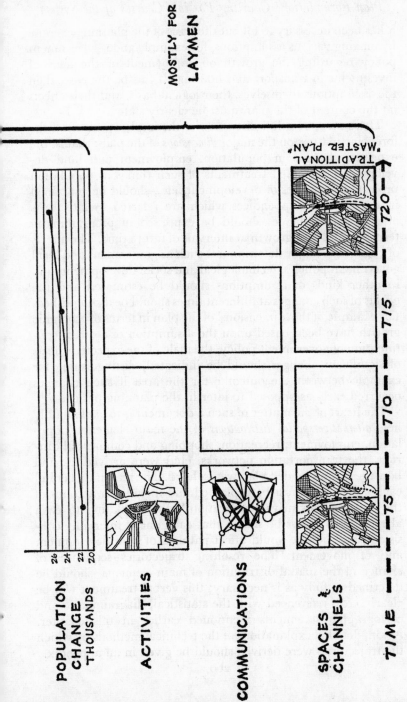

9.4 Simulation process output

it has been necessary to fill out the basis of the planning exercise by making various assumptions, for example about government policy regarding the growth of employment or the level of investments in transport and housing. If this be the case, then the assumptions themselves, their logical basis, and their effects on the content of the plan must be clearly stated.

There must be a full discussion of the implications of all the foregoing matters on the major *dimensions* of the plan; that is, the expected changes in population, employment and land development. (Detailed treatments of such things as population projection, densities of development, etc., should be contained in the technical appendices which are referred to later.) As always, these changes should be expressed in programmatic terms – as stages of growth at intervals of future time. The effects of changes in major determinants such as government and local government policies, technological and social developments and in other kinds of assumptions should be estimated and the effects of such changes at different times should be distinguished. For example, if the 'dimensions' of the plan in terms of economic growth have been based upon the assumption of a direct continuation of government policy, the scale of the expected effects of significant changes should be indicated, distinguishing for example between the outcome for the area if such changes occurred early as opposed to later in the planning period.

The heart of the matter in such a document is to explain fully how *alternative spatial distributions* of the main elements (population, employment, recreation, shopping and commercial districts, the transportation networks, etc.) were arrived at, and how the recommended plan was isolated. The reasoning behind each alternative must be explained and include an account of the public policy/private aspiration 'bundle' relating to each alternative. It must be shown that each one is internally consistent, and how it would affect patterns of land development and of movement. The resulting trajectories – sequences of change in the spatial distribution of main elements – should be described as fully as is necessary; this verbal treatment will be clearly cross-referenced with the statistical, diagrammatic and cartographic statements mentioned earlier in this chapter. Again, detailed explanations of the technical methods by which the trajectories were derived should be given in an appendix.

The criteria by which the alternatives were tested and evaluated should be listed and arguments advanced for each in turn, and for all the criteria collectively. The exclusion of any particular criterion which might seem obvious should be explained. The relationships between the chosen criteria and planning objectives should be indicated. Finally, the 'weighting' given to each criterion when combined to produce a final selection should be the subject of reasoned argument, which should include a demonstration of the effects of altering the weighting and a discussion of the implications for choice. For example, the recommended plan may have emerged because of a particular combination of 'weights' for, say, total travelling time and amount of land used for new residential development. It may be that slightly different weighting of these criteria would result in another plan alternative being the 'winner' (Hill, 1968). Obviously, then, the basis for the choice of these criteria and their degree of emphasis needs full and cogent argument. If the problem of weighting has been approached by attempting to reduce as many measurements as possible to terms of money, then the basis of assumptions about unit costs and the conversion of expenditure to capital sums should be carefully explained.

Finally, a full verbal account of the sequences of change in the patterns of land use and movement should be given. There should be a brief review of the evolution of the area over a period (of say, 50 years) in broad outline, drawing attention to any salient features (e.g. the effects of a technological development in the area's principle industry, the building of an important new road or the discovery of a new mineral resource).

Next, the 'state of the system' at the datum year, the year to which most of the factual information relates, should be described, drawing out the principal problems which physical planning is capable of tackling. Then, the narrative should continue with a clear but flowing treatment of the stage-by-stage evolution of the area as recommended in the plan (cross-referenced always with the maps and figures described earlier). Particular mention should be made of the major public works which are proposed, the sequence in which they occur and their approximate timing. Also, the ways in which household, industrial, commercial and other preferences about location, development, movement and the quality of living and working environments will be catered for by the plan must be explained. For example, if restraint is to be placed on an expected demand for housing at certain locations then this should be explained and justified as should the encouragement of, say, commercial growth in other parts of the planning area.

The text should avoid in these sections mere re-statement in words of what has been set out clearly in numerical and map form elsewhere. It should concentrate on those aspects which are most suitably explained by the written word; it should not duplicate but rather *complement* the maps and figures.

A series of appendices will be necessary to cover technical details of data sources and methods, survey, analysis, projection, simulation and evaluation. A full account of recommended techniques of implementation, control and review operations will also be necessary (see Chapter 11). This section might also cover data-management recommendations and suggestions for a 'research agenda'—items needing further investigation either by the planning authority itself or by specialised research agencies—to improve data, projection, simulation, control and so forth.

In summary, the form and content of the general land use and communications plan should be designed so as to satisfy the following conditions:

(1) to give a clear indication of the sequence of states which the urban system should take up at specified times;

(2) to enable the layman, the elected representative and the professional planner to understand precisely what is intended;

(3) to make clear the arguments and assumptions on which the plan is based, including an explicit statement of goals and objectives and the degree to which these are achieved;

(4) to provide the operational means for implementing the plan by a continuous process of management of the urban system;

(5) to do all these things with the maximum clarity of communication using the most appropriate media (including cartographic, pictorial, diagrammatic, statistical/numerical and verbal means).

IO

Plan Selection: Choosing the Desired Course

The process discussed here is the final evaluation of fully worked-out alternatives. But that is not the only point at which evaluation, judgement and choice occurs. As we said in Chapter 4, there are no neat and tidy sub-divisions of the planning process: goal-seeking interacts with simulation which itself is inseparable from survey information; development control is closely linked at intervals with review and the reformulation of goals and objectives. Evaluation occurs at many points in the design of the alternatives themselves. The 'short list' which is subjected to the fuller treatments discussed in this chapter will have evolved from a long process of trial-and-error simulations. From time to time, partial evaluations, small quantitative tests and judgements on intangibles will have led to the rejection of one alternative, the modification of another, the combination of two or more to create a better, perhaps more feasible 'starter'.

In earlier chapters we saw how the individual and the group —be it a household, a company, a social club or other body—investigate alternative courses of action and evaluate these in order to make a choice. We noted that very often the process of drawing up different possible plans of action and their selection of one of them was informal, indeed sometimes unconscious. Also, that the processes were frequently based on imperfect information both as to the opportunities available and as to the true costs and benefits of each. Nevertheless, the problem for a particular person or group is bounded; it has limits because the implications considered are in very large measure those affecting the person or group alone; seldom if ever are wider repercussions considered.

Plan Selection: Choosing the Desired Course

The planner is in a very different situation. His job is to consider the *social* costs and benefits of each alternative. It is the very difficulties of defining social costs and especially social benefits, together with the logical and practical difficulties inherent in welfare decisions which make plan selection such a major challenge. Put as simply as possible the problem is this: in classical economics the distribution of a scarce good among freely competing consumers is governed by the price at which that good is offered and the relative abilities of the consumers to pay; but theoretical and practical difficulties arise when we consider the allocation or distribution of 'goods' in the public or social interest—in conditions where there is no equivalent free-market mechanism and where the entrepreneur's criterion of maximising profits does not apply. It has been demonstrated that two ice-cream vendors on a beach with an even distribution of potential customers along its length would both tend to locate side-by-side at the mid-point. By contrast, a public official concerned to minimise the total amount of walking to obtain ice-cream would ask the vendors to set up their stalls one quarter and three-quarters of the way along the beach respectively (Alonso, 1964b).

A more fundamental difficulty arises from the nature of modern societies which, rather than consisting of a minority élite of leaders and a majority of the led is a much more complex structure than in previous periods. The spread of universal primary and secondary education in Great Britain was completed after the Second World War and the number of people proceeding to higher education is growing quickly. More people are better informed and more discriminating. Social welfare legislation and its administration must therefore take account of the fact that they serve not one but many different 'publics' with diverse views, aspirations and senses of priority. Physical planning, along with the many other arms of modern governmental activity has therefore a very difficult task in estimating the effects of alternative plans on the public interest so as to choose between them.

These problems are receiving increasing attention among practitioners and theoreticians, but so far the debate is not conclusive. Some work is at a highly philosophical level in the realms of social and political theory. Other workers are concerned with more practical aspects in the realm of welfare economics and yet others with detailed operational problems in the definition and measurement of social costs and benefits either in general or in relation to specific case studies.

This is, therefore, neither the place nor the time to attempt a summary or a clarification. The issues are raised in order to caution the reader of the intricacies of the problem and to give him a proper perspective of the degree of authority which the professional planner can properly assume when pronouncing on what is best for people. The technical methods discussed below should be viewed against this background of uncertainty, although they represent without doubt an advance on previous practice with its naïve paternalism inherited from the nineteenth-century origins of modern planning.

We have already discussed the goals-and-objectives stage of the planning process and it is from there that we can get the guiding principles of evaluation on which to grasp. The first derives from Friedmann's notion of *comprehensiveness* which he defines as pertaining to the system as a whole, rather than to any part or sub-system (Friedmann, 1965). The second is that the goal and objectives are ultimately expressed as *performance standards* for the system and it is from these that we must derive the criteria by which to judge, test and evaluate the alternatives set up. We can therefore state as the over-riding principle that evaluation of alternative plans must be based on attempts to show *how far each plan satisfies all the objectives which have been adopted for the planning exercise*–where these objectives are expressed as specifications of the performance of the urban or regional system.

We will now outline three techniques which have been offered for plan selection. They differ in complexity and in the degree to which non-quantifiable subjective judgements enter into their workings. They are respectively the cost/benefit method, the balance sheet method and the goals/achievements method.

The cost/benefit method
This method derives from the theory of the firm and has the simple aim of finding the most efficient among several solutions –i.e. that which minimises the cost/benefit ratio (Prest and Turvey, 1965; Mao, 1966). It therefore relies heavily on quantifiable elements in the analysis. In order to explain this we will

use an imaginary situation in which six alternative trajectories have been devised. For the sake of simplicity we will also imagine that five objectives have been adopted for the planning exercise and which therefore determine the criteria for plan selection. These are:

(a) to increase average residential rateable values from £100 per dwelling in 1961 to £130 per dwelling by 1986 (at constant prices);

(b) to reduce the overall urban density from 11·3 persons per acre in 1961 to 10·4 persons per acre by 1986;

(c) to minimise the total personal travel involved in the daily journey from home to work;

(d) to maximise the freedom of choice of roads for moving between all parts of the city and its surroundings;

(e) to preserve and where possible to enhance the special character of the cathedral area, the riverside and the view of the town as a whole from the north.

Taking the criteria above and the beginning with (a) the process would begin with the estimation of all the costs of residential development (including the acquisition of land, the preparation of sites, the costs of building, etc., etc.) for each of the alternatives developed by examining the state of the system at 1986. The 'benefits' are scaled by the extent of the increase in rateable values – either in absolute terms or as percentages of the £30 increase demanded by the objective. Turning to item (b) all the costs of reducing densities would be estimated. In addition to the kinds of costs already studied for (a) above these would include the costs of redevelopment and other measures taken to reduce densities. The benefits accruing from each alternative would be the extent of the reduction of overall densities below 11·3. Item (c) would prove more difficult than the previous two because of the problem of trying to isolate the actions proposed in order to reduce journeys to work. Such reductions might be attributable to relocations of employment and to alterations in the pattern of residential areas – both of which might have occurred for reasons not directly connected with journeys to work. The only way out of this difficulty is to adopt the best possible rules-of-thumb in assessing what actions are attributable to this objective, then to identify these and to estimate the costs of each consistently for all alternatives. The benefit side of the ratio might be expressed as total person-miles, person-minutes, or some other suitable measure of total travel to work. The cost element of item (d) could be estimated by such a measure as the total capital costs of road construction and improvement, but preferably it would include also the assumed costs of the capital development plus maintenance costs. The benefit could be expressed as the coefficient of network 'connectivity' mentioned in Chapter 6. Traditional cost analysis would not be easily applied to item (e) which involves a considerable amount of subjective judgement and non-quantifiable elements or intangibles. We will therefore pass over it here since the point is fully covered in discussing the other techniques of plan selection.

Having now considered each of the five objectives in turn as they relate to each of the six alternative plans, it is necessary to try and amalgamate these results into a single 'score' for each. Consider objective (a) first of all. For each alternative plan the costs of increasing rateable values can be compared with the extent to which such increases are achieved. The result might be expressed as the cost of raising the average rateable value by £1 at 1986, thus:

Plan alternative:	A	B	C	D	E	F
Cost of raising average residential R.V. by £1 (£m)	10·3	11·2	9·8	9·7	10·1	10·5
Total costs of residential development (£m)	63·7	70·1	62·6	63·3	65·2	69·3

For objective (b) the costs might be related to a reduction in overall density of 0·1 persons per acre, thus

Plan alternative:	A	B	C	D	E	F
Cost of lowering average density by 0·1 (£m)	6·2	7·1	6·4	6·9	6·6	7·0

The method of tackling the evaluation of plan performance with respect to objective (c) will depend on how detailed is the information about movement. If, for example, it is confined to a simple statement of the patterns of origins, destinations and volumes (with or without assignment to networks) then a simple figure of person- or vehicle-miles will be all that is available to be compared with another crude figure of total capital and operating costs for each plan alternative. If on the other hand more refinement has been used, the assignments of movements to the network may have taken congestion costs, reduced travel speeds, increased journey times and different operating and capital costs in different parts of the networks. The resulting totals are likely to be more accurate than if simple units have been used throughout, and especially will enable the total costs of travelling to be estimated more reliably.

The objective adopted states simply 'minimise the total personal travel' and this responsibility must be discharged. But it would be prudent to give also the results of any further analyses of the costs of these journeys thus in effect suggesting a re-formulation and re-statement of this particular objective. The results might take this form:

	A	B	C	D	E	F
Total personal travel (million person-miles per day)	2·1	2·2	1·9	1·9	1·8	2·0
Total personal travel (million vehicle-miles per day)	1·7	1·8	1·5	1·5	1·4	1·6
Annual cost of travel (£m 1966 prices)	3·2	3·2	3·0	3·0	3·9	3·1
Total capital costs of road and public transport (£m)	56·2	59·7	63·1	72·3	68·4	62·0

Alternative calculations based on
detailed study of travel patterns and costs

	A	B	C	D	E	F
Annual cost of travel (£m., 1966 prices)	3·1	3·3	3·4	3·6	3·6	3·2
Total capital costs of road and public transport (£m)	55·3	60·1	64·7	68·3	73·9	64·7
Ratio of costs of travelling	26·4	27·3	34·0	36·0	41·1	40·4

The 'benefit' element in each alternative plan attributable to the 'freedom of choice of roads' required by objective (a) may be measured by the coefficient of connectivity β mentioned in Chapter 6.

	A	B	C	D	E	F
Capital and operating costs of road network (£m)	41·3	43·4	48·6	52·7	50·2	49·1
Coefficient of connectivity, β	1·38	1·41	1·36	1·40	1·29	1·35

Finally, the fifth objective 'to preserve and ... enhance the ... cathedral area ...' cannot be brought within the framework of cost-benefit analysis. The costs which are attributable to serving this and similar objectives might, with some difficulty, be estimated (for example, the rent and rate income lost because development has been refused, the costs of building preservation, and landscape works). But at present, it is not possible to express the respective benefits in any quantified way. Therefore, in cost-benefit analysis strictly applied we must exclude all such 'intangibles' from the purview of the method, even though these differences between alternative plans are apparent. (The relaxation of this iron rule in the balance sheet and objectives/ achievements methods will be discussed below.)

The next step attempts to combine these separate measures of the success of each alternative into one measure which will then enable us to place them in rank-order of preference. Here we face the principal difficulty of this method, and indeed of all methods of the comparison of complex alternatives. This is, that whilst many or all of the *costs* may be expressable in common units, usually of money, the corresponding *benefits* cannot be expressed and therefore the 'scores' of each plan alternative on each of the several counts cannot be combined. For example, the benefit of an increase of £1 in the average residential rateable value cannot be combined or compared directly with the benefit of a 0·1 increase in the connectivity of the road network.

What then can be done to discover which is the best alternative? One approach is to place all the alternative plans in rank order from the point of view of each objective in turn, thus:

Objective	Plan:	A	B	C	D	E	F
Rateable value increase		4	6	2	1	3	5
Density Reduction		1	6	2	4	3	5
Personal travel – minimise		5	6	2	3	1	4
Choice of routes – maximize		3	1	4	2	6	5
Sum of rankings		13	19	10	10	13	19

The result of this is to indicate that the best alternatives are C and D, the next A and E, the worst B and F. But this assumes that each objective is equally important. This may not be the case—it may be accepted that some objectives have higher priorities than others. The differential importance of the objectives can be weighted in the usual way. Let us suppose that the order of priorities were density reduction, personal travel, choice of roads and rateable values, and that relative importance of these objectives could be reflected by numerical weights of 5, 3, 2 and 1 respectively. The table would then read:

Objective	Weight	Plan:	A	B	C	D	E	F
Rateable value	1		4	6	2	1	3	5
Density reduction	5		5	30	10	20	15	25
Personal travel	3		15	18	6	9	3	12
Choice of routes	2		6	2	8	4	12	10
Weighted sum of rankings			30	56	26	34	33	52
∴ Final rank order			2	6	1	4	3	5

This analysis confirms the cruder version's indication that plan alternatives B and F are the least satisfactory, that C is a good bet and that E has a middle position. But it 'promotes' A to a close second whilst 'demoting' D to fourth rank, although the differences between A, E and D are small and could well be completely altered by varying the system of weighting. Because this is so arbitrary, experimentation with different combinations of weights should be carried out (without altering the *order* of importance of objectives at this stage) to see how the final rankings vary; in this particular example the aim would be to clarify the closely-fought second, third and fourth positions in the final 'league table'.

But this consideration is limited to the benefits side of the problem; the costs which have to be incurred to yield these benefits have to be brought into account now. For each plan alternative we have estimated those costs as follows:

Objective		Costs in £m					
	Plan:	A	B	C	D	E	F
Creation of rateable value ⎤ Reduction of densities ⎦		63·7	70·1	62·6	63·3	65·2	69·3
Minimising personal travel		55·3	60·1	64·7	68·3	73·9	64·7
Maximising route choice		41·3	43·4	48·6	52·7	50·2	49·1
Totals (£m)		160·3	173·6	175·9	191·3	189·3	183·1

This indicates that A is by far the cheapest alternative followed by B, C, F and E whilst D is the most costly. But we are interested in *the relationships between costs and benefits*. The common measure of costs has been money but we saw that benefits were measured in such different ways that the only common units were rather arbitrary weighted numbers, expressing rank order of preference. Two forms of comparison of benefits and costs are now possible. First we can compare the rank orders of each plan from both points of view:

	Plan: A	B	C	D	E	F
Benefit rank order (weighted)	2	6	1	4	3	5
Cost rank order	1	2	3	6	5	4
Combined rank order index	3	8	4	10	8	9

Or, we can use the 'weighted-sum-of-rankings' numbers as indicators of the inverse of benefit (i.e. the lower the number the greater the benefit score of that plan alternative) and multiply these by the respective costs thus:

	Plan: A	B	C	D	E	F
Total Cost × Weighted sum of rankings index	160·3	173·6	175·9	191·3	189·3	183·1
	30	56	26	34	33	52
= Final cost/benefit index (rounded to 2 figures)	48	97	46	65	62	95

We could conclude at this point that in terms of the objectives by which the planning exercise is guided and by their priorities, and in so far as real or proxy measures of their degree of attainment and the respective costs incurred in each plan alternative, that which gives the greatest 'pay-off' in social terms in plan C, very closely followed by plan A. Plans E and D occupy a middle position whilst F and B are not worthy of further consideration because of the very high costs incurred for a limited progress towards objectives.

The distinction between the winner C and the runner-up A is a very fine one. Bearing in mind the crudities of the method, the coarseness of the measurements and the breadth of the assumptions, it would not be prudent to pronounce C to be the recommended plan on the basis of this analysis alone. If this is as far as cost-benefit analysis will go, then we must attempt to distinguish further by working at other elements in the alternatives–elements which cannot be considered in the cost-benefit method–especially those 'intangibles' which are not capable of quantitative measurement and comparison. One way of doing so is provided by the 'planning balance sheet'.

The Planning Balance Sheet Method

This method, first proposed by Lichfield (1956), greatly extends traditional cost-benefit analysis so as to examine *all* the effects for good and ill which are inherent in alternative courses of action; it also traces the incidence of these effects and quantifies the costs and benefits accordingly so far as possible. The object of the method is to enable the community to choose that plan which will maximise the achievement of community goals.

Lichfield's method in essence begins by regarding each plan as a series of development projects (Lichfield, 1964 and 1966). For each project the producers, operators and consumers are listed (both private and public). The costs and benefits arising from each project and their incidence on each section of the community are estimated. So far as possible each item is expressed in money or physical terms; intangible costs and benefits are noted. This preliminary set of social accounts is then inspected carefully to remove double counting and transfer payments to produce the final balance sheet.

The Planning Balance Sheet

	PLAN A				PLAN B			
	Benefits		*Costs*		*Benefits*		*Costs*	
Producers	*Capital*	*Annual*	*Capital*	*Annual*	*Capital*	*Annual*	*Capital*	*Annual*
X	£a	£b	—	£d	—	—	£b	£c
Y	i_1	i_2	—	—	i_3	i_4	—	—
Z	M_1	—	M_2	—	M_3	—	M_4	—
Consumers								
X¹	—	£e	—	£f	—	£g	—	£h
Y¹	i_5	i_6	—	—	i_7	i_8	—	—
Z¹	M_1	—	M_3	—	M_2	—	M_4	—

Source: Hill, (1968) Table 1

X, Y, Z are groups in the community considered as prod
whilst X^1, Y^1, Z^1 are the same groups in a consumer rôl
£ sign indicates an item expressed in money terms, the N
items measured in physical terms (output of minerals, u
electricity, passenger journeys per day, etc.) and the i
represent intangible costs and benefits. By converting r
costs and benefits to either capital or annual form, the n
items may be summed for each plan A and B. Physical iter
pressed in the same units of measurement may be aggregate
The result is a statement of total cost and total benefi
each plan being considered; these are expressed as monetary
other quantities and as intangibles in descriptive verbal for

Lichfield claims that the balance sheet lays the basis for :
rational decisions about alternative courses of action. The n
urement of costs and benefits although desirable, is not str
necessary; precise description is of the essence of the method
abling the planner to balance the monetary and physical
and benefits with the intangibles. At the same time a clear pic
is presented of *who* pays and on *whom* the benefits are bestov

In a recent review of methods of plan evaluation, Hill (1
criticises Lichfield's balance sheet because 'it does not appea
recognise that benefits and costs have only instrumental va
Benefits and costs have meaning only in relation to a w
defined objective. A criterion of maximising net benefits in
abstract is therefore meaningless. . . . It is meaningful to ad
compare benefits only if they refer to a common objecti
He goes on to add that if any objective 'is of little or no va
both for an entire community or for any sections within it, t
the benefits and costs referring to the objective are irrelev
for the community in question'. He cites the many differ
objectives implicit in Lichfield's case study of the San Franci
Mint (a building of architectural and historical interest) as an
ample of this difficulty and concludes that if a community sets
real store on the retention of historic buildings 'it is not legitim;
for an analyst to consider the elimination of a building of histo
value as a cost even though he personally believes it to be so

Cost/benefit analysis was developed for particular purpo
some thirty or more years ago, and suffers from the cardir
weakness of placing great emphasis on economic efficiency a:
criterion, with lack of concern, even neglect of other values. T

balance sheet is a considerable move in the right direction aiming at a comprehensive analysis; but perhaps it goes too far and fails to confine itself to explicit community objectives adopted for the planning exercise. Hill has put forward a method which he believes will overcome these criticisms and provide a sounder basis for the evaluation of alternative plans.

The Goals-Achievements Matrix

There are two outstanding features of Hill's method. First, the requirement that objectives (or specific *attainable* goals with instrumental value) should be put into operational form as far as possible. That is, they should be expressed in such a way that progress toward them, or retrogression from them, is measurable on some appropriate scale. Second, he introduces the requirement to give a numerical weighting to express the relative importance of each objective for each section of the community; these weights are used to multiply the appropriate costs and benefits of actions striving for the attainment of objectives.

This second feature requires also that the various sections of the community, or the various 'publics' who comprise the population of the area, be identified, This can be done by reference to 'income group, occupation, location, or any other preferred criterion'. The costs of actions which seek each particular objective or goal as borne by the several sections of the community are weighted to reflect the importance of each goal in the eyes of each group; benefits are weighted in similar fashion.

With the passage of time, it may be assumed that relative values will alter—goals once given primacy may be slipped to a median position whilst lowly objectives may have become issues of the first importance. These secular changes can be reflected in the analysis by altering the numerical weights used. As Hill says, 'the aggregated set of incidence weights applying to all the objectives can be considered as representing the community's conception of "equity" '.

Costs and benefits are defined in terms of goal-achievement—as retrogression from and progress towards objectives respectively. Where quantitative measures are used these should be in the same units for both costs and benefits.

The product of Hill's analysis for any particular plan is shown in the table opposite:

Goal: Description: Relative weight:	Incidence	α 2			β 3			γ 5			δ 4		
		Relative Weight	Benefits	Costs	Relative Weight	Benefits	Costs	Relative Weight	Benefits	Costs	Relative Weight	Benefits	Costs
	Group a	1	D	A	5	—	E	1	N	—	1	R	Q
	Group b	3	—	H	4	—	—	2	—	—	2	T	S
	Group c	—	J	L	—	S	—	3	—	M	1	W	V
	Group d	2	—	—	2	—	—	4	—	—	2	—	—
	Group e	1	K	—	—	U	T	5	P	—	1	—	—
				Σ					Σ	Σ		Σ	Σ

Source: Hill, 1968, Table 2

The goals α, β, etc. have relative weights of 2, 3, etc., which have been determined by study of the community's aspirations and problems. Groups of people a, b, c, etc. within the community have different strengths of feeling about each goal and these are again expressed by relative weights. For instance, the concern felt by group c for goal β is expressed by 3 whereas group a's concern for the same goal is expressed by a weight of 5. The letters A, B, etc., are the costs and benefits expressed in monetary, physical or qualitative terms. Where all the costs and benefits for any goals can be expressed in the same quantitative terms, summation can be performed (as indicated by Σ in the table above); obviously this cannot be done where intangibles are involved. In the very rare cases where all the costs and benefits for all the goals can be expressed in the same quantitative units, a grand summation is possible. In these rare cases, monetary units seem the most probable.

Hill then faces the question of how to compare tangibles with intangibles and points out that to some extent, the distinction between them is arbitrary. 'For instance, the specification of the colour of an object implies no more than the specification of the wave-length of the light reflected from it.' Although advances towards the measurement of present intangibles are being made all the time; these 'require qualitative judgements relating to the development of valid scales of measurement. . . .' He goes on to stress the importance of the correct identification and use of different scales (nominal, ordinal, interval and ratio in ascending order of complexity) and gives useful examples of the sorts of planning objectives which can be measured along each scale.

The final part of his article discusses ways in which the results can be presented to the political decision-makers. First, the planner can submit the results (as in the table above) for each alternative without attempting a synthesis and leave the 'politicians' to debate them with particular reference to the weighting of objectives. Second, the summary result can be presented and the preferred plan indicated – i.e. that with the largest index of goals-achievement. Although this suffers from most of the criticisms levelled at Lichfield's balance sheet in that it sums costs and benefits related to different goals and objectives it does provide an easily determined summary of the effects of plans on the achievement of objectives by the community. Since the index is determined in a similar manner for all alternative plans under consideration, it does enable a comparison to be made. Finally, the simplest approach is to measure all costs and benefits on the ordinal scale—scoring $+1$ if the progress toward the objective is made, o if there is no effect and -1 if the action is detrimental, the weights acting as usual.

	Goal α : Weight = 2			Goal β : Weight 1		
	Group Weight	Plan A	Plan B	Group Weight	Plan A	Plan B
Group a	3	+6	-6	3	-3	0
Group b	1	-2	+2	2	0	-2
		+4	-4		-3	-2

Source: Hill (1968) Table 3

Plan A Score $= +4 - 3 = 1$
Plan B Score $= -4 - 2 = -6$
Therefore Plan A is preferable to Plan B

Hill admits that his proposed goals-achievement matrix is complex and costly. It does not give a quick answer but as he very rightly says 'it is more expressive of the complexity of the consequences of urban development'. He emphasises that the key to the method is the weighting system used, for it is 'not very useful if weights cannot be objectively examined or assumed'. Further, because the interdependence of objectives is not directly reflected in the method, it is restricted to single-sector plans.

What method of plan evaluation?
We said at the beginning of this chapter that the discussion would be inconclusive; in such a rapidly-evolving subject that is hardly surprising. We have looked in passing at three techniques which might be used as aids to plan selection. It is important to realise that their value is in *guiding* the selection process; such techniques, with all their freely-admitted shortcomings do not constitute methods by which choices are *determined*.

Both Lichfield and Hill are quite right in emphasising that the selection of a multi-purpose development plans from a range of alternatives is a very complex procedure. And when they and other writers (e.g. Bruck, Putman and Steger, 1966) say that their work is only an aid to decision-making they are not being falsely modest. Rather they are putting the half-formed tools they offer in the context of the job they are intended for; and that context is clearly the social and *political* process of reaching decisions.

Our century has seen the emergence of two increasingly powerful groups involved in such decisions: government and its professional advisers. It is in everyone's interest that the former group should be aided by the best possible guidance towards more responsible, educated and rational judgements through the provision of better and better information by the latter. But the rational analysis of highly complex systems can only go so far. Consumer groups have demonstrated this in trying to recommend the 'best buy' among groups of motor cars, refrigerators and services. They too face the problem of the selection and weighting of criteria; they too often conclude that in the final analysis, the choice must rest with the reader, *his* personal value scales and what *he* regards as useful and desirable.

Dyckman (1961) concluded a brilliant analysis of the literature on planning and decision theory with the point that we should not be dismayed by the awful problems of decisions about complex systems in a pluralistic society; we have three well-established pragmatic methods—the market, law and politics. This seems to be reinforced by one of Hill's suggestions of placing the goals-achievement account before the politicians and encouraging them to accept their rightful responsibility of resolving priorities among goals and objectives—the basis of the weighting system.

Another essential for research is Friedmann's comprehensive indices of urban/regional system performance which would parallel those for the nation as a whole; these already aid political discussions of goals and choices among alternatives at the national level.

But the overriding need is to develop strong lines of communication between the professional planners, armed with better evaluative tools, and the community and its representatives who should be helped and encouraged to make better inspections of the plans that are being offered 'for sale'.

11

Plan Implementation:
System Guidance, Control and Review

In this chapter we complete the cycle of the planning process outlined in Chapter 5 by dealing with the implementation of plans. As we saw in Chapter 4 this is essentially *a control activity* where 'control' is interpreted in the widest sense, implying not merely the use of the veto but including positive intervention. There, too, we learned how control is 'that . . . which provides direction in conformance with the plan, or in other words, the maintenance of variations from system objectives within allowable limits' and that this is of universal application (Johnson, Kast and Rosenzweig, 1963).

The same chapter outlined the control of cities and regions by comparing the actual state with the intended state at regular intervals and carrying out regulative actions on the basis of any divergence revealed. We can now expand that outline by virtue of what we have learned in succeeding chapters and go into more details of the everyday working of the plan.

We have seen in Chapters 8 and 9 that the essence of plans for urban and regional systems is a trajectory of intended states. Also the general form of the trajectory will be a set of matrices or tableaux—one for each future time. These will specify the intended activities and spaces and their associated communications and channels. The activities and spaces will be related to an array of geographical sub-areas (of the total planning area)—e.g. enumeration districts, wards, parishes, zones, kilometre grid cells, etc., etc. The communications and channels will be similarly referenced and will also be mapped in conventional manner to show the intended networks and the volumes they should be carrying at the various times. So much for the intended states of the system.

The actual states at most times can be known in part only. Information to match up one-for-one with that in the plan may be derived from a variety of sources: the censuses of population, distribution, production, road traffic, as they are taken and published; the statistics of the Ministry of Labour on the locations, sizes and types of employment; development and other public and private agencies' records of operation. To the extent that these are not adequate, the planning authority must attempt to remedy this by carrying out or commissioning its own surveys of the situation.

At the time of writing, information for the control function in planning is not satisfactory for all the reasons mentioned in Chapter 8. But there is good reason to hope that the national censuses will in future be taken at five-yearly intervals (1971, 1976 ...); also the results should be available much more quickly than in the past and that their content and specification will be far more suited to the operations of many public welfare agencies, including planning authorities. For example, we may hope for more stable definitions of such essential units as 'households', for stability of geographical units of analysis (multiples of the 100-metre square cell) and for much better information on employment, economic activity, car ownership and possibly incomes. Improvement in the quality of these important information sources is bound to go ahead more slowly than most planners would like. In the meantime they must try for the best compromise between the expense of extra surveys and more broadly-stated plans – tailored to suit the data which *can* easily be obtained.

Let us assume that as a starting point, the planning authority has succeeded in framing the operational documents in such a way that all the necessary information about *actual* states can be obtained within one year. In other words the plan's intended state for mid-1971 can be compared with the information about the *actual* state (from the 1971 census, etc.) by the middle of 1972; and by the middle of 1977 the actual and intended states for 1976 can be compared; and so on. Let us suppose that 1966 was the datum year for this plan – that is, the time at which all the basic information about the area was carefully established, mapped and tabulated and which served as a take-off point for the main projections of population, employment, dwellings, car ownership, etc.

Now we will imagine ourselves in the planning office during the period 1966 to 1971 and try to understand how the plan is implemented. Our system grows and changes by the alteration of its component parts (activities in spaces) and their connections (communications in channels). The essence of control then is to regulate those disturbances so that the system's actual trajectory matches the intention as closely as possible. Each disturbance–that is each development application, whether for new construction, demolition, change of use or whatever–must be examined for the total effect it is likely to have on the system and whether or not this would result in moving the system in the right direction.

The examination of applications is likely to follow a checklist consisting of a series of questions. Obviously these will fall into four main groups:

(1) *Activity*

is the *type* of activity proposed consistent with the intentions of the plan? (e.g. residential, economic activity specified by class, recreational, etc.)

is the *size* of activity proposed consistent with the intentions of the plan? (e.g. number of persons, numbers of jobs, volume of production, etc.)

are the other characteristics of the proposal consistent? (e.g. seasonal fluctuation, shift working, etc.)

(2) *Space*

is the *amount* of space proposed consistent with the plan? (e.g. number of dwellings or towns, floor area, parking spaces, total area of land used, etc.)

is the *location* of space used consistent with the plan? (e.g. is the proposal likely to cause difficulty with later development?)

is the *intensity* of space-use proposed consistent with the plan? (e.g. density in persons per acre, workers per acre, etc.)

(3) *Communications*

is the *amount* of communication proposed consistent with the plan? (e.g. the numbers of trips which are likely to be 'attracted' by a workplace or 'produced' by a residential proposal; are the rates of trip production and attraction likely to differ significantly from those assumed in the plan?)

are the *types and modes* of communication consistent? (e.g. private vehicles, public transport, air passenger or freight movements, goods vehicle movements, etc.)

are the *frequencies* of communication consistent? (e.g. time of day, peak, off-peak, weekly or seasonal variations)

are the *sensory qualities* of the proposal consistent with the plan? (e.g. massing and general arrangement of buildings, prominent structures, landscape treatment, noise levels, pollution of air and water, aspect, prospect, etc.)

(4) *Channels*

is this *type* of channel consistent with the plan? (e.g. 400 Kv overhead cables, dual two-lane limited-access road, 36-ins. diameter gas pipeline)

is the *location* (or routing) consistent?

are the *connections*, access points, and junctions consistent?

are the *sensory qualities* consistent? (e.g. design and spacing of turns, design of bridges and cuttings, form of embankments, landscape design, etc.)

Obviously this listing is illustrative only; in practice only some of these questions may be asked and others would be raised in addition. But essentially they would relate to these four broad groups.

Let us now consider in more detail the problem of comparing intention and actuality when confronted by a specific proposal. Suppose that in a particular part of the area the plan indicated a 1966 population of 1,200 rising to 2,000 by mid-1971. The 1966 census data showed that the actual population was 1,350 persons; in other words, the system had gone slightly off course. In late 1967 the planning authority is presented with a proposal to build 170 private houses on 30 acres of land in this area. Should permission be granted?

First the activity element is examined. The proposal is, of

course, expressed in terms of houses and so some estimate must be made of the number of persons likely to live there. The planning officer considers the type of houses, their location and layout and decides to use a conversion factor of 3·4, resulting in an estimate of about 580 additional persons by the time the development is completed. This would raise the population of the area at, say, 1969 to around 1,930 persons—consistent with the plan.

Turning next to the space element the addition of 170 dwellings would raise the total in 1969 to 590 from its 1966 figure of 420. This is found to be well within the plan's intended 700 dwellings by 1971. However, the total land in use in this area would rise to meet the plan's intention of 85 acres—and about two years before time. Further study and discussion with the applicant (a speculative builder) reveals that the intention is to build houses for the upper-income groups in a relatively spacious layout; this is the principal reason for the shortfall on persons and dwellings and the consumption of all the land estimated to be needed. The planning officer checks the information used in the preparation of the plan, paying particular attention to the density assumptions used to relate population and dwellings to land areas; this confirms his previous supposition. Also, he finds that the socio-economic composition of the area would be rather more 'white collar' than the plan's intention if the proposal were allowed. This could have implications for car ownership and spending power. But the visual aesthetic character of the area would not be noticeably different from that intended in the plan if the application were approved.

In considering the communications element of the proposal he notes that the increased car ownership might affect the volume of private car trips originating in the area. In its turn, the greater volume of traffic might cause problems from the 'channels' point of view, although the access point to the secondary road system shown in the proposal is consistent with the plan's intentions.

Looked at in the round, a proposal of this kind must be considered at two main levels. First, does it conform with the *strategic* intentions of the plan for the town as a whole in terms of population distribution, employment location, the pattern and volume of journeys on the primary and secondary networks and the physical fabric of the area? Secondly, is the proposal consistent with the intentions of the plan at the more *detailed* local level where physical questions predominate: road alignments, access, the location of local schools, shops, parks and playing fields, and the visual and other sensory qualities of the immediate environment?

Each proposal must be examined at both levels. At the strategic or 'urban structure plan' level the elements of activity and communication will tend to weigh more heavily than questions of space and channels which will predominate when the proposal is compared with more detailed plans for parts of the planning area.

In the example used, the planning officer has satisfied himself that on most counts the proposal conforms to the plan's in-intentions. He notes however that his assumptions about density, socio-economic composition, and therefore spending power and car ownership will be to some extent invalidated if he grants permission. He therefore decides to do some fairly rapid checks to see how far these divergences would affect the urban structure policy as a whole.

To do this he returns to the context of the models used in the process of plan design and evaluation. The changed spending power given for the sub-area is estimated and the model which was used to test the sales in major shopping centres is re-run. This shows a rise of about 1 per cent or less in the sales for the nearest suburban area; the effects on all the other centres in the city are imperceptible. This result is well within the range of $\pm 1 \cdot 8$ per cent error which, he is advised, is inherent in the model's design (largely because of imperfections in data on incomes, expenditures and journeys to shopping centres). The effect on traffic flow estimates of the higher level of car ownership is similarly trivial when the traffic model is brought back into use.

The planning officer thus concludes that if he were to recommend approval of the application he would not be departing from his urban structure plan. It follows that the decision will be based primarily on the consideration of the proposal as it affects the immediate locality. Questions of physical detail, appearance, design of houses, the treatment of landscape, access and relationships with existing development will be the main criteria.

If the area is not one for which detailed designs have been prepared–such as in the 'action areas' proposed in the recent British legislation–then these issues will be examined in the light of the planning officer's knowledge, experience and judgement.

In his recommendation to the elected members of the planning authority he is able to distinguish between the quantifiable, and non-quantifiable effects and the implications of the proposals for the functioning of the area as a whole and for the immediate locality.

Similar principles apply in the special cases of control in areas where detailed physical plans have been prepared to co-ordinate developments in the period up to ten years ahead. In these cases it is relatively simple to see whether or not a proposal fits in with the plan's intentions for physical form–that is, from the points of view of spaces and channels. Checks will be made on building form, floor areas, parking space, access, landscape treatment and so on. But equally the activities and communications elements will be checked. Are the house and flat designs likely to accommodate the numbers and kinds of persons intended in the plan? Are the industrial buildings intended for those types of manufacture or distribution which were envisaged? How many private car and commercial vehicle trips are likely to be 'produced' by and attracted to the development? Notwithstanding the agreement of proposals with a detailed physical plan from the physical-form points of view, there may be divergences from the intended types of activity and communication. Once again, the models used in plan preparation can be brought into service to test the effects of these differences on the workings of the planning area as a whole.

So far, we have been discussing the regulation or control of our system by blocking or releasing private proposals for change. But the same principles apply to capital projects in the public sector–housing, hospitals, schools, swimming pools, roads, generating stations, transport termini, shopping centres and so on. These kinds of developments will usually be smaller in number but of greater unit size than most of the private developments, and differ from them in one particularly important respect. That is, their future occurrence will nearly always have been made known to the planning authority through consultations with the developing departments–central and local

of the real world, but when allowed by the model designer and operator to combine in different ways, paired elements from these two sets can generate the requisite variety because both structural and parametric elements have been based on careful study of the real world; the structural parts of the model express what are believed to be enduring relationships between human activities and communications in the spatial sense, whilst the parametric elements have set down (following conventional statistical analyses) the probabilities that each relationship will take up certain positions on a range of numerical values. For example, the structural element of the modelling may state that population will be disposed around employment nodes according to some inverse function of travel time; the parametric element will then embody a statistical statement about the range of values of parameters of the time/distance measure.

Conventional development plans, i.e. normative models of the real world, are crude and unreal. For in them 'relations exist which have no quantity, and numbers exist that stand in no relation to each other' (Beer, 1966, p. 319). The flexible approach to model design suggested here follows the important cybernetic principle, found in many controls for complex systems, of constructing a high-variety device by the free combination of low-variety components.

The model of the real world can now be used to obtain predictions or system trajectories as explained in Chapters 8 and 9. Consider the situation when, for the first time, it is possible to compare the model's prediction with that of the real world – i.e. between the first 'state' set out in the development plan and the actual state of the city or region. It is unlikely that a very good fit will be found but in this comparison lies the key to successful control. For if the relationship between real world and the model are analysed and the results *fed back* to the model's structural and parametric design elements, *its predictive powers are being amplified by a learning process*. The diagram opposite (Figure 11.1) might make clearer much of the preceding discussion.

The control operation is shown as C_1 and C_2 implementing the plan's sequence of intended states M_2 and M_3. (The diagram can be imagined as continuing indefinitely towards the right with the passage of time.) Control at C_1 must operate in

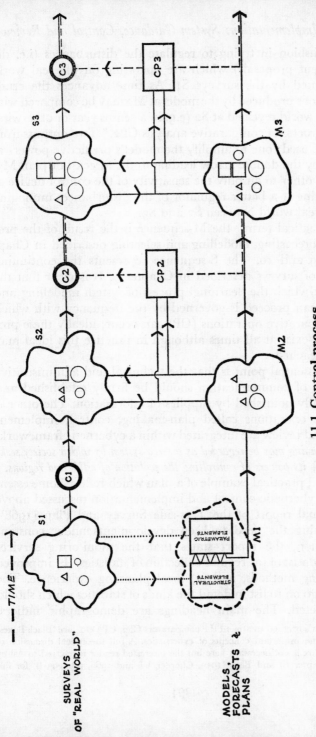

11.1 Control process

ad hoc fashion in trying to regulate the disturbances (i.e. development proposals) which are operating on the real world represented by the surveys S1. As time advances the crude predictions produced by the model at M2 may be compared with the real world revealed at S2 (e.g. in a census year or otherwise) in the process of comparative analysis CP2.* Two outputs from CP2 are used: one to amplify the model's predictive power—as shown by the double arrow leading to the forecast or plan M3, and the other to amplify the sensitivity of the control device at C2 making it a better regulator of the disturbances impinging on the real world between S2 and S3.

In practical terms, the M-sequence is the result of the process of forecasting, modelling and selecting described in Chapters 8, 9 and 10. The S-sequence represents the continuing process of surveys described in Chapter 7. It is clear that the speed at which the 'learning' process of system modelling and control can proceed is governed by the frequency with which the comparative operations (CP) can occur; ideally these processes co-exist at all times although in practice this ideal may not be reached.

One essential point is that the technical and administrative channels of communication should be firmly established and continually nourished by supplies of information. The other is that the operations called plan-making, control, implementation and review are integrated within a cybernetic framework; also, *planning may be regarded as a servo-system by which society seeks to amplify its powers of controlling the evolution of cities and regions.*

A good practical example of a plan which reflects some essentials of cybernetic control and implementation discussed above is the final report of the Tees-side Survey and Plan (1968). Mentioning the need to keep developments under constant observation, the report states that the monitoring services should consist of (a) regular collection of statistics, (b) improved forecasting methods, and (c) local planning experience. The authors go on to list in detail the kinds of statistics which should be collected. The main headings are demographic indices,

---

* In Beer's original treatment the comparators CP2, CP3 etc., are 'Black Boxes' —one of the important concepts of cybernetics. A full theoretical discussion of the Black Box is not necessary here but the interested reader is referred to Ashby (1956, Chapter 6) and Beer (1959, Chapter VI and 1966, pp. 293–8) for full accounts.

economic indices, housing indices, statistics of income, expenditure and retailing, and finally those concerned with transportation. The section concludes by reminding us how 'it is important that future data are in a form that is compatible with the data collected by Tees-side Survey and Plan. This applies to definitions, particularly the zoning systems' (i.e. areas to which the data relate).

In the context of planning of urban and regional systems as set out in this chapter, reviews of the plan are quite simply longer, harder, more fundamental periodic examinations of the relationships between intentions and actions. All the essential work is already being done from day to day by the control operations; there is no need therefore to mount a 'one-off' job consuming precious resources of skill and time as so often happens in British planning today; review becomes simply a longer beat in the rhythm of the whole process of implementation. There are two main outcomes possible if reviews show that the system is significantly 'off-course'. The first is to use all the aids at the planner's command (including the models of the system developed to prepare and test plans) to indicate what actions are needed to put the system back on course and what the various advantages and disadvantages of such activities are. The other possible outcome is to consider the desirablity of the deviant course in its own right and this involves thinking afresh about the major objectives of the plan and whether or not the time has come to recast them by deletion, addition or modification. In this case, as the Tees-side report states, 'the decision to change the objectives would be a vital political decision whose implications should be closely investigated before any action is taken. Once made, the new planning objective could make necessary substantial changes to the recommended planning proposals'. In other words, the cycle of the planning process comes full circle, returning from implementation and review to the re-examination and re-statement of goals and objectives.

Finally, the implementation of a plan depends wholly on the *will* of the planners and their 'clients' to do so. We have stressed the logical and practical frameworks of the planning office in this chapter; truly they are *necessary* conditions but not *sufficient*. Irreducible requirements include a clear definition of the rôles of central and local governments and other public bodies as

these affect the plan; the relationships between the public
bodies and private citizens, indicating their rights and responsibilities under statute law and administrative procedures; the
duties of preparing, executing, controlling and reviewing the
plan and how these devolve upon the bodies concerned, paying
particular attention to responsibilities for public investment
in buildings, plant, roads and so on. The 'hardware' of the
plan must be properly mated with the 'software' of the appropriate human organisation and relationships both within
and between the various political and professional groups concerned (Cherns, 1967).

Implications of a Systems Approach to Planning

The book opened with a discussion of man in a systems context; we close it by looking at the planning of urban and regional systems in its human context—the world of practice, professional organisation, teaching and research.

Planning Practice

A systems view of cities and regions and of their management can be of great benefit to the practice of planning. Such a view provides a single framework for the continuing task, providing useful links between the various parts of the process. All types of 'client' group may enter into discussions with planners and with each other. A systems view of their city might enable them to see better the extent of certain problems and opportunities, and certainly will make for closer discussion on the impact of different proposals. In the past, and to a great extent at present, such deliberations are seriously hindered because of the lack of an adequate and mutually acceptable frame of reference. To the industrialist, the developer, the amenity society or the private citizen, the views of many professional planners and their employers seem altogether too vague and imprecise when it comes to questions of the likely effects of different courses of action and of more specific proposals for change. Obviously there will always be considerable areas of doubt, a realm of uncertainty in anything as complex as a modern human settlement pattern. But for too long planners and their customers have tried to carry on their dialogue without a really practical basis for testing the possible outcomes of their views, aspirations and actions. This lack of the right operational tools has mirrored the absence of truly comprehensive theories of urban and regional change. At the same time, the profession in Britain may not have been sufficiently aware of how much progress had been made in these fields and therefore failed to carry these advances further (McLoughlin, 1966b).

It may be that the construction-and-design basis of the British planners' intellectual tradition goes some way towards an explanation. But in the 1950's increasing numbers of other kinds of people were entering the profession following a change in the admission regulations of the Town Planning Institute. These geographers, economists, social scientists and others began to influence discussions in the planning schools, in the offices and at meetings, conferences and seminars. In addition to being much-needed helpers to their overworked colleagues, they began to cast a number of doubts on some unchallenged assumptions and practices. But a major problem was the lack of a common language in which to discuss the phenomena and the processes involved in planning. Entrants to the planning schools from other skills and academic traditions faced a double problem: understanding the planning teachers' views and those of fellow-students from other backgrounds. To the extent that the Schools failed to provide a unifying framework, these difficulties were carried forward into practice where they were often exacerbated in a practical context.

But significant changes can be detected (e.g. Kitching, 1966). Once-separate strands of thought and action seem increasingly to lead in the direction of common ground where new, often unsuspected unities of concept and purpose are being discovered (e.g. Chisholm, 1966). That common ground is the systems view put forward in this book. It provides the links necessary between the aspirations of the client groups, the understanding and analysis of the social scientist, the ideas of opportunity and constraint provided by the architect, engineer, surveyor, valuer and accountant and the notions of implementation in the mind of the public administrator. If we read the signs correctly, the increasing awareness of this common ground is now beginning to make the combined effects of these mixes of skill far greater than the sum of their parts.

The major implication of these ideas is that the devising of plans for cities and regions should be centred in practice upon the fullest possible understanding of the system to be managed. This understanding will best be achieved and advanced by the development and continuous improvement of models which simulate the system's behaviour. The 'model package' will provide at all times the focal point for all the discussions, debate, experiment, analysis and innovation which must go into the exploration of a community's future. Equally the models will provide the key to the ongoing process of managing the system by public works and the control of development. They will do so by testing, either singly or in aggregate, all significant proposals for change whether arising inside or outside the system.

Models therefore must be the technical heart of the operations of the planning office. All of its personnel will be involved in their building, operation and improvement, though at different levels and frequencies and from varying points of view (Harris, 1967). The technical head of the organisation and his senior staff will maintain an overview. They will have decided in the past the models' main outlines and set in train more detailed work on the families of sub-models. From time to time they will guide major overhauls of the whole model package. Staff responsible for the production and review of strategic development plans will use the models in the process of exploratory plan design, testing and evaluation. Those in charge of more detailed plans will generalise the results of their work and convert these into terms acceptable for model input so that the effects of, say, a residential design or a coastal conservation policy may be tested for 'goodness of fit' with strategic plans. Development control staff will make the most frequent use of these tools, 'feeding' the appropriate models with the appropriate information about single large applications or aggregations (e.g. monthly, quarterly, annually) of smaller ones.

There should also be a group of skilled people to look after the detailed working and improvement of the models and to collect, process, transmit and dispense all the necessary information in the planning office. Very often in the past, this group has been called the 'research section' which misnomer flatters the staff whilst devaluing the word research. Some research (in the strict sense of the discovery of fresh knowledge) undoubtedly has been done in planning offices and more is likely in the future. A fitter name for this essential part of the planning office would be the 'information' section or group. It would include most of the skills appropriate to handling and interpreting large volumes of information: systems analysts, programmers, punch operators, keyboard operators, etc. Whilst a number of planning operations will not necessarily require very high capacity in data-processing, most planning offices now and in the future will need access to at least a small or medium-sized computer as well as more modest equipment such as automatic electric calculating machines.

The question arises whether this group should be part of the planning office, both administratively and physically, or part of a larger information department of the local planning authority, handling information needs for all its services; health, education, roads, housing, markets, libraries, etc. Three points argue in favour of the big unit. First, the economies of scale, second the overriding need for uniformity in definition and interpretation within a 'universe' of information – especially in the service of important public policies where consistency is vital among strategic decisions, and finally the fact that many if not most of the facts which planners must handle are also relevant to the operations of other related areas of the public service. This is not the place, nor have we the time to discuss this question in detail (Hearle and Mason, 1956). But two things seem certain. In the first place there is the need for a large central computing and information service for all departments of an authority. This could be organised around a 'data bank' on which all departments could draw, and into which everyone would deposit. But each operating department will need constant access to information for its own purposes of day-to-day working or more protracted investigation; not all of this will be useful to the authority as a whole. Furthermore, departments will frequently need to use data in a form (e.g. of definition, or geographical coding or date of recurrence) which is unsuitable for storage in the central facilities. It therefore seems desirable that at least some departments should maintain their own information sections of the kind we mentioned above. Great care should be taken to ensure that relationships between the central and departmental groups are clear.

The basis of these arrangements might be suggested by a few selected illustrations. The finest grain of demographic, economic and land data for the administrative area could be held centrally within the main data bank. This would be updated regularly by all departments of the authority. The planning office might co-operate with the public health inspectors in the recording of all building developments, changes of use, etc., as they occurred. The detailed methods of description, storage and retrieval would have been settled by negotiation between the central and departmental information staffs.

By contrast, the strategic modelling effort in the planning office might need a much coarser grain of demographic and economic information (which could be obtained from the central bank by aggregation before output) and in addition similar data for a number of past census years. Moreover, there may be a need for comparable data for areas outside the authority's jurisdiction and for other data not held in the central bank. Experimental model design and testing based on such information could best be carried on in the planning office; from time to time full prototype model runs could be executed on the central computer. But the overriding need for an information service within the planning office arises from the continuous monitoring and control function. Obtaining the best possible descriptions of the current state of the system, modelling the effects of recent planning permissions and developments and their interpretation in a policy context provide the justification for an information group in the department itself.

The main result of adopting a systems approach is a move towards greater integration of the several parts of the planning process in the office. The shared family of models and the sustaining information supply provide both the opportunities and the need for comprehensive, synoptic attitudes and integrated practices. The lines of demarcation which now exist between the typical sectors of a planning department—'plan', 'research', 'control' and 'design' are the most common—would certainly become much more blurred even if they did not vanish entirely. Because no office has yet been run wholly on a systems basis it is too early to be more than speculative. But it may well be that a better form of organisation would be to relate the staff hierarchy and functions to the nature of the urban system and its control. Thus, junior professional staff would work on particular sub-systems (e.g. recreation, housing, public road transport, manufacturing industry) in detail, led by intermediate staff members with a particular skill or bent in that field; as one moved upwards in the organisation more generalised responsibilities for understanding and controlling the system would be encountered. Thus the typical 'vertical' division of most British planning offices, which separates the principal elements of the planning process would be succeeded by 'horizontal' divisions reflecting a hierarchial view of the job permitting the fullest integration of all parts of the planning exercise (Figure 12.1).

At the same time, a systems view of cities and regions, and the contribution this makes to the requirement for improved management practices throughout the public services, would foster a greater degree of integration between the planning operations and those of many other public welfare activities. By these means, physical planning which serves the community's welfare largely from the *spatial* point of view may become more closely meshed with the work of many others whose task is to serve individuals, families and groups in the *non-spatial* parts of their life (Bolan, 1967; Webber, 1965).

A great deal has been said elsewhere about the geographical definition of local government areas and their powers and functions; there is no need to summarise it here because for the most part the reforming attitudes expressed and the suggestions put forward most recently are broadly congruent with another of the implications we wish to record. It is commonplace to say that local government areas should be defined for land-use and transport planning purposes so that areas with common social, economic and environmental problems are not divided and that all the area dependent upon a town or city for its main employment, educational, commercial, recreational and cultural needs should form an administrative unit. Another way of putting the same point is to say that administrative units should each encompass a recognisable urban or regional system.

The arrangements made under the 1960 Local Government Act applied this sort of requirement but were rightly criticised for being too selective in singling out only the largest urban systems (the big conurbations and their environs) for treatment as 'Special Review Areas'. Derek Senior (1966) took a more balanced view and suggested the division of the provinces into 30 or 40 'city regions'—very largely the urban systems defined

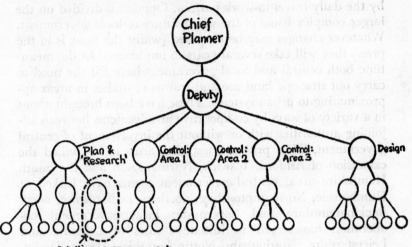

Intelligence service weak and remote from top management; no direct influence on control actions

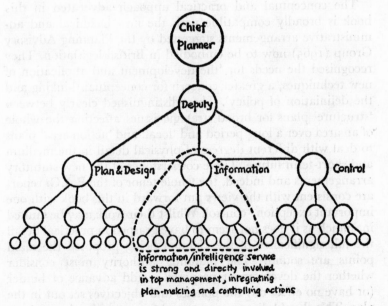

Information/intelligence service is strong and directly involved in top management, integrating plan-making and controlling actions

12.1 Staffing: traditional and suggested frameworks

by the daily travel-to-work pattern. Opinion is divided on the larger complex issues of the whole future of local government. Whatever changes may be proposed (whilst this book is in the press) they will take several years to implement. In the meantime both central and local government have felt the need to carry out strategic land use and transport studies in areas approximating to urban systems. These have been brought about in a variety of ways by co-operative arrangements between adjoining authorities with or without the involvement of central government. Thus private consulting firms have studied the expansion of Ashford, Ipswich, Northampton and the South Hampshire area; central government teams have looked at Humberside, Northamptonshire, northern Bedfordshire, north Buckinghamshire and Severnside; local government co-operation has served to initiate studies of Leicester and Leicestershire, Nottingham–Nottinghamshire–Derby–Derbyshire, and Coventry and Warwickshire. That such steps have already been taken is evidence of the widely-felt need to treat urban and regional systems in a sensible way, even if this means some *ad hoc* arrangements in the short run.

The conceptual and practical appoach advocated in this book is broadly compatible with the new technical and administrative arrangements suggested by the Planning Advisory Group (1965) now to be embodied in British legislation. They recognised the needs for 'the development and application of new techniques, a greater concern for conceptual thinking and the delimiation of policy'. They distinguished clearly between 'structure' plans for broad strategic issues affecting the whole of an area over a long period and 'local' and 'action area' plans to deal with different degrees of physical detail in the medium and short-term future. These cornerstones of the new statutory arrangements and indeed, the whole tenor of the P.A.G. report are consistent with the views put forward in this book with one important exception–control. Whilst their work may be faulted inasmuch as it does not seem to have grasped in practical detail the full significance of the changes being proposed the main points are sound. 'The planning authority must consider whether the development proposed would advance or hinder (or have no effect on) the policies and objectives set out in the plan. This should discourage control for control's sake, and encourage authorities to use their powers of development control not in a negative way but positively and imaginatively to advance the objects of the plan' (Planning Advisory Group, 1965, paragraph 7:9); the techniques we have outlined in previous chapters provide a practical basis for doing so.

People for Planning

What sort of people will be needed to operate planning based on a systems approach? (Reade, 1968). There can be no doubt that an operation as complex as planning, touching as it does some of the most deeply-held values of individuals and communities, cannot be the monopoly of one particular skill or background. But this is true of virtually all activities of similar scale, be they industrial, commercial, educational or otherwise. Health services are not the monopoly of doctors, education is not the exclusive preserve of teachers nor the oil industry of petrologists and analytical chemists. In the very nature of modern society, the manifold purposes and actions require the constant combination and re-combination of many different skills and aptitudes. In different contexts a person with a particular skill will play as many different roles. But in each context, because of the central purposes, objectives and procedures, one kind of skill will play the leading rôle, ensuring the right 'mix' of others and their effective co-operation.

A good deal of nonsense has been uttered in the past about planning being a job for 'a team of specialists' or words to that effect. In one way, the statement is superfluous, inasmuch as this is true of any complex job. But the tone of such statements implied that the skills which had been drawn into planning over the years *and they alone* could provide teams, of varying composition, to do all the different kinds of planning jobs called for. They were also defensive in attitude to some extent, being unsure of the significance of the 'planning generalists' entering the profession from courses which trained people *ab initio* as planners, in contrast with the long-established method of entry via a previous qualification in architecture, surveying, and latterly, the social sciences.

Of course, comprehensive planners, like all other 'generalists' are open to a special kind of criticism: that in taking up an integrating rôle they are in danger of telling a host of people with other skills how to do their jobs. How could anyone, even after the best sort of education, simultaneously oversee the operations of an architect, a sociologist, a landscape designer, a geographer, an engineer and a host of others, like some preposterous puppet-master? (Altshuler, 1966). These and similar questions were based on a fundamental misunderstanding. It arose from the failure to define the planning process and the systems it sought to control (McLoughlin, 1965).

Comprehensive planners have a good deal to answer for here; they have been guilty of sins of omission and commission. On the one hand somewhat visionary claims were made for comprehensive planning, without being backed up by sufficiently rigorous argument. On the other, the syllabuses of many courses of training might have been designed to cause disquiet. It was difficult for many people to see how rag-bag collections like 'Principles of Architecture', 'Elements of Sociology', 'Essentials of Economics', 'Outlines of Geography' and 'Planning Practice' and the like amounted to a new comprehensive approach or were the foundation of a different kind of skill. The specialists in these fields quite rightly turned the old joke against themselves round the other way, seeing a generalist as someone who knew less and less about more and more until finally he knew nothing about everything.

The way out of these dilemmas was obscured by the intellectual isolationism of many planners, their belief that planning was somehow unique and could not be usefully compared with current problems and developments in other fields of high-level decision making. General medicine is credible and accepted because the human body has long been regarded as a system in its own right; modern industrial and commercial management is developing through the clarification of the firm as a system too (Beer, 1959; Johnson, Kast, and Rosenzweig, 1963).

Generalists in any field are not supermen who know how to do everyone's job; they are simply *specialists in the higher-order systems in the given context*. Clear definitions of these systems and their sub-systems provides the operating framework for the generalist as well as illuminating the rôles and relationships of other skills involved (see for example Loeks, 1967 and Mocine, 1966). Generalists may be defined as people who can:

 (i) understand the nature and behaviour of the appropriate
     system;
(ii) distinguish elements and sub-systems within it and how
     their problems are approached by people with other
     skills;
(iii) co-operate in the setting of goals and objectives for the
     system;
(iv) devise the best methods of improving system performance;
 (v) carry continuing responsibility for the performance of the
     whole system.

These criteria may be interpreted so as to refer specifically
to the planning of towns and regions and provide a profile of
the comprehensive or generalist planner. The revised education
policies of the Town Planning Institute provide more details of
the sort of training required (Kantorowich, 1966). In planning
'the chartered town planner plays the central and crucial
professional rôle. His special skill, a command of the planning
process as a whole, qualifies and entitles him to organise and
co-ordinate all planning operations as well as to design and
control the implementation of the plan or policy.

In addition to the chartered town planner, there are numerous persons in other disciplines or professions who participate in the planning process and make essential contributions
to it ... it is important clearly to distinguish between the
work in planning of the chartered town planner and that of
skilled contributors. The chartered town planner must understand the contributory operations and their implications
for planning sufficiently well to integrate them into the preparation of the scheme for the area being planned for which
he carries the professional responsibility. With this under,
standing, he would be able, during the build-up of the plan-
to profit from the interactions with contributors and, at the
stage of implementation, to provide both the framework and
scope for those concerned in development. On the other hand,
it is not necessary for the planner to be expert in the skills of
each contributory discipline.'

Under the revised scheme for the Institute's final examination, each candidate would be asked to show:

 (i) that he has a sound knowledge of the historical, social,
economic, and physical background to planning;

(ii) that he has adequate knowledge of the theories, techniques and procedures of planning, especially those for formulating, directing and integrating planning operations in the build-up and implementation of a physical plan;

(iii) that he appreciates the importance of social activities and functions (such as shopping, transport, the supply of utilities and services, etc.) in an overall system of land-use and settlement, and understands how contributory operations related to these can be used in planning it;

(iv) that he has the knowledge and skill to design a comprehensive physical plan or policy;

(v) that he is well-versed in the law relating to planning, and understands the planners' professional rôle and responsibility.

Obviously the training of such people is a demanding business for both teachers and students. Not only does it ask for a deep theoretical understanding of urban and regional systems and their control and guidance, but also for *practical skill in doing so*. The necessary level of ability can only be achieved by experience – in the case of students this must of necessity be simulated experience. Only protracted contact with a wide range of such problems and exposure to the difficult questions of value inherent in decision-making, to the criticism of teachers, fellow-students and practitioners can produce the required competence. Courses, however soundly-based and up-to-date in their theoretical foundations and treatment of background material, cannot be regarded as providing a training for planners unless the essential element of practical 'clinical' training in decision-making is there.

One final point on education. A systems approach to cities and their planning suggests that however different the landscapes we call 'town', 'metropolis', 'countryside' or 'region' may be, and no matter how different their activities and communications, they are systems of the same general class, manageable by similar procedures. As a French colleague put it recently, 'regional planning is planning at an intermediate level, between the national level and the local level. But the differences between those levels is fading away: in the economic field, national planning is gradually assuming some characteristics of regional planning . . . for physical planning the boundary between town planning, conurbation planning, and regional planning is not clear and will be less clear' (Piquard, 1967). The Town Planning Institute should once more consider the gains in understanding which might accrue to a change of name; and some of the recent educational developments and proposals going by titles such as 'regional planning' and 'regional studies' should do likewise. For both, it might be best to be verbose yet unambiguous.

The relationships between the planners and the contributory skills might now be clarified by reference to our system description. The other personnel involved will of course depend on the nature of the area being planned and its particular problems and objectives. But in general they will fall into categories depending on whether their principal skill is concerned with activities, spaces, communications, channels or sub-systems which unite these. For example:

1. 'activities' contributors:
   demographers, economists, persons with knowledge of special activities such as extractive industries, recreation, tourism, shipbuilding, etc.
2. 'spaces' contributors:
   architects, landscape architects, engineers, land surveyors, valuers, agriculturalists, geographers, geologists, etc.
3. 'communications' contributors:
   transport engineers, specialists in air traffic, telecommunications, public transport, etc.
4. 'channels' contributors:
   engineers of many kinds, also architects, landscape architects, etc.
5. contributors providing a general service to the organisation:
   goal-setting: sociologists, political scientists, etc.
   simulation, modelling and 'information services': systems analysts, mathematicians, programmers, etc.
   evaluation: economists, sociologists, pyschologists, etc.
   implementation: public administrators, public works experts, etc.

In the confusion which for so long surrounded education for planning, the need for special kinds of courses to orient the intending contributor towards planning has been overlooked. Let us hope that now we are beginning to have a firmer notion of the planning function itself and the training of planners, we can look forward to more courses which attempt this vital job; it is heartening to see the collaboration to this end between the Town Planning Institute and bodies representing the contributory skills.

Planning Research

The most immediately obvious effect on research of the adoption of a systems view is to focus attention on the nature of urban and regional systems themselves. So long as planning has lacked a unified 'core' theory, so long as it has been a hotch-potch of poorly-related ideas deriving from utopianism, paternalism, public health, civic design, applied economics and human geography, for so long has its so-called research been scanty and fragmented. And perhaps the planners' inability to outline the possibility of such central theories of urban systems and their control has been a partial explanation of the lack of financial support for planning research. Fortunately this is no longer the case; the establishment of the Social Science Research Council and the Centre for Environmental Studies has transformed the situation. Both bodies have a great interest in clarifying concepts of planning and in fostering discussion and writing for this purpose. The C.E.S. effort is noteworthy here, placing considerable emphasis on the need to hasten slowly, to avoid commitment of resources to what might prove to be yet more research into minutiae when the overview is lacking. A search for firmer concepts of urban and regional systems and their control figures prominently in the Centre's ideas (Llewelyn-Davies, 1967; Wilson, 1969).

But this fundamental research, oriented to conceptual advances, needs to be complemented by applied research into the practical problems of system simulation and evalution. A huge effort is needed to provide practitioners with the tools they need for experimenting and devising plans, and for testing and choosing between them. These operational exercises could best be carried out by co-operative ventures involving research workers and practitioners to their mutual benefit. The empirical testing of ideas would feed back to more fundamental questions of concept whilst the practitioners would benefit by exposure to more general problems which underlie their specific day-to-day worries. Some model-building is already under way both in research organisations and in planning offices; most of it seems to accept either explicitly or implicitly a systems framework. But far more work, more co-operation and more dissemination of results is needed. The new-style British planning system was designed to encourage the use of new techniques; the government should play its full part is seeing that planners have the right tools for the job.

The area which is virtually untouched by research concerns the control function. There is now a voluminous literature of general control theory and its application to specific fields—especially to industrial automation, telecommunications and military systems. The acceptance of the systems view put forward in this book calls for a great deal of effort in applying general theories of control—especially cybernetics, the control of very complex systems—to the planning of cities and regions. If the power and elegance of these general theories can so transform such fields as petrochemicals and ballistic nuclear weapons, what benefits could their application to the management of the human habitat produce?

By far the most taxing research needs follow from all this. These are the problems of evaluation in which we have turned full circle to the starting point—*human values*. The narrow 'technical' problems of how to carry out evaluation are receiving increasing attention. The continuing research into the development and refinement of cost-benefit type methods is to be welcomed. Almost no work has been done though on the development of indicators of system performance for cities and regions—measures, however crude initially, of certain aspects of the whole quality of life in an area. The results of such badly-needed research could begin to transform discussions of goals and objectives in practice as well as having important links with research into evaluation of alternatives.

A sense of proportion

Finally, the most important implication of a systems view of planning may be to induce a greater degree of humility in the planners themselves. However tenuously, the self-image of the planner can be traced back to its origins in middle-class paternalists, utopians and the professional advisers of the rich and powerful. The postures of knowing best what others need and making people happy through improved physical forms are now confined to a small minority. Yet as we probe deeper and deeper into the systems we treat, we become increasingly aware of the labyrinthine nature of human motivations, choices and actions. We realise too that the physical planner's unique skill is in the manipulation of only the spatial element of life—a small facet of the kaleidoscope of human existence. Even then, with systems so large and complex, if we can raise their performance levels by but a few degrees we can congratulate ourselves.

There is much more to life than location and interaction. And yet 'as the barest minimum, the task is to seek that spatial distribution of urban populations and urban activities that will permit greater freedom for human interaction while, simultaneously, providing freer access to natural amenities and effective management of the landscape and of mineral resources.

'This is no mean task—and probably the meanest part of the task will be to disabuse ourselves of some deep-seated doctrine that seeks order in simple mappable patterns, when it is really hiding in extremely complex social organisation instead' (Webber, 1963).

References

ALEXANDER, CHRISTOPHER (1964) *Notes on the synthesis of form* Cambridge, Mass.

ALONSO, WILLIAM (1964a) *Location and land use* Cambridge, Mass.

ALONSO, WILLIAM (1964b) Location theory. John R. Friedmann and William Alonso (eds.) *Regional development and planning* Cambridge, Mass.

ALTSHULER, ALAN (1965a) The goals of comprehensive planning *Journal of the American Institute of Planners 31*, 186–95

ALTSHULER, ALAN (1965b) *The city planning process: a political analysis* Ithaca, N.Y.

ANDERSON, JAMES R. (1962) The dilemma of idle land in mapping land use *The Professional Geographer, 14*

APPLEYARD, DONALD, KEVIN LYNCH and JOHN R. MEYER (1964) *The view from the road* Cambridge, Mass.

ARTLE, ROLAND (1959) *Studies in the structure of the Stockholm economy* Stockholm

ARVILL, ROBERT (pseud.) (1967) *Man and environment* Harmondsworth

ASHBY, W. ROSS (1956) *An introduction to cybernetics* London

ASHWORTH, W. (1954) *The genesis of modern British town planning* London

BARROWS, H. H. (1923) Geography as human ecology. *Annals of the Association of American Geographers, 13*, 1–14

BECKERMAN, W. and Associates (1965) *The British economy in 1975* Cambridge

BECKMANN, MARTIN and THOMAS MORSCHAK (1955) An activity analysis approach to location theory. *Kyklos, 8*

References

BEER, STAFFORD (1959) *Cybernetics and Management* London

BEER, STAFFORD (1966) *Decision and Control* London

BEESLEY, M. E. and J. F. KAIN (1964) Urban forms, car ownership and public policy; an appraisal of 'Traffic in Towns' *Urban Studies 1*, 174–203

BEESLEY, M. E. and J. F. KAIN (1965). Forecasting car ownership and use. *Urban studies, 2*, 163–185

BERMAN, BARBARA R., BENJAMIN CHINITZ and EDGAR M. HOOVER (1959) *Projection of a metropolis* Cambridge, Mass.

BERRY, BRIAN J. L. and WILLIAM L. GARRISON (1958) Recent developments in central place theory. *Papers and proceedings of the Regional Science Association, 4*

BERRY, BRIAN J. L. and WILLIAM L. GARRISON (1959) The functional bases of the central place hierarchy. Mayer and Kohn (eds.), *Readings in urban geography* Chicago

BERRY, BRIAN J. L. and A. PRED (1961) Central place studies: a bibliography of theory and applications *Regional Science Research Institute, Bibliographic Series, 1*

BERRY, BRIAN J. L. (1964) Cities as systems within systems of cities *Papers and proceedings of the Regional Science Association, 10*

von BERTALANFFY, LUDWIG (1951) An outline of general system theory *British Journal of the Philosophy of Science, 1*, 134–65

BOLAN, RICHARD S. (1967) Emerging views of planning *Journal of the American Institute of Planners 33*, 233–45

BOR, WALTER (1968) Milton Keynes–The first stage of the planning process *Journal of the Town Planning Institute, 54*, 203–8

von BÖVENTER, EDWIN (1964) Spatial organisation theory as a basis for regional planning. *Journal of the American Institute of Planners, 30*, 90–100

BROWN, MAURICE The time element in planning *Journal of the Town Planning Institute, 54*, 209–13

BRUCK, H. W., STEPHEN H. PUTMAN and WILBUR A. STEGER (1966). Evaluation of alternative transportation proposals: the northeast corridor *Journal of the American Institute of Planners, 23*, 322–33

BUCHANAN, COLIN in association with ECONOMIC CONSULTANTS LTD. (1966) *South Hampshire Study: A report on the feasibility of major urban growth.* 3 vols. London

BURGESS, ERNEST W. (1925) Growth of the city; in R. E. Park et al. (eds.) *The city* Chicago

References

CARROTHERS, GERALD P. (1956) An historical review of the gravity and potential concepts of human interaction *Journal of the American Institute of Planners, 22,* 94–102

CATANESE A. J. and A. W. STEISS (1968) Systemic planning–the challenge of the new generation of planners *Journal of the Town Planning Institute 54,* 172–6

CHADWICK, GEORGE F. (1966) A systems view of planning *Journal of the Town Planning Institute 52,* 184–6

CHAPIN, F. STUART (jr.) (1965) *Urban land use planning* Urbana, Illinois

CHAPIN, F. STUART (jr.) and SHIRLEY F. WEISS (eds.) (1962) *Urban growth dynamics in a regional cluster of cities* New York

CHAPIN, F. STUART (jr.)and SHIRLEY F. WEISS (1962a) *Factors influencing land development* Chapel Hill, N.C.

CHAPIN, F. STUART (jr.) and HENRY C. HIGHTOWER (1965) Household activity patterns and land use *Journal of the American Institute of Planners, 31,* 222–31

CHERNS, A. B. (1967) *The use of the social sciences* (inaugural lecture) Loughborough

CHILDE, V. GORDON (1942) *What happened in history* Edinburgh

CHISHOLM, MICHAEL (1962) *Rural settlement and land use: an essay in location* London

CHISHOLM, MICHAEL (1966) *Geography and economics* London

CHORLEY, RICHARD J. and PETER HAGGETT (eds.) (1967) *Models in geography* London

CHRISTALLER, WALTER (1933) *Die Zentralen Orte in Süddeutschland* Jena

CHURCHMAN, C. W., R. L. ACKOFF, and E. L. ARNOFF (1957) *Introduction to operations research* New York

CLARK, COLIN (1967) *Population growth and land use* London

CLAWSON, MARION and CHARLES L. STEWART (1965) *Land use information* Baltimore Md.

COLBY, CHARLES C. (1933) Centrifugal and centripetal forces in urban geography *Annals of the Association of American Geographers, 23,* 1–20

COMMITTEE ON HIGHER EDUCATION (1963) (The 'Robbins committee') *Higher Education* London

COWAN, PETER (1966) Institutions, activities and accommodation in the city *Journal of the Town Planning Institute, 52,* 140–1

References

CRIPPS, ERIC and DAVID FOOT (1968) Evaluating alternative strategies *Official Architecture and Planning 31*, 928–941

CULLINWORTH, J. B. (1960) *Housing needs and planning policy* London

DONNELLY, THOMAS G., F. STUART CHAPIN (jr.) and SHIRLEY F. WEISS (1964) *A probabilistic model for residential growth* Chapel Hill, N.C.

DOXIADIS, CONSTANTINOS A. (1966) *Between Dystopia and Utopia* Hartford, Conn., and London

DUCKWORTH, ERIC (1965) *A guide to operational research* London

DUNN, EDGAR S. (1954) *The location of agricultural production* Gainsville, Florida

DYCKMAN, JOHN (1961) Planning and decision theory *Journal of the American Institute of Planners, 27*, 335–45

ELLENBY, JOHN (1966) *Research leading to a computer–aided town and regional planning system* (mimeographed) Dept. of Geography, London School of Economics

FAGIN, HENRY (1963) The Penn-Jersey transportation study: the launching of a permanent regional planning process *Journal of the American Institute of Planners, 29*, 8–17

FARBEY, B. A. and J. D. MURCHLAND (1967) Towards an evaluation of road system designs *Regional Studies, 1*, 27–37

FELDT, ALLAN G. (1966) Operational gaming in planning education *Journal of the American Institute of Planners, 32*, 17–23

FIREY, WALTER (1961) *Land use in central Boston* Cambridge, Mass.

FOLEY, DONALD L. (1964) An approach to metropolitan spatial structure, in Melvin M. Webber (ed.) *Explorations into urban structure* Philadelphia

FOSTER, C. D. (1963) *The transport problem* Edinburgh

FRIEDMANN, JOHN (1965) Comprehensive planning as a process *Journal of the American Institute of Planners, 31*, 195–7

FRIEDMANN, JOHN and WILLIAM ALONSO (1964) (eds.) *Regional development and planning* Cambridge, Mass.

FRIEDRICH, C. S. (1929) *Alfred Weber's theory of the location of industries* Chicago

316

References

GALBRAITH, J. K. (1962) *The affluent society* New York

GARRISON, WILLIAM L. (1962) Towards simulation models of urban growth and development *Lund Studies in Geography, Series B, (Human Geography,) 24,* 92–108

GEDDES, PATRICK (1915) *Cities in evolution* Edinburgh (Revised edition, edited by Jacqueline Tyrwhitt, London, 1949)

GODDARD, JOHN (1967) Changing office location patterns within central London *Urban Studies, 4,* 276–85

GOTTLIEB, ABE (1956) Planning elements of an inter-industry analysis: a metropolitan area approach *Journal of the American Institute of Planners, 22,* 230–6

GOTTMAN, JEAN (1961) *Megalopolis: The urbanized northeastern seaboard of the United States* New York

GREENHUT, MELVIN L. (1956) *Plant location in theory and in practice* Chapel Hill, N.C.

GUTTENBURG, ALBERT Z. (1959) A multiple land use classification system *Journal of the American Institute of Planners, 25,* 143–50

GUTTENBURG, ALBERT Z. (1960) Urban structure and urban growth *Journal of the American Institute of Planners, 26*

HAGGETT, PETER (1965) *Locational analysis in human geography* London

HALL, PETER G. (1966a) *The world cities* London

HALL, PETER G. (1966b) *Von Thünen's isolated state* London

HARRIS, BRITTON (1961) Some problems in the theory of intra-urban location *Operations Research, 9,* 695–721

HARRIS, BRITTON (ed.) (1965) Urban development models: new tools for planning. Complete issue of the *Journal of the American Institute of Planners, 31,* No. 2

HARRIS, BRITTON (1966) The uses of theory in the simulation of urban phenomena *Journal of the American Institute of Planners, 32,* 258–73

HARRIS, BRITTON (1967) How to succeed with computers without really trying *Journal of the American Institute of Planners, 33,* 11–17

HARRIS, CHAUNCY D. and EDWARD L. ULLMANN (1945) The nature of cities *Annals of the American Academy of Political and Social Science, 242,* 7–17

HEAP, DESMOND (1965) *An outline of planning law* London

References

HEARLE, E. F. R. and R. J. MASON (1956) *A data-processing system for state and local governments* Santa Monica, Cal.

HERBERT, D. T. (1967) Social area analysis: a British study *Urban Studies, 4,* 41–60

HERBERT, JOHN D. and BENJAMIN STEVENS (1960) A model for the distribution of residential activity in urban areas *Journal of the Regional Science Association* Fall.

HILL, MORRIS (1968) A goals-achievements matrix for evaluating alternative plans *Journal of the American Institute of Planners, 34,* 19–29

HIRSCH, WERNER Z. (1964) (ed.) *Elements of regional accounts* Baltimore, Md.

HOCHWALD, WERNER (1961) (ed.) *Design of regional accounts* Baltimore, Md.

HOOVER, EDGAR M. (1948) *The location of economic activity* New York

HOSKINS, W. G. (1955) *The making of the English landscape* London

HOYT, HOMER (1939) *The structure and growth of residential neighborhoods in American cities* Washington

ISARD, WALTER (1956) *Location and space-economy* New York

ISARD, WALTER and others (1960) *Methods of regional analysis* Cambridge, Mass.

ISARD, WALTER and THOMAS A. REINER (1962) Aspects of decision-making theory and regional science *Papers and proceedings of the Regional Science Association, 9*

JACKSON, JOHN N. (1962) *Surveys for town and country planning* London

JAMESON, G. B., W. K. MACKAY and J. C. R. LATCHFORD (1967) Transportation and land use structures *Urban studies, 4,* 201–17

JAY, LESLIE S. (1966) *The development of an integrated data system* London

JAY, LESLIE S. (1967) Scientific method in planning *Journal of the Town Planning Institute, 53,* 3–7

JOHNSON, R. A., F. E. KAST and J. E. ROSENZWEIG (1963) *The theory and management of systems* New York

References

JOINT PROGRAM, THE (1965) *Goals for development of the Twin Cities metropolitan area* St. Paul, Minnesota

KANTOROWICH, ROY H. (1966) Education for planning *Journal of the Town Planning Institute, 53,* 175–84

KITCHING, L. C. (1966) Regional and county planning–looking beyond P.A.G. *Journal of the Town Planning Institute, 52,* 365–6

KOOPMANS, TJALLING C. and MARTIN BECKMAN (1957) Assignment problems and the location of economic activities *Econometrica*

LEEDS SCHOOL OF TOWN PLANNING (1966) *Scunthorpe: a study in potential growth* Scunthorpe

LEICESTER CITY PLANNING DEPARTMENT (1964) *Leicester Traffic Plan* Leicester

LEONTIEF, WASSILY (1953) (ed.) *Studies in the structure of the American economy* New York

LEVEN, CHARLES L. (1964) Establishing goals for regional economic development *Journal of the American Institute of Planners, 30,* 100–10

LEVIN, P. H. (1966) The design process in planning *Town Planning Review, 37,* 5–20

LICHFIELD, NATHANIEL (1956) *The economics of planned development* London

LICHFIELD, NATHANIEL (1964) Cost-benefit analysis in plan evaluation *Town Planning Review, 35,* 159–69

LICHFIELD, NATHANIEL (1966) Cost-benefit analysis in urban redevelopment: a case study–Swanley *Urban Studies, 3,* 215–49

LICHTENBERG, ROBERT M. (1959) *One-tenth of a nation* Cambridge, Mass.

LITTLE, ARTHUR D. (INC.) (1963) *San Francisco community renewal program–purpose, scope and methodology* Santa Monica, California

LLEWELYN-DAVIES, RICHARD (1967) Research for planning *Journal of the Town Planning Institute, 53,* 221–25

LLOYD, P. E. and P. DICKEN (1968) The data bank in regional studies of industry *Town Planning Review, 38,* 304–16

LOEKS, C. DAVID (1967) The new comprehensiveness *Journal of the American Institute of Planners, 33,* 347–52

LÖSCH, AUGUST (1940) *Die Räumliche Ordnung der Wirtschaft* Jena

LOWENSTEIN, LOUIS K. (1966) On the nature of analytical models *Urban Studies, 3,* 112–19

References

LOWRY, IRA S. (1964) *A model of metropolis* Santa Monica, Cal.

LOWRY, IRA S. (1965) A short course in model design *Journal of the American Institute of Planners, 31,* 158–66

LUTTRELL, W. F. (1962) *Factory location and industrial movement* London

LYNCH, KEVIN and LLOYD RODWIN (1958) A theory of urban form *Journal of the American Institute of Planners, 24,* 201–14

LYNCH, KEVIN (1960) *The image of the city* Cambridge, Mass.

MACKINDER, H. J. (1902) *Britain and the British seas* New York

McKENZIE, R. D. (1933) *The metropolitan community* Chicago

McLOUGHLIN, J. BRIAN (1965) Notes on the nature of physical change *Journal of the Town Planning Institute, 51,* 397–400

McLOUGHLIN, J. BRIAN (1966a) The P.A.G. report: background and prospect *Journal of the Town Planning Institute, 52,* 257–61

McLOUGHLIN, J. BRIAN (1966b) The current state of British practice *Journal of the American Institute of Planners, 32,* 350–5

McLOUGHLIN, J. BRIAN (1967) A systems approach to planning *Report of the Town and Country Planning Summer School,* pp. 38–53 London

MAO, JAMES C. T. (1966) Efficiency in public urban renewal expenditures through benefit-cost analysis *Journal of the American Institute of Planners, 32,* 95–107

MEIER, RICHARD L. (1962) *A communications theory of urban growth* Cambridge, Mass.

MEIER, RICHARD L. and RICHARD D. DUKE (1966) Gaming simulation for urban planning *Journal of the American Institute of Planners, 32,* 3–17

MEYER, J. R., J. F. KAIN and M. WOHL (1965) *The urban transportation problem* Cambridge, Mass.

MEYERSON, MARTIN and EDWARD C. BANFIELD (1955) *Politics, planning and the public interest* New York

MITCHELL, ROBERT B. and CHESTER RAPKIN (1954) *Urban traffic: a function of land use.* New York

MITCHELL, ROBERT B. (1959) *Metropolitan planning for land use and transportation* U.S. Government, Washington, D.C.

MITCHELL, ROBERT B. (1961) The new frontier in metropolitan planning *Journal of the American Institute of Planners, 27,* 169–75

References

MOCINE, CORWIN R. (1966) Urban physical planning and the 'new planning' *Journal of the American Institute of Planners, 32*, 234–237

MORRILL, RICHARD L. (1960) Simulation of central place patterns over time *Lund studies in Geography, Series B, (Human Geography) 24*, 109–20

MOSER, C. A. (1960) *Survey methods in social investigation* London

NATIONAL CAPITOL PLANNING COMMISSION (1962) *A policies plan for the year 2000: the Nation's Capital* Washington, D.C.

NATIONAL PARKS COMMISSION (1968) *Recreational use of the countryside* (Research Register No. 1) London

von NEUMAN J. and O. MORGENSTERN (1944) *Theory of games and economic behaviour* Princeton, N.J.

O.R.R.R.C. (Outdoor Recreation Resources Review Commission). *Public outdoor recreation areas: acreage, use and potential* U.S. Government, Washington, D.C.

PALANDER, TORD (1935) *Beiträge zur Standortstheorie* Uppsala

PALMER, J. E. (1967) Recreational planning–a bibliographical review *Planning Outlook, 2*, (new series), 19–69

PETERSEN, WILLIAM (1966) On some meanings of 'planning' *Journal of the American Institute of Planners, 32*, 130–42

PFOUTS, RALPH W. (1960) (ed.) *The techniques of urban economic analysis* Trenton, N.J.

PLANNING ADVISORY GROUP (1965) *The future of development plans* London

PREST A. R. and RALPH TURVEY (1965) Cost-benefit analysis: a survey *The Economic Journal*, pp. 683 et seq.

RANNELLS, JOHN (1956) *The core of the city* Philadelphia

RATCLIFF, RICHARD U. (1949) *Urban land economics* New York

RATCLIFF, RICHARD U. (1955) The dynamics of efficiency in the locational distribution of urban activity; in Robert M. Fisher (ed.) *The metropolis in modern life*

READE, ERIC (1968) Some notes toward a sociology of planning –the case for self-awareness *Journal of the Town Planning Institute, 54*, 214–18

ROGERS, ANDREI (1966) Matrix methods of population analysis *Journal of the American Institute of Planners, 32*, 40–44

321

References

ROGERS, ANDREI (1968) *Matrix analysis of inter-regional population growth and distribution* Berkeley, Cal.

ROSE, JOHN (1967) *Automation: its anatomy and physiology* Edinburgh

ROTH, GABRIEL (1967) *Paying for roads* Harmondsworth

SCHLAGER, KENNETH J. (1965) A land use plan design model *Journal of the American Institute of Planners, 31,* 103–11

SENIOR, DEREK (1966) *The regional city: an Anglo-American discussion of metropolitan planning* London and Chicago

SIGSWORTH, E. M. and R. K. WILKINSON (1967) Rebuilding or renovation? *Urban Studies, 4,* 109–21

SMETHURST, P. R. (1967) The national travel surveys: a source of data for planners *Town Planning Review, 38,* 43–63

SMITH, D. L. (1967) The problems of historic towns in a period of population growth and technological change. *Report of proceedings of the Town and Country Planning Summer School,* 54–62 (Held at the Queens University of Belfast) London

SONENBLUM, SIDNEY and LOUIS H. STERN (1964) The use of economic projections in planning *Journal of the American Institute of Planners, 30,* 110–23

STARKIE, D. N. M. (1968) Business premises traffic-generation studies *Journal of the Town Planning Institute, 53,* 232–4

STEWART, CHARLES T. (1959) The size and spacing of cities. Mayer and Kohn (eds.) *Readings in Urban Geography* Chicago

STONE, RICHARD (1962a) *A computable model of economic growth* London

STONE, RICHARD (1962b) *A social accounting matrix for 1960* London

STONE, RICHARD (1963) *Input-output relationships 1954–66* London

TANNER, J. C. (1961) *Factors affecting the amount of travel* (Road Research Technical Paper No. 51) H.M.S.O. London

TAYLOR, JOHN L. and K. R. CARTER (1967) Instructional simulation of urban development *Journal of the Town Planning Institute, 53,* 443–7

TEES-SIDE SURVEY AND PLAN (1968) (Wilson and Womersley, chartered architects and town planners, in association with Scott, Wilson Kirkpatrick and Partners, consulting engineers) Volume 1: *Policies and proposals* H.M.S.O. London

References

VON THÜNEN, JOHANN HEINRICH (1826) *Der isolierte Staat in Beziehung auf Landwirtschaft und Nationalökonomie* Hamburg

TIEBOUT, CHARLES M. (1962) *The community economic base study* The Committee for Economic Development, New York

TOULMIN, S. (1953) *The philosophy of science* London

TUCKER, ANTHONY (1968) Research for survival *The Guardian* April 30, Manchester

ULLMANN, EDWARD L. (1941) A theory for the location of cities *American Journal of Sociology*

UNIVERSITY OF MANCHESTER, DEPARTMENT OF TOWN AND COUNTRY PLANNING (1964) *Regional shopping centres; a planning report on northwest England* Manchester

UNIVERSITY OF MANCHESTER, DEPARTMENT OF TOWN AND COUNTRY PLANNING (1967) *Regional shopping centres: a planning report on northwest England: Part 2, a retail gravity model* Manchester

VERNON, RAYMOND (ed.) (1959) *New York metropolitan region study* (10 volumes) Cambridge, Mass.

WAGNER, PHILIP L. (1960) *The human use of the earth* New York

WALKDEN, A. H. (1961) The estimation of future numbers of private households in England and Wales. *Journal of the Royal Statistical Society*, 174-86

WEBBER, MELVIN M. (1963a) Order in diversity: community without propinquity *Cities and Space, the future use of urban land* pp. 23-54 Baltimore, Md.

WEBBER, MELVIN M. (1963b) Comprehensive planning and social responsibility *Journal of the American Institute of Planners*, 29, 232-41

WEBBER, MELVIN M. (ed.) (1964) *Explorations into urban structure* Philadelphia

WEBBER, MELVIN M. (1965) The rôle of intelligence systems in urban-systems planning *Journal of the American Institute of Planners*, 31, 289-96

WEBER, ALFRED (1909) *Ueber den Standort der Industrien* Part I, Reine Theorie der Standorts. Tübingen

WIENER, NORBERT (1948) *Cybernetics* New York

References

WILKINSON R. and D. M. MERRY (1965) A statistical analysis of attitudes to moving (a survey of slum clearance areas in Leeds) *Urban Studies 2*, 1–14

WILSON, ALAN G. (1969) Research for regional planning *Regional Studies 3*, 3–14

WINGO, LOWDON (1961) *Transportation and urban land* Washington

WINGO, LOWDON and HARVEY S. PERLOFF (1961) The Washington transportation plan: technics or politics? *Papers and proceedings of the Regional Science Association, 7*

WINGO, LOWDON (1966) Urban renewal: a strategy for information and analysis *Journal of the American Institute of Planners, 32*, 143–54

YOUNG, ROBERT C. (1966) Goals and goal-setting *Journal of the American Institute of Planners, 32*, 76–85

ZETTEL, R. M. and R. R. CARLL (1962) *Summary review of major metropolitan area transportation studies in the United States* University of California, Berkeley, Cal.

Index

Accessibility
  goal, 108
  objectives for, 115–16
  in models, 239
Action, *see* Implementation
Activities, 20–2, 25–8, 38–9, 77–8
  information needs, 128
  contrasted with 'land use', 129–30
  linkages, 70
  place related, 77
  classification of, 130–1
  classification schemes, 133
  intensity of, 140
  projection of, 174
  in plans, 256, 279
Activity rates (in forecasts), 206
Activity systems, 30–68
  surveys of (information), 157
  use in forecasting/simulation, 215
Adaptation, 24–7, 34, 69
  information on, 136–9
Adapted spaces, *see* Spaces
Ad hoc control, 290–1
Administration (*see also* Government and Public Policies), 302–5
Aesthetics
  goal, 107
  objectives, 117–18
  in control, 264–5
Agencies (for change), 46–9
Aggregation (dis-), 132 n., 238
Alexander, Christopher, 251
Altshuler, Alan, 107, 110, 306
Analogue models, 221

Anderson, James R., 141
Anticipation, 64, 289
Appleyard, Donald, 118
Apportionment methods (forecasting), 178, 200
Architecture, 24, 70, 305–10
Areal units (information), 160, 211, 234–5
Artle, Roland, 203
Ashby, W. Ross, 75, 90, 119, 128, 290

Balance Sheet (Planning), 272–4
Banfield, Edward C., 106
Beckerman, W. *et al.*, 192, 194, 196–7
Beer, Stafford, 75–8, 94, 119, 290–4, 306
Beesley, M. E. and Kain, J. F., 192
Behaviour patterns, 25, 28, 34–5, 95
  in transport plans, 66–7
  in location theory, 68–70
  place-related, 77, 129
  information on, 157
  assumed in simulation, 236 *et seq.*
Behavioural change, 38–41, 48, 53, 56
Benefits (and Costs) 39, 49–53, 56–7, 264
Berman, Barbara R., Chinitz, B. and Hoover, E. M., 206
von Bertalanffy, Ludwig, 75
Biological sciences, 84, 119, 289
'Black Box', 294

Bolan, Richard S., 302
Bor, Walter, 120
Boundaries, 133
Bruck, H. W., Putman, S. H. and Steger, W. A., 278
Buchanan, Colin, 79, 84, 118, 189, 200, 206
Burgess, Ernest W., 61

Capacity of communication channels, 149
Car ownership, 192, 216
Carter, K. R., 228, 240
Central Place theory, 62
Centre for Environmental Studies (C.E.S.), 310
Chadwick, George F., 18, 70, 231
Channels, 35, 38, 79, 129, 148, 162, 219–20, 279
Chapin, F. Stuart, 30, 34, 68, 77, 104, 142, 158, 174–6, 178, 201, 237, 254
Cherns, A. B., 296
Chicago, University of, 61
Childe, V. Gordon, 19
Chisholm, Michael, 298
Choice, range of, 98
Christaller, Walter, 62
Churchman, Ackoff and Arnoff, 75
City regions, 302–4
Clawson, Marion, and Stewart, Charles, 129 *et seq.*
Climax ecology, 29, 289
Cohort-survival method (population forecasts), 184–90
Colby, Charles C., 62
Committments, 212–13
Communications, 27, 29, 38, 77–8
    information about, 128, 144–52, 161
    interchanges, land use, 138–9, 151–2
    intensity of, 146
    forecasting, 214–19
    simulation of, 240
    in plans, 256, 279
Communication theory, 78, 144

Complexity, *see* System
Comprehensive ideal, 107, 109–12
    vs. specialism, 110
    in evaluation of plans, 265
Computer, 66–8, 82, 238–9, 242 *et seq.*, 250, 252
Concentration (*vs.* dispersal), 116, 231, 233
Connectivity, measures of, 120, 267
Conservation, 16, 233
Constraints, 43–6
Contributors (skills), 305–9
Control
    in complex systems, 17, 59, 75, 81, 84–5, 89–91
    error-controlled regulation, 85, 279, 282–4, 288, 294–6
    in history, 92–3
    of human environment, 21–3, 70, 94, 311
    information needed for, 280, 288
    methods in practice, 281–8
    'structural' *vs.* detail, 283–4
    requisite variety, 290–4
    monitoring, 281, 294–6
Correlation, 170
Cost/benefit analysis, 56–7, 264–73
Costs (*see also* Benefits)
    of communications/channels, 151 264
Cowan, Peter, 79
Cripps, Eric, 245, 250
Cullingworth, J. B., 192
Cultural activities (forecasts), 210
Cybernetics
    promise of, 17, 89–91
    principles of, 75
    as control element of planning, 101, 289–96

Data-processing, *see* Information
Davies, H. W. E., 18
Decisions, 34, 36, 43, 57
    on locations, 61, 69
    rationality of, 63
    sequential, 65
    effecting changes, 98, 227
Decision theory, 16, 65

Index

Density (*see also* Intensity)
information on, 140–1
Desire lines, 226
Destinations, *see* Origins
Determinism, 70, 85, 169
Development(al change), 35–41, 47, 52–4
Development control, 86 (*see also* Control)
significance of, 101, 299
Dialogue (professional/political), 107, 120–3
Disciplines (skills), 305–10
Dispersal, *see* Concentration
Disturbances, 290
Doxiadis, Constantinos, 22
Duke, Richard D., 220, 240
Dyckman, John W., 69, 96, 109, 278
Dynamic plans, *see* Plans
Dynamic system, *see* System

Ecological school in location theory, 61–2
Ecology, eco-system, 20–8, 34–6, 64, 69–70, 75, 94–5, 311
Economic 'health', 108
goals/objectives, 113
projection, forecasts, 192–209
base methods, 198–200
Education, forecasting, 209
Elite groups, 92
Engineering, 24, 305–10
Enumeration Districts (Census), 159
Environment, 19–23
Equilibrium
in location theory, 51, 60–3
'one-shot' plans, 66, 231, 245 *et seq.*
Evaluation, 29, 38, 51, 84
by individuals/groups, 95
of alternative plans, 100, Chapter 10 generally

Fagin, Henry, 226
Farbey, B. A., 112, 253
Feedback, 70, 87–9, 289, 292
Flexibility, objective of, 118–20
Flow (of communication), 80

Foley, Donald L., 16, 157
Foot, David, 245, 250
Foster, C. D., 217
Friedmann, John, 106, 110, 265, 278

Galbraith, J., 194
Gaming Simulation
in setting goals/objectives, 123–4
as modelling device, 228, 240–2
Gans, Herbert, 69
Geddes, Patrick, 24, 125
General system theory (*see also* System), 17, 75
Gill, David C., 18
Goals (*see also* Objectives)
formulation, Chapter 6
individual, 95
community, 97–8
hierarchy of, 104–5
types of, 107–9
methods of clarifying, 120–3, 311
in simulation, 233
in evaluation, 254–5, 274–7
flexibility, reviews of, 295–6
Gottlieb, Abe, 201
Gottmann, Jean, 22
Government, powers of, 20, 94, 208, 257–60
Grid, National, 135
references, 135–6, 159–60
Guttenburg, Albert Z., 129

Habitat, 19–20, 25–7
Haggett, Peter, 16, 112, 117
Hall, Peter, 18, 22
Harris, Britton, 16, 68, 167, 223, 227, 299
Harris, Chauncy D., 63
Healthy conditions (goal of), 108
Heap, Desmond, 45
Hearle, E. F. R. and Mason, R. J., 300
Herbert, D. T., 192
Hightower, Henry C., 157
Hill, Morris, 261, 273, 278
Hirsch, Werner Z., 112
Homeostasis, 289
Hoover, Edgar M., 61

Hoskins, W. G., 93
Households, 192
Hoyt, Homer, 62

Idle channels, 150–1
Idle land, 141–2
Impact analysis, 228
Implementation (action), 101
Improvements (land), 136
Incomes (and expenditure), 141,
    192
Incremental view/approach, 67
Information, Chapter 7, 42, 51,
    64–5
  in control, 89, 164, 280, 288
  misuse of, 125, 291
  simplifications, 152 *et seq.*
  on activity systems, 157
  modelling needs, 224–5, 232, 242–
    243
  in evaluation of plans, Chapter 10
    generally
  staff organisation for, 300–1
Information systems, design of, 163–
    165, 235
Input/Output methods, 201–4
Intangibles, 272–4
Intensity
  of activity, 140
  of communication, 146
Intuitive control, 89
Isard, Walter, 16, 176, 178, 182,
    192, 195, 202
Isomorphism (of control with sys-
    tem), 95–6, 101
Iteration, 247

Jackson, J. N., 163
Jamieson, G., Mackay, W. and
    Latchford, J. R., 253 n.
Jay, Leslie, 129, 165, 229
Johnson, R. A., Kast, F. E., and
    Rosenzweig, J. E., 85, 124, 279,
    288, 306

Kantorowich, Roy H., 18, 307
Kast, F. E., *see* Johnson, R. A.
Kitching, L. C., 298

Land use, 62, 65–6, 80–1
  weakness of definitions, 129–30
  'traditional' map, 152
  and transport (interrelationship
    between), 66, 80–1, 226
Land values, *see* Values
Learning process in control device,
    292–4
Leicester City Planning Depart-
    ment, 217
Leven, Charles, 107, 113
Lichfield, Nathaniel, 16, 39, 43, 52,
    272–4
Linear programming, 33, 251–2
Little, Arthur D., 212
Living systems, 119–20
Llewelyn-Davies, Richard, 86, 310
Location, information, 133
Location theory, Chapter 3
Locational change, 35–41, 47, 53–5,
    63
  opportunities for, 139
  behaviour, 157
Loeks, David C., 306
Lösch, August, 63
Lowry, Ira S., 223–5, 246–50, 287
Luttrell, W. F., 42
Lynch, Kevin, 118

Malthus, 19
Manchester, University of, 17
Mao, J. C. T., 265
Mathematical models, 222 *et seq.*,
    238 *et seq.*
Matrix methods (population fore-
    casting), 190–2
  as information stores, 128, 228–30
McLoughlin, J. Brian, 34, 70, 85,
    298, 306
Megalopolis, 22
Meier, Richard L., 228, 240
Melville, Ian S., 18
Merry, D. M., 41
Metropolitan regions/areas, 63, 66–7
Meyer, John R., 118
Meyerson, Martin, 106
Middle-range planning, 107
Migration, 182, 184, 187–9

Mitchell, Robert B., 65, 80, 83, 87, 226, 253
Mocine, Corwin R., 306
Modal split (choice), 66, 218, 253
Models (*see also* Simulation), 67, 81, 83, 220–30, 299
  in plan-making, 252–5
  in control, 87, 101, 284–5
  traffic, 216–18, 239, 253
  descriptive, 222
  predictive, 222
  planning, 223
  examples of, 235 *et seq.*
  design and calibration, 243
Monitoring
  goal formulation, 121
  in plan implementation, 195, 281, 294–6
Monte Carlo routines, 242
Morgenstern, O. *see* von Neumann
Moser, Claus, 163
Murchland, J. D., 112, 253

National Capitol Planning Commission, 234
National Grid, 135, 159–60
National Parks Commission, 211
Networks
  information on, 148
  in modelling/simulation, 244, 253
  in plans, 256, 279
von Neumann, J. and Morgenstern, O., 64

Objectives (*see also* Goals)
  in relation to goals, 106–7
  problems of definition, 111–12, 311
  examples of operational forms, 113–21
  multiple, 113, 277
  residential, 114
  flexibility, 118
  aesthetics, 117–18
  accessibility, 114–16
  in evaluation of plans, 264–5, 274–277
  flexibility, review, 295–6

Occupations, 192
Office organisation, 301–2
Operational (operations) research, 17, 33, 49, 75
Ordnance Survey, 135
  information source, 149
  for grid references, 159
Origins (and destinations), 144, 229
Outdoor Recreation Resources Review Commission (O.R.R.R.C.), 210
Ownership
  of land, 134, 143
  of channels, 151

Palmer, J. E., 211
Parcels (units of land), 134–6
Park, R. E., 61
Participation, *see* Public policies
Penn-Jersey Transportation Study, 67, 226, 244–5
Perloff, Harvey S., 67, 105, 226
Permissions (approvals), 284–8
Pfouts, Ralph W., 203
Physical forms, 234
Physiography, 134
Planning
  process, Chapter 5, summary 102–3
  in Britain, 15–16
  in North America, 16
  'urban' *vs.* 'regional', 23, 308–9
  'physical' *vs.* other forms, 97, 194, 286, 302
  decision to adopt, 96
  Planning Advisory Group (P.A.G.), 87, 290, 304
  in relation to wider social purposes, 96, 294, 302
  systems approach to (*q.v.*), 70, 75, 81–3
  Balance Sheet, *see* Balance Sheet
  control, *see* Control
  as a social servo-mechanism, 294
  practice, 297
  professionalism, education, 305–310
  research needs, 310

Index

Plans
    nature of, 83-4
    alternative courses, 98-9; evalua-
        tion of, Chapter 10
    system trajectories as basis for,
        229-30
    formulation of, Chapter 9, 252-5
    form and content of, 255-62
    presentation of, 257-62
    implementation, review, etc.,
        Chapter 11
    structural, detailed, 284-5
Political science, 70
Population, 19
    forecasting, 175-92, 205-9
Potential capacity of a channel, 149-
    150
Power over decisions, 92
Prediction, *see* Simulation
Prest, A. R., and Turvey, R., 265
Probabilism, 70, 170
Probability, 65, 85
Productivity, 196-7
Projection (*see also* Simulation)
    simple *vs.* analytical, 169
Public interest, 59, 120-3
Public policies, 82, 87
    in plan design (assumed), 99, 231
    in goal formulation, 122
    in simulation/forecasting, 208, 228
    in plan documents, 257-60
    in implementation, control and
        review, 295-6

RAND Corporation, 246
Random processes, 65, 77
Ranking (in order of merit), 269-72
Rapkin, Chester, 65, 80
Ratio methods (forecasts), 178, 200
Rationality, 63-4
Reade, Eric, 305
Recreation
    objectives for, 114
    forecasts for, 210-11
Recursive (models), 227, 235, 243
Redundancy (cybernetics), 119
Regional accounts, 204
Regional analysis, 16

Regional planning, *see* Planning
Research needs, 310
'Research' misnomer, 299
Resource management, 16, 22, 23
Review
    as part of planning process, 102,
        Chapter 11
    role of forecasts in, 195
    as part of whole control process,
        294-6
Robinson, David G., 18
Rogers, Andrei, 190-1
Rose, John, 85
Rosenzweig, J. E., *see* Johnson, R. A.

Sampling, 158-9
Scarcity, 69
Schlager, Kenneth, 251-2
Schonegevel, M. C., 18
Scientific method, 167
Sectors of economy (forecasts), 197
    et seq.
Senior, Derek, 302
Simulation (*see also* Models, Chapter
    8)
    need for, 81-2
    in control, 87, 101
    in plan design, 98-9, 229-30, 231
    in goal formulation, 123
    examples, 235 *et seq.*
    manual, 236-42
    mechanical (computer), 242-5
Smethurst, P. R., 162
Snow, Charles (Lord), 90
Social Science Research Council
    (S.S.R.C.), 310
Social Sciences, 24, 70, 298, 305-10
Social welfare activity, 210
Socio-economic groups, 192, 216, 240
Sonenblum and Stern, 195
Spaces ('adapted'), 26, 38, 78
    information about, 128, 133
    forecasting, 211-14
Spatial, 133
Standards (statutory), 94
Starkie, D. N. M., 162
Stewart, Charles, *see* Clawson,
    Marion

Index

Stewart and Warntz, 116
Stock (e.g. of buildings), 80
Stone, Richard, 204
Strategies, in games, 65
Structure, 79
Surveying, 24, 305–10
Surveys, *see* Information, Activities, Spaces, Communications, Channels
System
  performance criteria of, 111, 265, 311
  description of, 126–8
  of roads, 65–6, 80
  city/region as, 67, 70, 75–7, 80–3, 226, 297, 302–4
  view of planning, 70, 75, 81–3, 297, 302–4
  problems of identifying, 77–80, 234–5
  trajectory (as information), 165
  simulation, Chapter 8
  future states of (in modelling), 224
  complexity of, 234–5
  homeostasis in, 289
Systemic change, 37, 95
Systems analysis, 17, 75

Tanner, J. C., 192
Taylor, John L., 228, 240
Technology, 19, 35
Tees-side Survey and Plan, 294–5
Tenure, *see* Ownership
Theory, role of, 167, 223
Theory of planning, 16, 24
von Thünen, H. W., 60
Time, treatment of
  in simulation/forecasting, 171–4
  in mathematical models, 223–4
Toulmin, S., 60
Town Planning Institute, 15, 298, 307
Traffic, *see* Models, Communications, Simulation, etc.
Trajectories
  of urban/regional change, 67
  of alternative plans, 99–100, 171, 228

of urban systems, 128–9, 163–5
  in forecasting methods, 207, 228
  in control and implementation, 281
Transmission (communications), 145, 214–16
Transport, 78
Transportation plans, early U.S., 65
Travel behaviour, 192
  forecasting, 214–19
Trip generation, 65, 216, 226, 253
Tucker, Anthony, 23
Turvey, R. A., 64

Ullmann, Edward L., 63
Unused land, *see* Idle land
Urban geography, 61
Urban planning, *see* Planning
Urban sociology, 16, 62

Vacant land, *see* Idle land
Values (ethical), 23, 305, 311
  about environment, 34, 311
  of land, channels, 143
  in simulation/models, 237
Variety (Law of Requisite), 290; *see also* Control
Volume of communication, 146

Wagner, Philip, 34
Walkden, A. H., 192
Warnzt and Neft, 116
Webber, Melvin M., 16, 77, 123, 312
Weber, Alfred, 61
Weiss, Shirley F., 242 n.
Wiener, Norbert, 75, 90
Wilkinson, R., 41
Wilson, Alan G., 310
Wingo, Lowdon, 67, 105, 226

Yates, W. M. F., 18
Young, Robert C., 105, 107

Zettel, R. M. and Carll, R. R., 216
Zones, in transportation plans, 66